LAW WRITERS AND THE COURTS

Da Capo Press Reprints in

AMERICAN CONSTITUTIONAL AND LEGAL HISTORY

GENERAL EDITOR: LEONARD W. LEVY

Claremont Graduate School

LAW WRITERS
AND THE COURTS

*The Influence of Thomas M. Cooley, Christopher
G. Tiedeman, and John F. Dillon upon American
Constitutional Law*

BY CLYDE E. JACOBS

DA CAPO PRESS • NEW YORK • 1973

Library of Congress Cataloging in Publication Data

Jacobs, Clyde Edwards, 1925-
    Law writers and the courts.

    (Da Capo Press reprints in American constitutional
and legal history)
    Bibliography: p.
    1. Cooley, Thomas McIntyre, 1824-1898. 2. Tiedeman,
Christopher Gustavus, 1857-1903. 3. Dillon, John
Forrest, 1831-1914. 4. United States—Constitutional
history. I. Title.
KF367.J33   1973   342'.73   73-251
ISBN 0-306-70570-2

This Da Capo Press edition of *Law Writers and the*
Courts is an unabridged republication of the
first edition published in Berkeley and Los Angeles
in 1954. It is reprinted by special arrangement
with the University of California Press.

Published by Da Capo Press, Inc.
A Subsidiary of Plenum Publishing Corporation
227 West 17th Street, New York, New York 10011

Manufactured in the United States of America

Law Writers and
the Courts

CLYDE E. JACOBS

Law Writers and the Courts

The Influence of Thomas M. Cooley,
Christopher G. Tiedeman, and
John F. Dillon Upon American
Constitutional Law

UNIVERSITY OF CALIFORNIA PRESS
BERKELEY AND LOS ANGELES · 1954

UNIVERSITY OF CALIFORNIA PRESS,

BERKELEY AND LOS ANGELES, CALIFORNIA

CAMBRIDGE UNIVERSITY PRESS, LONDON, ENGLAND

LIBRARY OF CONGRESS CATALOGUE CARD NUMBER: 54-7474

COPYRIGHT, 1954, BY THE REGENTS OF THE UNIVERSITY OF CALIFORNIA

PRINTED IN THE UNITED STATES OF AMERICA

DESIGNED BY A. R. TOMMASINI

Preface

IT HAS BEEN SAID that the law writers, as distinguished from the judges and the practicing lawyers, have played only minor and relatively insignificant roles in the formulation and development of American legal principles. It is true that the publicists have exercised somewhat less influence upon the courts of countries where the common law prevails than upon those of countries whose legal systems are based upon the civil law. But some law writers have enjoyed, at various times, tremendous prestige in the United States and, as a result, their ideas have been impressed upon our law.

During the period immediately following the Civil War the number of law writers in America was very great, and their works were voluminous. Most of these writers were of no special importance, however; and their works, although impressive for their magnitude and scholarship, lacked originality. But a few writers made outstanding contributions to the growth and development of important constitutional principles. Thomas M. Cooley, Christopher G. Tiedeman, and John F. Dillon, not less than the judges and the lawyers, were responsible for the popularization within their profession of constitutional principles which encompassed the laissez faire policies demanded by industrial capitalists. The object of this work is to describe and evaluate the contributions made to our constitutional law by the more important text writers of the post-Civil War period.

For purposes of this study I have selected two legal principles which were developed during the years after the Civil War and which were incorporated into our state and federal constitutional law largely through the efforts of the publicists. Upon the basis of my research I concluded that the works of Cooley and Tiedeman were instrumental in the formulation, development, and application of the liberty of contract principle as a limitation upon the police power of the states and the commerce power of the national government, and that the treatises of Cooley and Dillon were of equal importance in making the public purpose maxim an important restriction upon the taxing and spending powers of state and local governments. The substance of this book has been organized around these two principles. In the introductory chapter I have sketched, largely upon the basis of secondary source materials, the historical background and significance of constitutional principles which protected property rights before the Civil War. The second and third chapters are a discussion of the development and application of the liberty of contract principle. In the fourth and fifth chapters I have analyzed the origins, growth, and decline of the public purpose restriction on the taxing and spending powers. The sixth, and final, chapter is an evaluation of the work of these publicists in relation to the over-all development of laissez faire constitutional ideas during this period.

If my enterprise is in any measure successful, credit must be, and is gladly, shared with those who gave generously of their time, energies, and facilities. A research fellowship provided by the Horace H. Rackham School of Graduate Studies of the University of Michigan enabled me to initiate the work. Special facilities and indispensable materials were made available to me by the officers and staffs of the following institutions: William W. Cook Library of Legal Research of the University of Michigan, Kansas State Law Library, California State Law Library, California State Archives, and Illinois State Archives. Mr. Heber Harper of Haverford College provided me with copies of documents in the Philadelphia Bar Association Library. Mr. Jason L. Finkle of the University of Michigan and Miss Bess Ellen Backes of the University of California read the manuscript at various stages of development and made valuable suggestions as to form and style. The permission of the following publishers to use quoted material is acknowledged: Little, Brown & Co.; Harvard Law Review; The Macmillan Co.; Marshall Jones Company; and Princeton University Press.

My deepest gratitude is expressed to Professor Harold M. Dorr of the University of Michigan who was a constant and unfailing source of inspiration, information, and advice throughout the course of my work. To those mentioned and to others I am sincerely grateful. Their contributions have improved this work. Whatever errors it may contain are my own.

C. E. J.

Davis, California
March, 1953

Contents

ix

1

Conservative Principles and Liberal Reforms Before the Civil War

AMERICAN POLITICAL INSTITUTIONS, from the times of the first settlements, have been profoundly influenced by theories of limited government. In the pre-Revolutionary period limitations derived from various "higher law" and natural-rights concepts. Later, written constitutions, either as sources of governmental powers or as declarations of governmental limitations, were adopted at all political levels. The earlier higher-law and natural-rights doctrines were gradually supplanted by or incorporated into these written instruments.

For a time the idea of limited government was emphasized largely by liberal and revolutionary theorists. But, as government came increasingly under popular control, conservatives accepted the concept and derived from it the "preconditions" of majority rule. As enunciated by conservatives, these preconditions quite naturally included the sanctity of private-property rights, and numerous specific principles whereby these rights received protection from legislative impairment were gradually developed.

The present chapter was written with two general objects in view: (1) to sketch the development and to indicate the significance of certain constitutional and legal principles which served propertied interests before the Civil War and (2) to demonstrate the partial decline of these principles under the impact of Jacksonian democracy.

I

Conservative Principles Before the Civil War

During the early Colonial period of American history the more articulate theorists, most of them New England clergymen, emphasized the concept of divine law as the source of secular authority and the regulator of individual conduct;[1] but these writers were not primarily concerned with the rights of individuals vis-à-vis their political institutions. Although any discussion of a higher law which is binding upon rulers would seem to imply the existence of an area of individual or corporate rights derived from that law, the first generation of New England theorists did not address itself to this question.[2] The influence of then contemporary European theories of a more secularized orientation had not yet been felt, and the higher-law doctrines of Protestant churchmen, both in England and on the Continent, were of dominant influence in New England.

In the latter part of the seventeenth century and the first years of the eighteenth century the volume of political literature, both systematic and occasional, declined substantially in the American colonies. New England clergymen continued to write on politics and on related subjects, but the number of writings was not great. Still, this literature is important in the development of American political and legal thought because it bears clear impressions of secular influences. Locke and Pufendorf, as well as traditional sources—the Bible, Luther, and Calvin—exercised considerable influence on political speculation in America at that time.[3] Unlike the early generation of theorists, those of the later era discussed not only divine law but also ideas of inherent natural rights. These ideas became a ready and powerful weapon which the colonists were to use in the impending political struggles with England. Under the impact of difficulties with the mother country, particularly after 1760, philosophical and political discussion was revitalized and stimulated.

Although utilization of natural-rights concepts for revolutionary purposes was initiated in New England, writers in the middle and southern colonies soon accepted the doctrine.[4] Indeed, it was Virginia which contributed most by way of practical application of the theory.[5]

---

[1] For notes to chap. I, see pp. 171–176.

As a result of the revolutionary orientation of principles of natural rights, a few extreme conservatives began to reject these theories altogether.[6] But most Loyalists accepted Locke's social compact, although in doing so they emphasized the duty of passive obedience to duly constituted authority. On the other hand, a few, including the noted clergyman Jonathan Boucher, maintained the high-Tory position and rejected Locke's concepts altogether.[7] For Boucher the doctrines of consent and of human equality were subversive of all government and, consequently, must be categorically denied. Other conservatives, however, discerned that there was nothing inherently revolutionary in the doctrine of natural rights and that with proper emphasis it might well become a bulwark of conservatism. To many revolutionists natural rights might justify a radical alteration in existing relationships between the mother country and the American colonies, but at the same time these conservative revolutionists could invoke the same theory, orientated differently, to justify socioeconomic arrangements favorable to propertied interests. Temporarily, it is true, a radical interpretation of natural rights was ascendant, and not a few of the revolutionary leaders discerned that they were fighting two battles—one to preserve their lives (because they were traitors to England), and another to preserve their property and vested interests from assaults by radical state legislatures. In both struggles these conservatives were ultimately successful.

Even during the war itself radicalism ebbed gradually. State price-fixing laws had disappeared by 1780, and legal-tender legislation had been repealed in all states by 1782.[8] The reasons for the revival of conservative influence at this time are difficult to discern. In some measure explanation may rest upon the fact that radical leaders had spent themselves in battle or had become conservative as the result of newly created opportunities for personal fortune.[9]

A partial victory for conservatism was registered with the adoption of the Articles of Confederation.[10] As a frame of government this document did not completely satisfy propertied interests, but at least it provided for a *de jure* general government. It was a step, although admittedly a hesitant one, in the direction of national stability. The severe depression which followed in the wake of the Revolutionary War discredited the new government, and it was widely supposed that the economic crisis directly resulted from the

lack of a strong central authority. It is certain that the failure of the
government to cope adequately with the commercial warfare among
the states was a contributing factor, but contemporary scholars point
to other causes as well, not the least of which was the overexpansion
of domestic production.[11]

Conservatives were thoroughly alarmed by this economic stagna-
tion and the radical agitation that accompanied it. Outbreaks such
as Shays' Rebellion seemed to challenge the fundamentals of the
social, economic, and political order. Suggestions for a new or, at
least, a revised system of government received more serious consideration by men of property. In 1787 a convention was assembled
in Philadelphia for the ostensible purpose of proposing amendments
to the Articles of Confederation. Dominated by commercial and
landed interests, and scarcely representative of even that restricted
segment of the population which then constituted the qualified
electorate, the delegates chose to go beyond their instructions and
to draw up a new instrument of government. The conservative origin
and character of the document were ably demonstrated many years
ago by Professor Beard, and the essential elements of his thesis are
now widely accepted.[12] The new government was endowed with extensive commercial and financial powers which might be utilized so
as to benefit the interests of the propertied classes. Under the influence of Alexander Hamilton the new government embarked upon
an economic program favorable to the interests of property owners.
The funding of the national debt, the assumption of state debts, the
establishment of the United States Bank, and the tax program
favored those interests which had framed and actively supported the
Constitution.

In addition to strengthening the national government, the Constitution, particularly by virtue of Article I, section 10, imposed very
real checks upon the states, which at that time were regarded as the
strongholds of radicalism. Nevertheless, these rather broad safeguards with which property rights were surrounded did not prove
completely satisfactory to conservatives. Shortly after their creation,
the federal courts, both in their reasoning and in their *dicta,* began
to invoke extraconstitutional limitations upon state power. It was
alleged that these limitations derived from natural rights and from
fundamental principles of republican government. But the "natural

rights" and "republican principles" of which the courts spoke were not those of the Revolution. Rather the emphasis was upon property rights, upon rights said to be vested. "Natural rights" and "vested rights" were made virtually synonymous by the judiciary.

In *Vanhorne's Lessee v. Dorrance*,[13] a federal circuit court, speaking through Justice Paterson, declared invalid a Pennsylvania enactment which vested ownership of disputed land in one party after the land had been granted to another. The court declared that "the right of acquiring and possessing property and having it protected, is one of the natural inherent and unalienable rights of man."[14] Such a law, said the court, "is contrary to the principles of social alliance in every free government."[15] And, in order to justify further the decision, the court invoked the contract clause of the Constitution. Three years later, in 1798, Justice Chase in his oft-quoted *dicta* in *Calder v. Bull* declared:

> I cannot subscribe to the omnipotence of a *State Legislature,* or that it is *absolute and without control;* although its authority should not be *expressly* restrained by the *Constitution* or *fundamental law,* of the State. The people of the *United States* erected their Constitutions, or forms of government, to establish justice, to promote the general welfare, to secure the blessings of liberty; and to protect their *persons* and *property* from violence. The purposes for which men enter into society will determine the *nature* and *terms* of the *social* compact; and as *they* are the foundation of *legislative* power, *they* will decide what are the proper objects of it: The *nature* and *ends* of *legislative* power will limit the *exercise* of it. This *fundamental* principle flows from the very nature of our free *Republican* governments, that no man should be compelled to do what the laws do *not* require; *nor to refrain from acts which the laws permit.* . . . There are certain *vital* principles in our *free Republican governments,* which will determine and over-rule *an apparent and flagrant* abuse of *legislative* power; as to authorize *manifest injustice by positive law;* or to take away that security for *personal liberty* or *private property,* for the protection whereof the government was established. An ACT of the Legislature (for I cannot call it a *law*) contrary to the *great first principles* of the *social compact,* cannot be considered a *rightful exercise* of *legislative* authority.[16]

This is the classic statement of the principle of vested rights. Although gradually supplanted and absorbed by specific constitutional guarantees, this principle was from time to time invoked until long after the Civil War, especially by state courts.[17] But it was rarely, if ever, utilized by the United States Supreme Court as the sole basis for the invalidation of legislation. In *Terrett v. Taylor*[18] the Court, speaking through Justice Story, came perilously close to resting its decision upon this ground alone; but, actually, it did not go that far, and it was content to refer to the "great principle of republican government" as well as the "letter and spirit" of the Constitution. Justice Story failed to specify what constitutional provision was alluded to, but it is almost certain that he was referring to the contract clause.

Both the state and the federal courts continued to invoke the doctrine of vested rights during the early decades of the nineteenth century, but at this time other limitations upon legislative authority were gradually developed. Probably the most important of these was that provision in Article I, section 10, of the Constitution which provides that "no State shall pass any law impairing the obligation of contracts." By its interpretation of the contract clause in *Fletcher v. Peck*,[19] the Court imposed severe restrictions upon state power. And, in later cases, these restrictions were made still more rigorous. In the *Fletcher* case, one may discern the begininngs of an important transition in constitutional doctrine. Chief Justice Marshall, who delivered the opinion of the Court, seemed to vacillate between the vested-rights principle and the contract clause in his quest for a satisfactory ground upon which the statute in question might be invalidated. He argued at some length that a state legislative grant was a contract which could not be impaired by subsequent repeal. Apparently the chief justice himself was not entirely satisfied with his reasoning, for as a further justification of the decision he added:

It may well be doubted whether the nature of society and of government does not prescribe some limits to the legislative power; and if any be prescribed, where are they to be found, if the property of an individual, fairly and honestly acquired, may be seized without compensation?[20]

Fletcher v. Peck illustrates the close association of vested rights with a specific constitutional guarantee; and it marks, better than any other single case, the increased tendency of the courts to make the contract clause the principal receptacle for the vested-rights doctrine. The growth and decline of the contract clause subsequent to the *Fletcher* case is too well known to need detailed description. *New Jersey v. Wilson*,[21] decided two years later, indicated that whatever original doubts the chief justice may have entertained concerning the scope of the contract clause had since been dispelled. In this case the Court reached the rather surprising conclusion that a tax exemption granted by a state to the Delaware Indians on certain lands was a contract attached to the land itself. Consequently, the state might not tax the land even after its sale by the original grantees to other parties.

In 1819 the Court decided two cases involving the obligation of contracts. *Dartmouth College v. Woodward*,[22] the first of these, became the most important of the contract cases in terms of later constitutional history. The importance of the case was not generally perceived at the time the decision was rendered,[23] but its later ramifications with respect to American financial and economic development can scarcely be overemphasized. In a broadly phrased opinion, Marshall declared that corporate charters were within the meaning of the obligation-of-contract clause, and that, as a result, a state legislature had no authority to amend or repeal such charters. At this time the corporate form of organization was rapidly coming into its own as a means of pursuing economic and financial activities. The Marshall decision, although it was subjected to two modifications in later years,[24] afforded private business enterprise an opportunity to grow unhampered by legislative supervision. In some respects the decision was an unfortunate one because the people of the several states were apparently subjected in perpetuity to the errors of their legislators. Eventually, however, this undesirable result was largely avoided. A few state legislatures had already adopted the practice of inserting in corporate charters clauses reserving to themselves the powers of repeal and of amendment. By 1819 this practice had not yet become widespread, but the decision in the *Dartmouth College* case encouraged it considerably. Later the states included such reservation clauses either in their constitutions or in general incorporation laws, and the state legislatures thus retained their authority over corporations chartered in the future.[25]

The opinion of the Court in *Sturges v. Crowninshield*[26] was rendered only two weeks after the *Dartmouth College* case had been decided. Unlike its predecessor, this case received much attention. It was widely believed that the Court, under the terms of the contract clause, had interdicted all state insolvency laws—whether they be prospective or retrospective in their operation upon contractual obligations.[27] Certain ambiguities in Marshall's phraseology might justify such an interpretation; but, actually, the decision went no further than to hold that insolvency laws were void insofar as they affected contracts made before their enactment. The precarious condition of business at that time probably disproportionately magnified the significance of the case.

An overwhelming number of Marshall's colleagues supported his views in these cases. However, in 1827, Marshall, for the first and only time in his lengthy judicial career, delivered a written dissent in a constitutional case. In *Ogden v. Saunders*[28] a bare majority of the Court, with seeming reluctance, refused to extend the contract clause in such a way as to inhibit state insolvency laws which were prospective in their operation. The dissenting opinion of the chief justice is a remarkable one because it embodies not only elements of the doctrine of vested rights but also a reasonably explicit statement of the doctrine of liberty of contract. He maintained that "individuals do not derive from government their rights to contract, but bring that right with them into society; that obligation is not conferred by positive law, but by the act of the parties."[29] According to his view, "this results from the right which every man retains to acquire property, to dispose of that property according to his own judgment, and to pledge himself for a future act."[30] Marshall, it is true, equivocated somewhat by adding that the remedy, individual coercion, had been surrendered when men entered society, and that, consequently, the states might properly legislate with respect to remedies for the violation of contracts. But the argument that the obligation itself was a creation of the parties and that it existed apart from positive law closely resembles the individualistic concepts of John Locke, and it presaged the eventual development of the liberty of contract doctrine. The opinion is somewhat perplexing, however, because Marshall also stated:

> The right to regulate contracts, to prescribe rules by which they may be evidenced, to prohibit such as may be deemed mischievous, is unquestionable, and has been universally exercised. So far as this power has restrained the original right of individuals to bind themselves by contract, it is restrained; but beyond these actual restraints the original power remains unimpaired.[31]

By way of example, Marshall in his *dicta* defended the validity of legislative prohibition of usurious contracts. Perhaps he, like the commentators and judges of a later time, was maintaining not only that the general rule was liberty of contract but also that the legislature might impose restraints upon this liberty, if the courts agreed that the contract was mischievous and the restraint was desirable.

Ogden v. Saunders marks a turning point in the interpretation of the contract clause. Until that time, the scope of the clause had been steadily expanded, and it had come to embody a large part of the vested-rights doctrine. But as a result of this decision its further extension was definitively checked. Later judicial decisions tended to restrict somewhat the application of the clause, and after 1830 the tendency to insert reservation clauses in charters, in general incorporation laws, and in the constitutions of the states became quite general. Moreover, the Court's ruling in *Charles River Bridge v. Warren Bridge*[32] that public grants must be construed strictly against the grantees and in favor of the public undermined somewhat the extreme ramifications of *Dartmouth College v. Woodward*. Although an inkling of this development appeared in Marshall's opinion in *Providence Bank v. Billings*,[33] to a conservative like Story the Court's decision in the *Bridge* case seemed to fly in the face of earlier precedents and to portend most serious peril.[34]

At the time of the expansion of the contract clause another important development beneficial to conservative interests was taking place, largely within the states. In New York, James Kent, who served from time to time in several judicial capacities, was engaged in the constructive task of writing into the law of his state the principles of the common law and of equity. It has been generally supposed that the English common law obtained in this country from the time of the first settlements. Actually, it was not until the middle of the eighteenth century that the courts in the colonies began to follow English legal principles systematically.[35] The publication, in 1765, of the first edition of Blackstone's *Commentaries* contributed materially to the adoption of these principles by colonial courts.[36] And then, too, an increasing number of colonists journeyed to the mother country for legal training, and upon their return worked, either as judges or lawyers, for the reception of English law. This reception was retarded somewhat by the bitterness engendered against the English institutions by the Revolutionary War.[37] In 1796, when Kent received his first judicial appointment, the New York law was sufficiently unsettled that his whole judicial career was largely devoted to applying principles of English law and equity, in a slightly modified form, to American conditions. It was not long until the New York reports became most prominent in the world of citation, but popular resistance to the application of common-law principles was not lacking. New Jersey, Pennsylvania, and Kentucky legislated against the citation of English cases. Opposition to the common law was evidenced in other states as well.[38]

The conservative character of the common law had been recognized for some time. By subjecting legislative enactments to common-law interpretation, the courts might temper or undermine any legislation subversive to vested rights. During the time when Kent was a member of the Council of Revision, which exercised a suspensive veto over state legislation—a veto combining both political and legal considerations—he strove to establish the common law as a virtual standard whereby the validity of statutes might be measured.[39] The great treatises of both Kent[40] and Story[41] indicate the emphasis each of them placed upon the common law as a source of principles affording protection to property rights.

By the 1830's the common law had been sufficiently applied and systematized in American practice that it came to exercise tremendous influence upon legal development and public policy. Indeed, one of the rules of statutory construction, "statutes in derogation of the common law are to be construed strictly,"[42] constituted for many years a check on legislative innovation far more subtle but scarcely less stringent than written constitutional limitations. As one writer on the Jacksonian period emphasized, "in the hands of judges like Peter Oxenbridge Thacher the common law became a bottomless reservoir of reasons why no one should do anything."[43] The effect of the glorification of judge-made law has been aptly summarized by Dean Pound:

As late as 1905 a leader of the American bar, thoroughly imbued with the ideas of the historical school, told us that it was a wise doctrine to presume that legislators intended no innovations upon the common law, and assume so far as possible that statutes were meant to declare and reassert its principles. As no statute of any consequence dealing with any relation of private

law can be anything but in derogation of the common law, the social reformer and the legal reformer, under such a doctrine, had always to face the
situation that the fruits of their labors would find no sympathy in those who
applied it, would be construed strictly, and would be made to interfere with
the *status quo* as little as possible."

The common law, like the contract clause, absorbed much of the
natural-rights doctrine; and it was assumed by many jurists that the
common law, as a product of the reasoning of centuries, was declara-
tory of immutable principles of right and justice. Gradually, as the
legislatures concerned themselves with a wider range of issues, the
scope of the common law diminished, but even in the twentieth
century its influence is very real.

None of these protections, from the conservative viewpoint, was
completely satisfactory. Although the contract clause was a notable
guarantee, conservative interests might well be dissatisfied with the
outcome of *Ogden v. Saunders*. After 1827 the scope of the clause
underwent gradual, but definite, diminution.[45] The vested-rights
doctrine, as construed by the courts and standing apart from any
specific constitutional limitation, was too vague to prove entirely
satisfactory. Moreover, after 1830, it came to be clearly recognized
that the legislative power of the states was restricted only by written
limitations in the state and federal constitutions. The state constitutions were, then, essentially negative documents, permitting the legislatures to do all that was not prohibited to them.[46] The courts were
already subject to considerable criticism by liberal elements. The
number of constitutional opinions rendered by the Supreme Court
under Marshall which were well received by the populace at large
was extremely small,[47] and many state courts were faring little, if
any, better. Under such circumstances resort to vested rights, natural
justice, and republican principles as a basis for invalidating statutes
might well arouse hostility. There can be no doubt that after 1830
the doctrine declined rapidly in importance although it was subsequently resuscitated.[48]

The common law was likewise unable to afford conservative interests all the protection that they desired. The effect of statutes
might be tempered by resort to common-law interpretation. Legislative intent might be tortured, even frustrated, by the practice.
Nevertheless, if the legislature was assertive, if it persisted in its at-

tempts, the courts could scarcely construe its enactments as inferior
to the common law, unless some constitutional provision incorporat-
ing the common law into the fundamental law of the state was
discovered.

A movement for codification of the laws had begun in the 1820's,
and it gained momentum after the inauguration of Jackson.[49] Here
again was a direct challenge to conservative interests; and those interests, in general, vehemently opposed such projects. As one might
suppose, both Kent and Story were not in sympathy with such proposals, although the latter served on a committee established in Massachusetts for the purpose of inquiring into the expediency of
codification.[50] Where the supporters of codification concerned themselves with statutory compilation and arrangement, they were generally successful, but they made far less progress in their efforts to
systematize the common law. Probably the most notable development which occurred in almost all states was the simplification of
procedure in the courts.[51] This, from the standpoint of liberals, was
a very real gain. Conservatives, then, had been able to prevent any
general changes except in a few isolated instances; but the experience
had been thoroughly alarming because it portended the possible decline of the common law as a morass of precedent which justified
judicial protection of vested interests.

Democratic Reforms as a Challenge to Conservatism

The election of Andrew Jackson to the presi-
dency in 1828 marks the beginning of a new era in the economic and
political development of the United States. The period was one of
intense political feeling, and it posed for the statesmen of the time
some of the most vital problems in American history. Universal suffrage, public education, temperance and prohibition, public improvements, the tariff, banking, the status of corporations, and slavery were
difficult issues leading to perhaps unparalleled controversy and vitu-
peration. They were problems which created wide and distinct cleav-
ages between conservative property holders and the "radical" masses.
In addition, this period was characterized by economic changes
which were not to have their full impact upon the nation until after
the Civil War.

The reform movement which preceded the Civil War generally stirred conservative fears. The legislatures had become increasingly the instruments of the white male population as the result of the incessant broadening of the electorate and the reduction of suffrage requirements. This trend toward universal manhood suffrage began with the Revolution, but it was accelerated during the Jacksonian era as Western ideals of democracy successfully invaded the eastern states. The perils inherent in legislative activity were accentuated, in conservative opinion, by suffrage trends. As a result of the altered character of the electorate, conservative politicians were forced to change their tactics.[52] Conservatism was no longer openly identified with the interests of the propertied classes. Rather the appeal was popularized: the successful campaign of the Whig candidate, William Henry Harrison, in 1840 contrasted most sharply with the campaigns conducted by the Federalist party thirty years earlier. By such techniques, the conservative minority might hope to control the popular branches of government, at least occasionally. On the whole, however, Jacksonianism successfully challenged conservative influence, until its energies were divided and dissipated in the antislavery agitation.[53]

As reform movements gained the support of many state legislatures, conservatives, with the aid of bench and bar, began to cast about for limitations upon governmental authority—limitations which would safeguard their interests from impairment by legislative enactments which reform had stimulated. But in some instances the restrictions which were formulated were products of liberal, rather than of conservative, efforts.[54]

Among the problems which troubled statesmen of the Jacksonian period was that of public improvements. The eventual resolution of this problem, which was dictated by popular feeling (or as conservatives would have said, by the agitation of the "radicals"), played into the hands of propertied groups and came to subserve these interests. State activity in this field had been encouraged, if not necessitated, by the official attitude of the Jackson administration toward federal support of such projects. After the Maysville Road veto message,[55] the states supported public improvements in various ways. For example, the state of Georgia assumed full responsibility for the construction and operation of a railroad. In other instances the states merely purchased stocks, or they authorized their subdivisions to do so.[56] The states which were most active in financing these improvements, either directly or indirectly, were those of the frontier where transportation was urgently needed and where private capital was unequal to the task. A large number of canals and most railroads were speculative, because they were built not to satisfy the needs of an already existing market but to encourage settlement in frontier areas.[57] Such ventures were, at the very least, risky; and revenue from these enterprises was not immediately forthcoming. In the meantime, state indebtedness increased rapidly. As late as 1820 the states were free of financial obligation, but by 1838 their debts totaled $170,000,000 to which another $30,000,000 was added by 1840.[58] Over 90 per cent of this debt was contracted to pay the costs of the public-works program.

The panic of 1837 and the subsequent depression brought financial reckoning. By 1841 nine states had stopped paying interest on their debts, and three states—Mississippi, Florida, and Michigan—repudiated their obligations either in whole or in part.[59] The result was a decline of state activity in the public-improvements field. Most states liquidated all or part of their enterprises. In practically all of them constitutions were amended so as to prohibit state projects of this kind in the future.[60] There is little evidence that these amendments were the result of conservative agitation. Rather they reflected the popular temper of the time. Despite the popular origin of these amendments, conservatives ultimately gained, because governmental business activity then seemed discredited and new opportunities for profitable investments were opened to those having money. Private corporations profited from the experiences of the states, large-scale experimentation and attendant financial risks were no longer necessary, and the new enterprises enjoyed great success.[61]

The status of corporations was one of the most fruitful sources of political agitation during the Jacksonian era. Often disagreement arose about the status of the banking business. This controversy was very important, because it revealed the fundamental differences between conservative and liberal theories of the desirable relationship between government and the business community. Upon its outcome depended, in large measure, the course of American economic development in later decades.

To the democratic idealist of the time, the corporation—deriving its privileges and existence from a special charter—was incompatible with republican institutions.[62] For a time attempts were made to divert the trend in business organization away from corporations and into the direction of partnerships. These efforts were doomed to failure for two reasons. First, the corporation had already been firmly established as a legitimate form of business organization. Second, the economic necessities of the time demanded large capital outlays which only corporations could furnish.[63] Proposals were made to grant charters only to those business enterprises which could not be undertaken on an individual or partnership basis,[64] but eventually the opposition changed its line of argument. State governments found the question of limited liability for stockholders equally perplexing, and their policies were subject to much vacillation.[65] To the thoroughgoing democrat such a principle was most difficult to justify and to accept. In an age when ordinary bankruptcy laws were not popular, questions about such a privilege were inevitable. Nevertheless, the necessity of attracting capital for essential activities overruled the objections, and the principle was accepted.

Upon admitting the necessity, if not the desirability, of corporations, Jacksonians adopted another tactic. They urged the democratization of corporations through a system of general incorporation laws.[66] Here, they were more successful than they had been when they had opposed corporate organization *per se*. But the general incorporation law was eventually to operate to the advantage of propertied interests. In form, at least, such a proposal seemed to abolish the monopolistic and privileged character of corporations. If opportunities were opened to all through abolition of special charters, then the system would be more democratic and less corrupt. The proposal tended to cut across party lines, with some conservatives, like Webster, supporting it.[67] The reform, however, was initiated by liberals and, largely through their efforts, won widespread acceptance in the states. During the period few laws regulating corporations which were then already in existence were enacted. Although Massachusetts attempted to supervise corporate activity, such regulation was not popular elsewhere.[68] Not only did conservatives oppose governmental regulation as violative of their property rights, but Jacksonians tended to regard it as a transgression of man's liberty. The result

was that the number of corporations increased rapidly, and industrialization of the country's economy gained momentum.

The controversy over corporations in general and the United
States Bank in particular illustrates that fundamental cleavage which
existed between Jacksonians and the champions of Whiggery. It
became increasingly evident that the former were opposed to all
special privileges which the business community had come to expect
from government. Unlike liberals of a later time, Jacksonians favored a policy of laissez faire and were, for the most part, champions
of many Jeffersonian economic principles.[69] For Jackson the most
serious aspect of the bank war was the question: shall the government rule the bank or the bank the government? And, indeed, the
machinations of Nicholas Biddle made the question a legitimate
one. On the other hand, the proponents of Whiggery followed the
tradition of Hamiltonian paternalism. For them the government was
an instrument by which their interests were to be protected and
from which financial favors might be obtained.[70] The business community was shortly to protest its preference for laissez faire, it is true;
but it supported the doctrine only when its immediate interests were
thereby benefited.

Another proposal which most vitally affected certain property interests was prohibition. Of the various reform projects which commanded widespread support, that which looked to the prohibition
of the manufacture and sale of intoxicants most directly challenged
the property rights and business privileges of a certain segment of
the community. In terms of the individualistic political outlook
of the period, temperance, but scarcely prohibition, can readily be
justified. For a time the antiliquor movement was confined largely to
the demand for temperance, but in the 1840's appeals for outright
prohibition became more frequent. The movement gained great momentum in New England where the concept of community responsibility had long flourished, but it had little impact upon the South
where more individualistic philosophies prevailed.[71] In 1851 Maine
adopted the first prohibitory law, and other states soon followed with
similar legislation.[72] At first, conservatives regarded the program as
an example of the foreign "isms" which were believed to be invading
the country; but, eventually, the movement acquired respectability,
and even some conservatives supported it. It is perhaps significant,

however, that prohibition legislation resulted in one of the first explicit judicial statements of the doctrine of substantive due process, the opinion of Judge Comstock in *Wynehamer v. People*.[73] The implications of legislative prohibition of any business were not overlooked by conservatives, and the quest for judicial safeguards was intensified.

Tremendous progress was made in industrializing the economy of the United States during the thirty years which preceded the Civil War. This development had already taken place in England and in several countries of western Europe. It is said that by 1815 the typical English capitalist was an industrialist, while as late as 1840 the typical American capitalist was either a merchant or a banker.[74] Although the population of the United States had gradually shifted toward the cities between 1790 and 1840, this trend was most pronounced after the depression of 1837. Whereas in 1790 little more than 3 per cent of the population lived in urban places, in 1840 about 8½ per cent and in 1860 more than 16 per cent dwelt in such communities.[75] The slowness of American industrial development, as compared with that of England, may be attributed to several factors—the competition of foreign goods, commercial prosperity, and abundant opportunities for lucrative speculation in land.[76] These factors encouraged the investment of capital in commerce rather than in industry. Mercantile interests lost ground in the 1830's, however. The panic of 1837 and the ensuing depression, by undermining confidence in mercantile ventures, encouraged industrial expansion. In 1840 only $250,000,000 was invested in manufactures, but twenty years later the amount had increased to $1,000,000,000.[77] The progress of industry during this period need not be measured solely by the increase in capital investments. Unprecedented technological advances were made, and this, too, indicated that industrialization was under way.

In the wake of the American industrial revolution many economic and social problems arose. Trade unions had developed in a few communities during the first years of the century, but they were not in any sense the outgrowth of factory conditions. Rather they constituted a protest against the growing tendency within the merchant-capitalist system to reduce both the master and his subordinates to the status of wage earners.[78] The movement was extremely feeble and failed to challenge the substantial interests of the propertied classes. Still, the latter were very much alive to the potential dangers created by such organizations. Political action on the part of the workers was not very effective at the time because suffrage restrictions had not yet been liberalized. Economic action was hampered by judicial hostility, first evidenced in a decision in 1806 which held that a combination to raise wages was a conspiracy prohibited by the common law.[79]

This early labor movement was almost wholly ineffective until the time of Jackson. With the liberalization of suffrage requirements, however, it gradually gained political prestige, and labor unions exercised some influence in the general reform movement of the period. The political program of the unions during the 1830's, although feared by conservatives, scarcely challenged their immediate interests. Some labor activity, it is true, was directed toward realization of schemes of Utopian socialism; but of more permanent significance were demands for universal suffrage and education, for popular election of all officials, for a less expensive legal system, and for abolition of imprisonment for debt.[80] These demands were not characteristic of an industrial proletariat. Rather, they were a part of a general reform movement which derived much of its strength from its appeal to the middle classes. Eventually most of these proposals were accepted by the governments concerned.

Between 1832 and 1836 the unions were active on the economic front also, and this likewise excited conservative fears, possibly with greater justification. There were numerous strikes concerning wages and hours, but the courts again and again imposed stringent checks upon such activity.[81] It was not until *Commonwealth v. Hunt*,[82] decided in 1842, that the courts came to recognize the legality of labor organizations. The most serious blow to the trade unions of this period was the panic of 1837. By 1836 membership in the unions had reached nearly 300,000, and many organizations operated on a national scale. But these national organizations disappeared almost completely, and membership in the local unions dwindled to the vanishing point as the depression deepened and competition for jobs became more intense.[83] Most of the few economic gains which had been made in the preceding decade were completely lost. President Van Buren's executive order of 1840 (in which the national government established the ten-hour day for certain of its employees) and the ten-hour day in certain private shipyards were the only lasting gains of an economic character.[84]

Prosperity returned in the 1840's, and with it came renewed efforts by labor unions to improve the lot of the workingman. Demands for the ten-hour day became increasingly prevalent, and some progress, most of it resulting from economic rather than from political pressure, was made. By 1850 the average working day was eleven and one-half hours, considerably below that existing in 1800, and real wages had increased materially.[85] On the political front the gains made by labor were more modest. In the early 1840's the legislature of Massachusetts enacted a law prohibiting the employment of children under twelve years of age for more than ten hours daily,[86] and other states soon followed this example.[87] No previous decade had witnessed such substantial progress in the betterment of the status of the workingman; and the aspirations and successes of the unions, unimpressive though they may be according to modern standards, were disquieting to conservatives of the period.

It is the decade before the Civil War from which Professor Commons dates the beginnings of the real trade-union movement in the United States.[88] The change in the character of the movement occurred in part because the social reformers who had previously dominated labor activity became absorbed in the antislavery crusade. Deprived of outside leadership, the workingmen had to discover leaders among their own membership.[89] It is also true that by the 1850's the industrial revolution had made a considerable impression upon America. With the development of the factory system a vigorous labor movement was well-nigh inevitable. Demands for better working conditions, shorter hours, and higher pay gradually replaced the idealistic projects with which the early labor movement had been identified. As a consequence of this change of emphasis, progress along economic lines was very real, although the modern conservative, unlike his ideological ancestor, might tend to scoff at the seemingly moderate program of the workers. In a few crafts hours were reduced to eight daily (although the general average was much higher), and real wages increased materially during this last decade before the war.[90]

The new industrial capitalists fought the program of labor vigor-
ously, but before the Civil War this segment of the propertied
classes was not politically dominant. Industry had generally failed
to capture the citadels of political power, and this failure was particularly evident with respect to the national government.[91] The
industrial entrepreneur was engaged in perilous battles against two
foes—the planter aristocracy of the South and the free laboring
masses of the North. The Democratic party, which usually dominated national politics, had come under the sway of Southern elements, but the newly formed Republican party offered interesting
opportunities. Despite the liberal, free-soil character of this group at
the time of its formation, it was soon invaded by the industrial capitalists and became more conservative.[92] The political dominance of
a new kind of conservatism was in the offing—a conservatism which
differed substantially from that advocated by the planter-merchant
element.

After the Civil War began, this new conservative class tightened
its grip upon the Republican party. The policies of the party (and
they generally became the policies of the national government) were
designed to realize the aspirations of the industrial capitalists. A
protective tariff was enacted, national banks were established, lucrative war contracts were negotiated, and tax laws favorable to industry were passed.[93] Each of these measures hastened the process of
industrialization immeasurably. Even the immigration policy (contract labor) and homestead legislation proved beneficial to the entrepreneur by guaranteeing him a cheap labor supply and by creating
new markets in the unsettled West.[94] There can be little doubt that
the Civil War, which initiated a revolution in the South, completed
another in the North. Industrial capitalism had come of age.

As industrial capitalism developed and as conservative fear of
radicalism increased, it became evident that the judiciary would be
called upon to provide additional safeguards for property rights.
Traditional guarantees of the rights of property, the vested-rights
principle and the contract clause, were still available, but they had
lost their dynamic quality. Something new was needed, something
that might fill up the constitutional hiatus which the transition from
a mercantile to an industrial economy had occasioned. The older

principles had afforded protection to traditional kinds of property, particularly tangibles. But would they adequately protect the kind of property generally associated with industrial capitalism? To a limited extent, the contract clause did do so because it was interpreted in a way that prevented the legislature from impairing the rights and privileges granted in corporate charters. Nevertheless, this guarantee was insufficient in itself, and it was further diluted by the fact that many legislatures had reserved to themselves the right to repeal and amend such charters. The vested-rights principle was even less satisfactory and was the object of much popular suspicion. Clearly, then, if the aspirations of the industrialists were to be judicially recognized, a new constitutional principle (or a new interpretation of an old principle) was required.

Before the Civil War, a few state courts had discovered a constitutional provision, found in most of the state bills of rights, which might be interpreted to limit legislative power. That provision was, of course, the "law of the land" clause or its more recent variant, "due process of law."[95] The provision possessed at least three qualities which made it a potential guarantee of industrial property rights. First, it was a *written* guarantee of both liberty and property. The courts could be fairly certain that their application of an express constitutional restriction upon governmental powers would occasion less indignation than would their use of extraconstitutional principles. Second, having its origin in Magna Charta and having enjoyed the tributes of Coke and Blackstone, the provision was a venerable one. Third, the provision was exceedingly vague. This latter characteristic particularly commended it to the attention of conservative judges and lawyers. Originally interpreted as a procedural guarantee only,[96] the clause was eventually made a guarantee of substantive rights. As early as 1857 in his opinion in *Scott v. Sanford,* Chief Justice Taney of the Supreme Court of the United States accepted, for certain purposes, the latter interpretation of the clause.[97]

The due-process clause could readily accommodate common-law principles and the doctrine of vested rights. And it might also be interpreted as an interdiction against any legislation which appeared unreasonable or capricious to the judges. Traditional kinds of property could receive protection; and, at the same time, new types of property, those associated with an industrial as opposed to a mercantile or agrarian society, might be plausibly recognized.[98] Due process could constitute, then, a shield not only for tangible property but also for private economic power.[99] This development did not occur until after the Civil War, but the prewar cases wherein substantive due process was recognized anticipated the later elaboration of the provision.

In the period following the Civil War the publicists and lawyers set about the task of developing a constitutional law favorable to the laissez faire economic philosophy which prevailed among industrial capitalists. Thomas M. Cooley, John F. Dillon, and Christopher G. Tiedeman were foremost among the legal commentators of the period. Drawing upon the precedents of the pre-Civil War era, interpreting them according to certain economic predilections, and projecting upon an industrial economy the ideals of a frontier society, these writers supplied the bar, and the bar in turn supplied the bench, with numerous principles which restricted the powers of legislative bodies.[100] The first impact of these doctrines was felt in the state courts, but eventually the federal courts accepted the principles. Cooley's works, in particular, enjoyed tremendous success. As his influence increased, as the doctrines of substantive due process and of economic liberty gained widespread acceptance, later editions of his principal work, *A Treatise on Constitutional Limitations,* justified upon the basis of an increasing number of more relevant (and more respectable) precedents, the principles enunciated in the first edition. Cooley and his fellow writers supplied the judiciary with the materials whereby due process of the Fourteenth Amendment was given life and whereby the corresponding clause of the Fifth Amendment was subsequently reanimated. And in this, at least, the publicists contributed to a constitutional revolution paralleling the industrial revolution which was then taking place.

It is the purpose of the following chapters to show how laissez faire constitutional principles, formulated by the publicists and embodying enormous restrictions upon the police and taxing powers of government, were written into the fundamental law of the land through judicial application of the Fourteenth and Fifth Amendments and of corresponding provisions in state constitutions.

2

Liberty of Contract: Genesis and Development

IN 1923, when dissenting in the case of *Adkins v. Children's Hospital,* Mr. Justice Holmes remarked:

> But in the present instance the only objection that can be urged is found within the vague contours of the Fifth Amendment, prohibiting the depriving any person of liberty or property without due process of law. To that I turn.

Earlier decisions upon the same words in the Fourteenth Amendment began within our memory and went no farther than an unpretentious assertion of the liberty to follow the ordinary callings. Later that innocuous generality was expanded into the dogma, Liberty of Contract. Contract is not specially mentioned in the text that we have to construe. It is merely an example of doing what you want to do, embodied in the word liberty. But pretty much all law consists in forbidding men to do some things that they want to do, and contract is no more exempt from law than other acts.[1]

During the fifty-five years which had elapsed between the adoption of the Fourteenth Amendment and the invalidation of the District of Columbia Minimum Wage Act, the Supreme Court of the United States had traveled, at the behest of conservative lawyers and state appellate tribunals, a long journey into previously uncharted territory. In the half-century since the decision in the *Slaughter-House Cases,*[2] the Court had in turn rejected, accepted, and delimited

---

[1] For notes to chap. 2, see pp. 176–183.

23

the liberty of contract. Mr. Justice Sutherland's now famous dictum, "freedom of contract is, nevertheless, the general rule and restraint the exception,"[3] might be, and is, criticized for its want of social and economic insights; but as a description of judicial attitudes prevailing at that time it contained an element of truth. Although statistical analysis indicates that only a small percentage of those statutes challenged as violative of due process were finally invalidated,[4] an examination of the substance of the opinions reveals that liberty—particularly economic liberty—was the judicial motif upon which decisions were generally constructed. The courts, it is true, were careful to point out that a presumption in favor of the validity of legislation inhered in the judicial function and that he who assailed a statute bore the burden of proof. Such principles, however, were honored more in their breach than in their observance. Economic liberty had become the underlying tenet of judicial philosophy. The *Adkins* case, in a sense, marks the apogee of a judicial epoch. The majority opinion of Justice Sutherland was a reaffirmation of the Court's determination to interpret the Constitution as a protective covenant of laissez faire, and the Holmes dissent was a succinct and critical summary of past developments whereby due process of law had been transmuted into the principal guarantee of corporate capitalism and of private economic power.

The development of the liberty of contract as a limitation upon the powers of both the state and the national governments was a judicial answer to the demands of industrialists in the period of business expansion following the Civil War. It constituted judicial acceptance of the economic theory of laissez faire and of the philosophic ideal of individualism. In the legal sphere, it represented not only a continuation but also a very substantial expansion of the principle of vested rights which the courts had applied since the formation of the Union. Under its various guises the vested-rights doctrine had been a powerful bulwark of the status quo. Property vested and contracts made were largely exempt from legislative interference:[5] the doctrine was a guarantee against numerous kinds of retrospective legislation. Liberty of contract had a much wider application. Where the principle of vested rights had protected only tangible property, liberty of contract—having been derived from the rights of liberty *and* property—afforded protection to intangibles associated with industrial capitalism. It protected private economic power and gave to that power a constitutional status.

In discussing the change in property concepts which industrial capitalism had worked upon the judiciary, Professor Commons quoted approvingly from the opinion of Judge Grosscup in *National Telephone News Co. v. Western Union Telegraph Co.*[6] Judge Grosscup asserted:

> Property ... is not, in its modern sense, confined to that which may be touched by the hand, or seen by the eye. What is called tangible property has come to be, in most great enterprises, but the embodiment, physically, of an underlying life—a life that, in its contribution to success, is immeasurably more effective than the mere physical embodiment.[7]

The "great enterprises" to which the judge alluded had at their disposal tremendous financial and human resources. The public had no practical alternative but to rely upon these businesses for essential goods and services. But the property rights of these enterprises had come to comprehend the right of the entrepreneur to dictate business policy, even if that policy imperiled the lives and well-being of both workmen and citizens. It was this power of the industrial capitalists which the courts, in the name of property, enforced upon the community. And when the legislature sought to intervene in the struggles between business and the public or between business and labor, the courts, as final arbiters, generally chose to enforce, under the guise of a constitutional right, the power of private enterprise. Private power, as wielded by corporate enterprises, was thus extended at the expense of public power, as wielded by the legislatures.

The doctrine of liberty of contract has its origins in the period following the Civil War, but those origins cannot be traced to any single judicial opinion, nor can they be ascribed to the work of any one legal thinker only. In the preceding chapter (pp. 8–9) it was shown that Chief Justice Marshall had formulated the principle in his dissenting opinion in *Ogden v. Saunders* but there was little, if any, inclination to resuscitate the contract clause as a guarantee of the right to make contracts. The earlier trend toward delimiting the scope of the guarantees afforded by this provision continued into the latter part of the century. The term, "liberty of contract," was not unknown to such Continental jurists as Grotius and Pufendorf; but, as a natural right, the liberty they mentioned applied not to the right to make promises, but to the sanctity of promises already made.[8] The Continental doctrine of liberty of contract did not go beyond (indeed, it did not go as far as), the settled application of the contract clause of the American Constitution, and it clearly cannot be regarded as the source of the American concept.

The term, "liberty of contract," will not be discovered in legal treatises published before the Civil War. As Professor Pound asserted, the untrammeled right to make promises was associated with the economic theory of laissez faire.[9] Its judicial recognition meant that a particular economic ideology, one supported by the entrepreneur but not always practiced by him, had become a part of the constitutional fabric of both the nation and the states. The doctrine had received the blessing of Adam Smith,[10] and in early cases the *Wealth of Nations* was occasionally cited as a leading authority for the proposition. But the economic foundations of liberty of contract scarcely sufficed for purposes of judicial rationalization. Although the careful reader may readily perceive that economic considerations were the underlying premise in scores of judicial opinions, only in a negligible proportion of these cases did the judges ignore altogether legal principles. The bench and the bar were confronted with the difficult problem of evolving a constitutional basis for laissez faire. It was this process of legal pathfinding which was to engage the energies of more than a generation of constitutional lawyers and judges.

The ratification of the Fourteenth Amendment in 1868 placed a general limitation upon the powers of the states, a limitation which was judicially enforceable. But there was wide disagreement as to the precise scope and purpose of the terminology therein employed; and this disagreement was, from the first, reflected in judicial utterances concerning the meaning of the amendment. The nebulous quality of its phraseology was more an asset than a liability, however. And with careful emphasis the amendment could readily become the covenant of laissez faire. The remainder of this chapter will examine the elements which, through judicial synthesis, came to make economic liberty, and especially the liberty of contract, a general rule of American constitutional law.

Six separate stages in (and they are elements of) the legal synthesis of liberty of contract will be considered:

(1) The publication, in 1868, of Thomas M. Cooley's *Constitu-*

tional Limitations, where he formulated the doctrines of class legislation, of implied limits on state legislative power, and of substantive due process.

(2) The early federal cases involving the initial interpretation of the Fourteenth Amendment, and the formulation therein, by certain judges, of the general principle of economic liberty.

(3) The state decisions from 1872 to 1884 wherein the courts distinguished between real and pretended exercises of the police power and wherein the liberty of contract was at last explicitly stated.

(4) The decisions of the federal courts from 1876 to 1884 wherein due process underwent a faint but important transformation.

(5) The state cases in 1885 and 1886 where constitutional laissez faire won decisive victories and where liberty of contract—perhaps the most important single tenet of the new economic-legal ideology—was, for the first time, applied.

(6) The publication in 1886 of Christopher G. Tiedeman's *Limitations of Police Power*—the most extreme defense of constitutional laissez faire principles ever written.

These cases and treatises were the fundamental materials with which the courts were to elaborate and apply laissez faire principles in the impending struggle between the entrepreneur and the public.

Cooley's Constitutional Limitations and the Foundations of Laissez Faire

If it were necessary to name the principal contributor to the cause of constitutional laissez faire in the era following the Civil War, Thomas M. Cooley would deserve such designation. Born on a farm near Attica, New York, Cooley was one of a family of fifteen children. His early life was marked by hardship but not by extreme poverty; he succeeded in obtaining a fairly good formal education. After attending the common schools in the community, he enrolled in Attica Academy. While in attendance there, he taught in the public schools in order to support himself.

Cooley was graduated from Attica in 1842, and, having previously made his choice of careers, moved to Palmyra, New York, where he commenced his law studies in the offices of Theron K. Strong. The latter, who was to become a judge of the state supreme court, was a man of ability, and young Cooley soon emulated his thorough and systematic habits. In 1843 Cooley set out for Chicago, but he lacked sufficient funds for the journey. Consequently, he settled in Adrian, Michigan, where he completed his preliminary law studies. At the same time he served as deputy county clerk. He was admitted to the bar in 1846, and married several months later.

Cooley's success as a lawyer was neither immediate nor easy. He tried his fortunes in other communities and in other enterprises (he was for a time editor of the Adrian *Watchtower*), and for nearly a decade he and his wife suffered hardship and privation. The turning point in his career appears to have occurred in 1855 when he formed a partnership with Charles M. Croswell. From that time on his law practice improved, and it was not long until he received recognition from both the university and the state.

The Michigan Senate chose Cooley to compile the state statutes in 1857. Within one year he had completed the task, and appointment as official reporter of the state supreme court followed immediately. This post, which Cooley held until 1865, proved to be but a steppingstone to a still higher office. In 1864 he was elected on the Republican ticket as a justice of the Supreme Court of Michigan, a post which he retained until 1885. During his tenure that tribunal became one of the most influential in the country. However, Cooley's distinguished colleagues on the bench—James V. Campbell, Isaac P. Christiancy, and Benjamin F. Graves—share credit with him for the court's preëminence.

Some years before his elevation to the bench, while still the court reporter, Cooley had undertaken new duties. In 1859 a law department was organized at the University of Michigan, and Cooley was asked to assume a professorship there. He accepted the post, although the monetary inducement was not great, and moved to Ann Arbor with his family. Cooley was a member of the law faculty for twenty-five years. During that time he presented courses on a wide variety of subjects, including constitutional law, real estate, trusts, domestic relations, wills, partnerships, and taxation. Although not a brilliant lecturer, he was noted for thoroughness and clarity of presentation.

Cooley resigned from the law faculty in 1884, but he accepted the chair of history and constitutional law in the Literary College in

1885. For two years his energies were divided between his academic duties and newly undertaken activities in railroad affairs. By 1887 he had severed all but nominal relations with the university, and in that year he assumed his last post in public life. President Cleveland appointed him a member of the Interstate Commerce Commission, and shortly after assuming the post he became chairman of the agency. For a period of four years Cooley applied himself to the novel and difficult tasks which his position entailed. But ill health and overwork forced him to resign before his term had ended. In 1891 he returned to Ann Arbor where, after several years of semiretirement, he died in 1898.

Cooley's reputation depends but little upon his careers as lawyer, judge, teacher, and administrator. Although the influence that he acquired in these capacities should not be discounted, it was Cooley the publicist who left an ineffaceable impression upon legal and political institutions in the United States. The first and greatest of Cooley's treatises was his *Constitutional Limitations*.[11] Published in 1868, only two months after the ratification of the Fourteenth Amendment, this work, although in no sense purporting to be an interpretation of that amendment, eventually served as a basic authority for its elaboration. The first edition of the treatise enjoyed immediate success in state tribunals; and new editions appeared in 1871, 1874, 1878, 1883, 1890, 1903, and 1927.[12] Each successive edition bears evidence of the popularity of his work and of the influence which Cooley's principles enjoyed in the courts. His prestige, to be sure, was more direct and immediate in the state tribunals than it was in the Supreme Court of the United States. Nevertheless, the latter tribunal eventually, albeit slowly, came to accept the fundamentals of the constitutional ideology which he enunciated.

One may speculate at length about the reasons for the unprecedented popularity of the work. Why did Cooley's treatise surpass even those of Kent and Story in prestige and authority? A number of reasons might be suggested, but two are of special importance. First, the *Constitutional Limitations* was the first systematic work of merit in the field of state constitutional law. It served, as no previous work had done, to bring order out of the confusion inherent in having a large number of separate, although basically similar, constitutional systems. It soon became the ready-made reference work, the handbook, of lawyers and judges. Second, the fact that the treatise, as its title indicates, emphasized limitations upon power rather than power itself made it readily compatible with prevailing economic and political ideas of the time. As was stated in the preceding chapter (pp. 20–22), a new constitutional law was in demand by industrialists, and Cooley's work went far toward satisfying the demand. In the preface to his work, Cooley himself had expressed, with extraordinary candor, his personal bias:

He will not attempt to deny—what will probably be sufficiently apparent—that he has written in full sympathy with the restraints which the caution of the fathers has imposed upon the exercise of the powers of government.

As a result the courts, particularly those of the states, were receptive. Not only did the treatise bring together the earlier precedents which delimited state legislative power, but also suggested principles which, although not completely original with Cooley, went against the weight of legal authority.

In some cases the *Limitations* could be, and often was, cited to support both sides of an argument. The courts, however, were generally inclined to accept those principles which restricted legislative power rather than those which sustained it. It is altogether possible, even probable, that the courts sometimes went somewhat beyond what Cooley had originally anticipated when he first set down his constitutional principles; but most of these judicial precedents were eventually accepted by the writer and became a part of the expanding footnotes by which one may differentiate the later editions of his work from that published in 1868. It seems completely fair to assert that the treatise was the most fecund source of laissez faire constitutional principles available during the period. Although Judge Cooley may not have been fully aware of the far-reaching economic and social implications of his principles, the eclecticism of bench and bar assured a capitalistic orientation for them.

Among the principles restrictive of legislative power which owe something of their development to Cooley was the liberty of contract. Nowhere in the treatise was the concept explicitly set forth, but several of Cooley's generalizations anticipated its formulation and contributed to its development. By 1884 Cooley was prepared to list among the five natural rights the right to make contracts[18]—a legal contribution made all the more remarkable by the fact that, as of that date, the doctrine had yet to receive unqualified judicial approbation. In the *Constitutional Limitations* Cooley had contented himself with a few generalizations wherein he scored "class legislation" as violative of the due-process guarantee. Of the passages in the *Limitations* which received judicial assent few were quoted more often than was the following:

The doubt might also arise whether a regulation made for any one class of citizens, entirely arbitrary in its character, and restricting their rights, privileges, or legal capacities in a manner before unknown to the law, could be sustained notwithstanding its generality. Distinctions in these respects must rest upon some reason which renders them important,—like the want of capacity in infants, and insane persons; and if the legislature should undertake to provide that persons following some specified lawful trade or employment should not have capacity to make contracts, or to receive conveyances, or to build such houses as others were allowed to erect, or in any other way to make such use of their property as was permissible to others, it can scarcely be doubted that the act would transcend the due bounds of legislative power, even if it did not come in conflict with express constitutional provisions. The man or the class forbidden the acquisition or enjoyment of property in a manner permitted to the community at large would be deprived of *liberty* in particulars of primary importance to his or their "pursuit of happiness."[14]

Although Cooley admitted that certain kinds of special legislation were unobjectionable, there was a pronounced tendency on the part of the courts to proscribe all special regulations unless confined to some class of persons who, at common law, lacked legal capacity. But citations to Cooley's works were by no means confined to those cases involving class legislation. Under certain circumstances general laws were also regarded as objectionable. Cooley had said:

On the other hand, we think we shall find that general rules may sometimes be as obnoxious as special, when in their results they deprive parties of vested rights. While every man has a right to require that his own controversies shall be judged by the same rules which settle those of his neighbors, the whole community is also entitled at all times to demand the protection of the ancient principles which shield private rights against arbitrary interference, even though such interference may be under a rule impartial in its application. It is not the partial character of the rule, so much as its arbitrary and unusual nature, which condemns it as unknown to the law of the land.[15]

It became not unusual, in later years, to condemn legislation regulating certain specified businesses and occupations as contrary to the due-process guarantee against class legislation. At the same time the courts frequently condemned general laws because, by virtue of their generality, they were regarded as so sweeping as to be utterly arbitrary in character. Legislators, in establishing social and economic policies, thus floundered between a Scylla and a Charybdis.

A careful study of the *Constitutional Limitations* indicates that the author never completely related the concepts of liberty and property, although certain relationships were rather vaguely suggested. Credit for the intermingling of these rights—the elaboration of the concept of economic liberty—is due more to the courts than to the publicists. Cooley's most notable contribution was his emphasis upon the law of the land (or due process of law) as a substantive limitation upon legislative powers.[16] Associated with the doctrine of implied limitations, due process—as elaborated by Cooley—became a general prohibition against nearly everything that conservative interests might regard as arbitrary or unreasonable. Other lawyers and judges were soon to engage in a futile effort to make the privileges-and-immunities clause of the Fourteenth Amendment the principal guarantee of laissez faire, but Cooley had already prepared the road which was later to be discovered and followed. Nevertheless, this writer, influential and prolific as he was, was not the sole contributor to the new ideology of economic freedom. The courts themselves were not idle, and the work of some judges, although at first not universally accepted, had far-reaching constitutional and political consequences.

The First Judicial Interpretations of the Fourteenth Amendment and the Genesis of Economic Liberty

It need occasion little surprise that John A. Campbell, former justice of the United States Supreme Court and counsel against the monopoly in the *Slaughter-House Cases,* placed greater emphasis upon the privileges-and-immunities and equal-protection clauses of the Fourteenth Amendment than upon the due-process provision in his memorable argument before the Court. As

Mr. Justice Miller remarked, when casually dismissing the due-process argument in his majority opinion, it "was not much pressed."[17] After briefly observing that the courts had precedents for the interpretation of that provision, Justice Miller remarked that "it is sufficient to say that under no construction of that provision that we have seen, or any that we deem admissible" can the legislation of Louisiana be regarded as a deprivation of property within the meaning of the clause.[18]

Even before the Civil War the concept of substantive due process had gained some currency, especially in the states. But, on the whole, the interpretations of that provision generally emphasized procedure rather than substance. Professor Corwin has indicated that on the eve of the Civil War the most conspicuous fact about our constitutional law was the virtual identification of the police power of the states with the sovereignty of state legislatures.[19] As was noted in the first chapter, the period from 1830 to 1850 witnessed a general decline of the doctrine of vested rights and a partial diminution of the contract clause and other checks on legislative power. Professor Corwin suggested, however, that there was a number of restrictive principles then in a state of "suspended animation."[20] Among these was the due-process clause, which, in his opinion, could claim vitality on a number of grounds. The elements of the post-Civil War doctrine of due process were present before the war, but they awaited a proper blending—a blending which Cooley had done much to accomplish when he associated implied limitations with due process of law. It is rather strange that in the early cases, wherein the United States Supreme Court interpreted the Fourteenth Amendment, Cooley was largely neglected; and it is reasonably clear that as a result of this neglect the emphasis was placed upon privileges and immunities rather than upon due process in both the arguments of counsel and the Court's opinions. On the other hand, in the state courts, where Cooley's influence was much more direct and immediate, greater emphasis was placed upon due process of law at this time.

The first federal case to deal extensively with the economic ramifications of the Fourteenth Amendment was *Live Stock Association v. Crescent City Co.*[21] Here Joseph Bradley, sitting as circuit justice, rendered an opinion which presaged the early importance of the privileges-and-immunities clause. The case involved a bill filed in equity by independent butchers of the city of New Orleans against the recently established slaughter-house monopoly and certain state officials in order to restrain the latter from instituting proceedings which would interfere with the complainants' businesses. Despite Justice Bradley's admission that the court over which he presided possessed no jurisdiction to grant the bill, he proceeded to discuss the merits of the case anyway. In the course of his opinion, he said:

> What, then, are the essential privileges which belong to a citizen of the United States, as such, and which a state cannot by its laws invade? It may be difficult to enumerate or define them. . . . But so far as relates to the question in hand, we may safely say it is one of the privileges of every American citizen to adopt and follow such lawful industrial pursuit—not injurious to the community—as he may see fit, without unreasonable regulation or molestation, and without being restricted by any of those unjust, oppressive, and odious monopolies or exclusive privileges which have been condemned by all free governments; it is also his privilege to be protected in the possession and enjoyment of his property so long as such possession and enjoyment are not injurious to the community; and not to be deprived thereof without due process of law. It is also his privilege to have, with all other citizens, the equal protection of the laws. Indeed, the latter privileges are specified by the words of the amendment.[22]

The tendency to intermingle due process and equal protection with privileges and immunities, as disclosed in the above passage, became a characteristic of early cases in both federal and state jurisdictions. This was of some importance because, in later cases, after the privileges-and-immunities clause had been accorded only a very restricted application, the economic rights which some judges had initially associated with that clause were readily subsumed under the due-process and equal-protection provisions.

A second passage of importance in the opinion reads as follows:

> There is no more sacred right of citizenship than the right to pursue unmolested a lawful employment in a lawful manner. It is nothing more nor less than the sacred right of labor. This right is not inconsistent with any of those wholesome regulations which have been found beneficial in every state.[23]

This passage is significant because it sets forth the concept of economic liberty as one of the most important rights possessed by the citizen. In later adjudications some judges were to maintain that the sacred right to labor was a major element of both liberty and property.

Three years after Justice Bradley's decision in the circuit court, several cases involving the same act of the state of Louisiana (that of March 8, 1869) were decided by the Supreme Court of the United States.[24] The importance of these cases was immediately recognized and the attorneys representing the parties were among the most eminent in the country. John Campbell, who had represented the antimonopoly interests in the circuit-court case, founded his objections to the monopoly law upon four distinct grounds: (1) the prohibition against involuntary servitude in the Thirteenth Amendment, (2) the privileges-and-immunities, (3) the due-process, and (4) the equal-protection clauses of the Fourteenth Amendment.[25]

The underlying hypothesis of the majority opinion was that the Civil War Amendments must be interpreted in the light of history and that according to such interpretations they were to be regarded as primarily applicable to the status of the Negro.[26] Throughout the majority opinion there was a more or less inarticulate assumption that the amendments were not calculated to revolutionize relations between the central government and the states. Although Mr. Justice Miller, in speaking for the majority, emphasized the Negro problem as the one to which the amendments were addressed, he admitted that their application, under certain circumstances, might be somewhat broader. But even if the Thirteenth Amendment proscribed the Mexican peonage and the Chinese coolie-labor systems, it was completely inapplicable to the kind of legislation enacted by the state of Louisiana.[27] With respect to the equal-protection clause the Court was even more emphatic: it was designed for the protection of Negroes, and it was unlikely that it could ever be claimed as a protection for other groups. The due-process argument was rejected summarily, but the privileges-and-immunities argument caused the majority judges more serious, although not insuperable, difficulty. Some privileges, Miller maintained, were derived from national citizenship and others from state citizenship.[28] The privilege of pursuing a business he associated with the latter. In that the Fourteenth Amendment prohibited the states from abridging only those privileges derived from United States citizenship, it was inapplicable to the Louisiana statute.

The restricted interpretation which Justice Miller accorded to the privileges-and-immunities clause has prevailed to this day. As a consequence of this interpretation, the clause was then, as it is now, relegated to a virtually useless role in American constitutional development.[29] Repeated efforts on the part of attorneys to obtain a more comprehensive application of the provision have invariably failed, although the vigorous dissents of minority justices have indicated that the Miller opinion has not yet gained universal acceptance.[30]

Four of the justices dissented in the *Slaughter-House Cases,* and the dissenting opinions are notable statements of the new ideology of economic freedom. Three separate dissenting opinions were rendered—one by Stephen J. Field, another by Joseph Bradley, and a third by Noah Swayne. Chief Justice Chase, who also was with the minority, concurred in the dissenting opinion of Field and wrote no opinion.

The Field dissent, in which concurred the entire minority, was of particular influence in later adjudications. In it many laissez faire arguments of John Campbell were reiterated and given judicial benediction. Justice Field admitted that certain parts of the law were valid exercises of the police power.[31] But he discovered that the primary purpose of the law was to create a monopoly and to grant exclusive privileges, and these were not exercises of the police power at all. The increasing inclination of the state courts in later cases to distinguish between exercises of the police power and exercises of arbitrary power under the guise of police regulations unquestionably owed something to the Field opinion. The justice was not certain that the Thirteenth Amendment was applicable, but he had no doubts that the Fourteenth Amendment afforded grounds for the invalidation of the legislation. Monopolies, he maintained, were an invasion of the privileges of United States citizenship because they "encroach upon the liberty of citizens to acquire property and pursue happiness."[32] Equality of right, "with exemption from disparaging and partial enactments, in the lawful pursuits of life, throughout the whole country, is a distinguishing privilege of citizens of the United States."[33] Field's argument that everyone enjoyed equal rights—subject only to restrictions based upon age, sex, or condition—to choose and follow lawful callings, contributed materially to the development of liberty of contract in later cases. The justice concluded his dissent by describing the right to labor as one of the "most sacred and imprescriptible rights of man,"[34] a proposition which he supported by quoting from the *Wealth of Nations* as follows:

The property which every man has in his own labor, as it is the original foundation of all other property, so it is the most sacred and inviolable. The patrimony of the poor man lies in the strength and dexterity of his own hands; and to hinder him from employing this strength and dexterity in what manner he thinks proper, without injury to his neighbor, is a plain violation of this most sacred property. It is a manifest encroachment upon the just liberty both of the workman and of those who might be disposed to employ him. As it hinders the one from working at what he thinks proper, so it hinders the others from employing whom they think proper.[35]

In this passage, which was appended to the margin of the opinion, are set forth at least two ideas which became a part of the judicial stock in trade in due-process litigation. First, liberty and property are related by means of the economic hypothesis that labor as the source of property is property. Therefore, economic freedom (which encompasses the right to labor) is not only a part of one's liberty but it is his property also. Earlier concepts of property had emphasized tangibles or, at the very most, the intangible qualities of the tangible thing. Here the emphasis was clearly otherwise. Applied to the individual workman such a property concept was constitutionally significant but scarcely revolutionary. When applied, however, to far-flung corporate enterprises such a theory of property served to promote the aggrandizement of private economic power, unchecked by governmental control. Second, there is an identification of the interests of the employee with those of the employer. The encroachment upon the liberty of the one is an infringement upon the freedom of the other. Later the courts were to invalidate legislation restrictive of the rights of the employers upon the arresting ground that the legislation invaded the rights of his workers. Thus, Justice Field sought to incorporate economic freedom and a particular economic ideology into American constitutional law. Despite his immediate failure he established something of the content of a new constitutional order, which within fifteen years was to be accepted by a majority of his colleagues.

It would appear that the direct influence of the Bradley dissent was not equal to that of the dissent rendered by Justice Field. But in many respects Justice Bradley stated a clearer case for the cause

of economic liberty than did his more conservative colleague although, in general, his appeal was not as ardent as was Field's. According to Bradley the right to choose an occupation was a part of
one's liberty and the right to follow that occupation, after the choice
had been made, was a property right. The obvious implication was
that an occupation, once it had been chosen, became a vested right.
At one point he observed:

> In my view, a law which prohibits a large class of citizens from adopting
> a lawful employment, or from following a lawful employment previously
> adopted, does deprive them of liberty as well as property, without due process
> of law. Their right of choice is a portion of their liberty; their occupation is
> their property. Such a law also deprives those citizens of the equal protection
> of the laws contrary to the last clause of the section.[36]

Justice Bradley, it is true, placed greater emphasis upon privileges
and immunities than upon the other guarantees of the Fourteenth
Amendment, but he seems to have understood the possibilities of
the due-process provision better than did his colleague, Justice Field.
To Bradley belongs the very real distinction of being the first Supreme Court Justice to discover, at least partially, the changing
content of due process of law.[37]

The dissenting opinion of Justice Swayne is of only incidental
interest. Like Bradley he placed some emphasis upon due process,
but he appears to have confounded the procedural with the substantive concept.[38] Of some interest was his statement that "life is the
gift of God, and the right to preserve it is the most sacred of the
rights of man."[39] A few state courts, in later cases, held that restrictions on the right to work and to engage in lawful business constituted a deprivation of the means of subsistence—of life itself—
without due process of law, but this proposition was never as fully
developed as were liberty and property due process.

The dissents in the *Slaughter-House Cases* became a part of the
materials with which the judges created the liberty of contract. The
principles of economic liberty which Field and Bradley had so ably
defended were soon written into state constitutional law and were
finally accepted by the Supreme Court of the United States. But
the state courts were also to make a contribution to the liberty of
contract. While the federal courts were engaged in the process of
interpreting the Fourteenth Amendment, the state tribunals were

following, in their quest for a new constitutional order, a reasonably distinct and independent course. In the period from 1870 to 1885 a number of cases involving the extent of the police power came before these courts with the result that the power underwent substantial diminution. Later, these state cases and the dissents in the *Slaughter-House Cases,* along with Cooley's interdiction against class legislation, were to be brought together, for the first time, in defense of a completely formulated doctrine of laissez faire constitutionalism.

The State Courts and Implied
Limitations on the Police Power

The proponents of laissez faire constitutionalism enjoyed, during the immediate post-Civil War period, far greater success in the state courts than they did in the United States Supreme Court. While the latter tribunal was extremely reluctant to accept the constitutional principles which advocates of the new order demanded, the state judiciaries were more sensitive to the pressures of corporate capitalism. That is not to imply, however, that the state courts invariably upheld the constitutional principles of laissez faire. For more than a decade after the ratification of the Fourteenth Amendment the outcome of the struggle between proponents of legislative sovereignty and the supporters of laissez faire remained very much in doubt. Some tribunals were far more receptive than others, and not until the middle 1880's were decisive victories registered in favor of laissez faire. But even in those cases where the old principles prevailed over the new, judicial attitudes underwent a pronounced alteration.

In 1872 the Supreme Judicial Court of Massachusetts rendered its opinion in *Watertown v. Mayo.*[40] The case involved a state statute prohibiting, in communities having more than four thousand inhabitants, the erection and occupation of buildings for the pursuit of the slaughter-house business and other noxious trades. The court sustained, without hesitation, the validity of the law; but its opinion was not without laissez faire implications. While admitting that all constitutional rights, including that of property, were subject to the police power, the judges nevertheless declared that the "law will not allow rights of property to be invaded under the *guise* of a police regulation."[41] When preservation of health and protection against threatened nuisance do not appear to be the real objects of the law, then "the courts will interfere to protect the rights of the citizen."[42] The court did not, in this case, review the facts in order to determine whether or not this was a real exercise of the police power. Apparently the well-known nature of the business convinced it that no such examination was necessary. But the salient feature of the court's *dicta* was its assertion of the distinction between real and pretended exercises of the police power. Judicially enforced, the distinction was tantamount to a substitution of judicial judgment for that of the legislature. The courts might well protest that the expediency and wisdom of legislation were never their concern, but the principle enunciated in the *Watertown* case and thereafter reiterated by other courts went far toward undermining the validity of this statement of judicial functions.

During the following year the Supreme Court of Illinois, a tribunal which distinguished itself by its laissez faire decisions, carried the principle enunciated by the Massachusetts tribunal a step further. In *Lake View v. Rose Hill Cemetery*[43] the plaintiff, an incorporated city, sought to restrain the company from using certain lands, situated within the city but owned by the company, for burial purposes on the ground that the city had, by ordinance, prohibited the use of land outside a certain area for such purposes. In its answer to the complaint the company contended that its charter (which was issued prior to the ordinances in question) endowed it with the authority to acquire and use lands in the city for cemetery purposes. Quoting Cooley to show that all contracts and rights were held subject to the police power,[44] the court added, however, that it was unlawful to deprive a corporation of any of its essential rights under the mere guise of police regulations. In support of this latter proposition, the court cited the *Constitutional Limitations*.[45] The judges voted four to three in favor of the company, and the minority wrote a vigorous dissent in which they pointed out that Cooley himself had recognized that "church yards which prove, in the advance of urban population, to be detrimental to the public health, or in danger of becoming so, are liable to be closed against further use for cemetery purposes."[46] Moreover, the minority, again quoting Cooley, emphasized that corporate privileges were not more sacrosanct than those of natural persons.[47]

The *Lake View* case is a significant one in the development of laissez faire constitutionalism. As in the *Watertown* case, a court had accepted the principle that the judiciary could decide whether a statute was a real or a pretended exercise of the police power and for the first time this principle resulted in the invalidation of a law. From another standpoint also the case is of interest. It illustrates and emphasizes the increasing reliance of the state tribunals upon the works of a constitutional commentator—a reliance unparalleled in American judicial history.

The advocates of laissez faire suffered occasional setbacks in their quest for a new constitutional order, however. *Commonwealth v. Hamilton Manufacturing Co.*,[48] decided by the Supreme Judicial Court of Massachusetts in 1876, became one of the most embarrassing state cases so far as the proponents of laissez faire were concerned. Here the court was called upon to determine the validity of a state law limiting the work of women in laboring and manufacturing establishments to sixty hours per week. Counsel for the company argued that the law was void because it violated his client's charter of incorporation by limiting its capacity to make contracts, a right which was inferred from the general language of the charter. The court answered this argument by observing that the corporation possessed the power to contract for all lawful labor, but that the charter guaranteed nothing more.[49] According to the court the law did not violate the right to work nor the right to employ workers. It merely limited the number of hours one might be employed in certain establishments. Presaging future developments was the company's contention that the law violated the rights of the employee. The court replied that the law imposed no general limitation upon the working hours of women but was merely a restriction on excessive hours in certain kinds of occupations. Moreover, the court indicated some doubts as to the propriety of the contention as well as to its validity, when it observed that, having decided that no substantial rights were impaired by the law, it need not inquire whether supposed injuries to employees "is a matter of grievance of which this defendant has the right to complain."[50]

In later cases, state courts proved less sensitive to the anomalous practice of the employer urging, supposedly on behalf of the employees, the invalidation of legislation enacted for the express purpose of improving the latter's economic and social status. The authority of the *Hamilton* case, as to the validity of maximum-hours legislation for women, was widely accepted, and only in exceptional cases did the courts strike down statutes of this kind.[51]

Of the state courts which influenced the development of constitutional laissez faire during the last thirty years of the nineteenth century none was more important than the New York Court of Appeals. That tribunal had already acquired a certain eminence in due-process litigation before the Civil War,[52] and its later decisions reveal its jealous guardianship over private rights. Although the decision in *Bertholf v. O'Reilly*[53] was favorable to the statute, the judges enunciated a number of laissez faire constitutional ideas in their opinion. In this case the defendant was sued under certain provisions of a civil-damages act which gave a right of recovery to any person whose property was injured by an intoxicated person against the person on whose premises the intoxicant was obtained. The court stated that the principal guarantee against unjust legislation was the due-process clause of the state constitution, and it pointed out that that guarantee must not be strictly nor technically construed. The liberty guaranteed by that clause included, according to the court's definition, the right to exercise one's faculties and to follow lawful callings.[54] The property right encompassed in the clause included "the right to acquire power and enjoy it in any way consistent with the equal rights of others and the just exactions and demands of the State."[55] This economic interpretation of the terms, liberty and property, and the assertion that the due-process clause was the chief guarantee against unjust legislation became potent ammunition in the arsenal of laissez faire and far overshadowed the fact that the court decided in favor of the statute. The proponents of legislative sovereignty might win victories, but throughout the period these forces lacked the initiative. A new order was surely emerging.

Another of those cases in which the courts accepted laissez faire principles but at the same time sustained regulatory legislation was *Shaffer v. Union Mining Co.*[56] In 1880 the legislature of Maryland had enacted a statute requiring mining, manufacturing, and railroad corporations operating in Allegheny County and employing ten or more persons to pay their employees in the lawful money of the United States.[57] Deductions were prohibited except for rent, medical expenses, and fuel. The act purported to invalidate all contracts in conflict with its provisions. In this case the plaintiff had been assigned, by certain employees of the defendant corporation, a part of their wages. The defendant refused to honor these assignments and the assignee brought suit to recover. Two questions were presented for determination: (1) Did the legislature have the power to limit the contractual capacity of these corporations, and (2) did the law restrict the rights of the employees and, if so, was the legislature competent to enact it? The judge readily answered the first question in the affirmative after observing that the legislature had reserved the right to repeal and amend corporation charters,[58] but the second question created greater difficulty for the court. It quoted approvingly from Cooley's *Constitutional Limitations* to the effect that the legislature could not deprive any one class of the capacity to make contracts,[59] but it concluded that for this very reason the legislature should not be presumed to have intended to restrict the employees' capacity in this respect. The court did not explicitly state that legislative interference with the individual's right to contract would have been unconstitutional, but that assumption seems to underlie much of the opinion. Liberty of contract merely awaited an opportunity for explicit formulation and application.

The Supreme Court of Missouri was the next tribunal to make a contribution to the cause of laissez faire. The validity of certain provisions of the Notary Act of 1881 was challenged in *State ex rel. Harris v. Herrmann.*[60] This case involved the ouster of a notary public who had obtained his commission before the enactment of the legislation but whose position, under the terms of the new legislation (applicable to cities having a population of more than 100,000) had been abolished. Although the substance of the law raises some doubts as to the good faith of the legislature in passing it, the court's opinion went well beyond the necessities of the situation. Challenged as a special law, the statute was proscribed by the court as a species of class legislation. The judges argued that this was so because the provision in question (section four) applied only to notaries whose commissions were obtained before the passage of the law. Said the court:

> If such a law is worthy of the title of a *general law,* then assuredly one would be equally deserving of such title, which would designate notaries by the distance they reside from the court house, and their stature, or the color of their hair, or other individual peculiarities.[61]

This admixture of *reductio ad absurdum* and *argumentum ad horrendum* became a familiar weapon of the courts in cases where social and economic legislation was invalidated. Following the brief of counsel, the court quoted a passage from Cooley on the subject of class legislation and concluded that the provision of the law under attack did precisely what Cooley said was forbidden.[62] The court admitted that the law was general in form, but it added that "courts of justice cannot permit constitutional prohibitions to be evaded by dressing up *special laws* in the garb and guise of *general* statutes."[63] This latter proposition, although admittedly unobjectionable in principle, was fraught with serious implications. In later cases the courts not infrequently engaged in minute analyses of challenged statutes in order to discover their partial character although the laws were, on their face, general. In such a way the judiciary acquired additional power as the supervisor of relations between the state and the private economy.

The liberty of contract limitation on the police power was explicitly formulated for the first time by the Supreme Court of Illinois. Although *Jones v. People*,[64] decided in 1884, did not result in the invalidation of any law, the opinion there indicated that the Illinois tribunal had fully embraced the doctrines of laissez faire. In this case the appellant, a coal-mine operator, had been indicted for his refusal to comply with a law requiring the owners and operators of coal mines to furnish track scales upon which all coal taken from the mine was to be weighed. The act further provided that such weight was to be the basis for the computation of wages. Counsel for the appellant based much of his argument upon passages from Cooley's works. The latter's edition of Blackstone's *Commentaries,* Volume I, page 137, was cited to support the argument that the law was unconstitutional because, if sustained, the operators would lose their right to contract on a certain basis for the payment of wages.[65] The *Constitutional Limitations* was cited to prove that the law was void.[66]

In its opinion, the court succeeded in evading the issue of the constitutionality of the law. Instead, it chose to emasculate the legislation by interpreting it to mean that, in the absence of specific contracts to the contrary, weight, as determined by the track scale, should be the basis upon which wages were to be computed. The court said:

Although section 2 does provide the weight determined by weighing on the scales furnished shall be considered the basis upon which the wages of persons mining coal shall be computed, we do not regard this as requiring that in all contracts for the mining of coal the wages of the miners must be computed upon the basis of the weight of the coal mined. That would be a quite arbitrary provision—seemingly an undue interference with men's right of making contracts; and we can not ascribe to the legislature the making of such an enactment, unless it be plainly declared, which is not done in this case.[67]

The Illinois court thus assumed the validity of the liberty of contract principle. In support of its position no authorities or precedents were cited, but it is probable that counsel's repeated references to Cooley had not passed unnoticed. Later cases more clearly disclose the debt which the Supreme Court of Illinois owed to the *Constitutional Limitations.*

Twelve years had elapsed between the decision of the Massachusetts tribunal in *Watertown v. Mayo* and the opinion of the Supreme Court of Illinois in the *Jones* case. The progress made by the advocates of laissez faire had been most remarkable. The state courts had not taken the final step: liberty of contract had yet to be made a ground for the invalidation of a law. But that development was not long in coming. Meanwhile, the federal courts were also engaged in writing laissez faire into the Constitution, but their progress was less spectacular than was that made in the states. The subtle changes which due process underwent at the hands of federal judges had important effects in later adjudications, however; and the history of the development of laissez faire would be incomplete without reference to the cases decided by the United States Supreme Court between 1873 and 1884.

The Federal Courts, Due Process, and Economic Liberty

After the decision in the *Slaughter-House Cases* a majority of the justices of the Supreme Court made a valiant effort, against increasing pressures, to maintain the position taken in the

Miller opinion. For more than a decade the Court refused to make the Fourteenth Amendment a stringent restriction on state legislative activity. But even in the cases in which regulatory statutes were sustained, laissez faire principles received inarticulate acceptance. Like the *Slaughter-House Cases,* the opinion in *Munn v. Illinois*[68] revealed the continuing reluctance of the Court to assume supervisory authority over state economic legislation. The case involved the validity of a state law fixing maximum charges for the storage of grain in certain classes of elevators in Chicago.

Counsel for the plaintiffs in error relied rather heavily upon Cooley's works in the argument against the legislation. Seven references to the *Constitutional Limitations* appeared in the brief to support various propositions[69]—to show that the law violated the due-process and equal-protection clauses,[70] to prove that it was class legislation,[71] and, finally, to demonstrate that the law was not within the scope of the police power.[72] Counsel for the state countered with one reference to the same work, but he relied primarily, and perhaps advisedly, upon other authorities. Chief Justice Waite rendered the Court's opinion upholding the law on the ground that the business regulated had become, by virtue of the magnitude and character of its operations, affected with a public interest. Such a ruling, of course, was a genuine setback for the advocates of laissez faire. But had not the chief justice implied by his public-interest argument that occupations not so affected were immune from such regulation by virtue of the due-process clause? The Court failed to answer this embarrassing question, and speculation as to the ramifications of the decision was justified.

Justice Field wrote a dissenting opinion in which Justice Strong concurred. The dissent rested upon two correlative grounds. First, the business regulated under this statute could not, according to principles of Anglo-American law, be regarded as one which was affected with a public interest.[73] Second, the regulation of this business was unconstitutional because it was a deprivation of property without due process of law.[74] Property, according to Field, was taken from the owner when, against his will, its uses or the prices for its use were prescribed by the state on the pretense of promoting the public good. He argued that title and possession were of little value when the essential attributes of property were destroyed. In a sense, Justice

Field was merely reiterating the views which he had expressed in the *Slaughter-House Cases;* but, significantly, his reasoning was more explicit. The due-process clause, not privileges and immunities, was emphasized. Due process was emerging as the basis for judicial supervision of economic legislation. The majority opinion in the *Munn* case was not subsequently overruled, but the steady crystalization of the concept of substantive due process and the later emergence of the principle of reasonable return eventually sublimated its social and economic implications.[75]

That a change in the Court's interpretation of due process was in the making was further indicated in *Davidson v. New Orleans.*[76] In this case counsel challenged, as violative of due process, legislation under which assessments had been made for the drainage of swamp lands. Justice Miller, speaking for the majority, expressed some impatience with the growing tendency to invoke that clause as a limitation on state legislative powers. He asserted:

It is not a little remarkable, that while this provision has been in the Constitution of the United States, as a restraint upon the authority of the Federal government, for nearly a century, and while, during all that time, the manner in which the powers of government have been exercised has been watched with jealousy, and subjected to the most rigid criticism in all its branches, this special limitation upon its powers has rarely been invoked in the judicial forum or the more enlarged theatre of public discussion. . . . There is here abundant evidence that there exists some strange misconception of the scope of this provision as found in the fourteenth amendment. In fact, it would seem, from the character of many of the cases before us, and the arguments made in them, that the clause under consideration is looked upon as a means of bringing to the test of the decision of this court the abstract opinions of every unsuccessful litigant in a State court of the justice of the decision against him, and of the merits of the legislation on which such a decision may be founded.[77]

But the Court itself suffered from something of the same misconception which its spokesman, Justice Miller, had criticized. In this very case the majority declared that the transfer of property from A to B by legislative act would constitute a deprivation of property without due process of law.[78] The Court thus admitted the applicability of the substantive interpretation of due process in one extreme instance at least. Justice Bradley concurred separately and argued that the Court was entitled to take notice of the "cause and object" of any taking in order to determine if the law satisfied the due process requirement.[79] The majority justices were not yet prepared to go that far, however.

In 1884 the Supreme Court was again called upon to dispose of certain issues concerning the slaughter-house business in New Orleans. Three years before the decision in *Butchers' Union Co. v. Crescent City Co.*[80] the city had granted the appellants, under the terms of the constitution of 1874, the privilege of landing and slaughtering livestock. By granting these privileges the city had apparently violated the terms of the appellee's corporate charter, which vested in the latter exclusive privileges to land and to slaughter livestock within the city. It was alleged that the new grant impaired an obligation of contract and, hence, was void under Article I, section 10, of the federal Constitution. The Court, speaking through Justice Miller, rejected this contention and held that the police power (in pursuance of which the charter had been granted) could not be bartered away by the legislature.[81]

The Court was unanimous in its decision, but four of the justices agreed for reasons other than those given by Justice Miller. Justices Field and Bradley wrote separate opinions in which they reiterated the views expressed in their *Slaughter-House* dissents. Both maintained that the charter of the monopoly was void *ab initio* under the terms of the Fourteenth Amendment. Field again stressed that among the "inalienable" rights was the pursuit of happiness which meant, among other things, the pursuit of lawful callings. Pursuit of the common vocations, thought Field, "is a distinguishing privilege" of United States citizenship.[82] Seeking once again to establish a firm relationship between liberty and property, he quoted from the *Wealth of Nations* the same passage which he had appended to his dissent in the *Slaughter-House Cases* (see p. 37).

Justice Bradley, with whom Harlan and Woods concurred, also emphasized the privileges-and-immunities clause, but he rested part of his reasoning upon the due-process and equal-protection clauses. He said:

> But if it does not abridge the privileges and immunities of a citizen of the United States to prohibit him from pursuing his chosen calling, and giving to others the exclusive right of pursuing it—it certainly does deprive him

(to a certain extent) of his liberty; for it takes from him the freedom of adopting and following the pursuit which he prefers; which, as already intimated, is a material part of the liberty of the citizen. And, if a man's right to his calling is property, as many maintain, then those who had already adopted the prohibited pursuits in New Orleans, were deprived, by the law in question, of their property, as well as their liberty, without due process of law.[83]

The principles set forth in the dissents in the *Slaughter-House Cases* had been reiterated, and—by force of circumstances quite beyond the control of the majority—had acquired additional dignity through their inclusion in concurring opinions.

Before 1885 the federal courts and the state tribunals had pursued reasonably distinct and independent courses in the development of laissez faire constitutionalism. As was previously noticed, the progress of state courts was more rapid than was that of the United States Supreme Court. In the cases decided after the *Slaughter-House Cases* and before 1885 the Court had made some progress, but nothing really spectacular had occurred. Due process was undergoing a slight, but important, transmutation, and the Court was wavering on the threshold of a new era in American constitutional history. It was not to accept unreservedly the new principles, however, until a substantial alteration in its personnel had occurred.[84] On the other hand, by 1884, one state court had expressly accepted the doctrine of liberty of contract,[85] and another had done so implicitly.[86] But in neither case was a statute actually invalidated on this basis. To a large extent the rapid development of laissez faire in the state courts was due to the influence of Cooley, for that writer exercised far greater influence upon those tribunals than upon the United States Supreme Court. In 1885 the results of previous litigation in both the state and federal tribunals were temporarily merged in a crucial case decided by the New York Court of Appeals, *In re Jacobs*.[87] Here for the first time was a synthesis of laissez faire ideas—economic liberty, substantive due process, and the prohibitions against "class legislation" and pretended exercises of the police power. The result of this synthesis was an opinion giving sweeping approval to the tenets of laissez faire.

Years of Decision in the Struggle for
Laissez Faire, 1885–1886

Among the most serious and prevalent evils of
the nineteenth century was the sweating system whereby labor was
exploited under conditions which, even for that time, were substand-
ard. Under this system entire families were employed in the manufacture of scores of products in their homes. In these sweatshops
thousands of indigent workmen and their families gained the barest
livelihood. Wages were unusually low, child labor was common, and
living, as well as working, conditions were miserable. The evils inherent in the system became more serious and evident as urbanization
proceeded. As metropolitan areas became more congested, home
manufacture of certain products directly endangered the public health
and welfare. It was for this reason that the first legislative measures
directed against the sweatshop system were passed. Such a law was
that enacted by the legislature of New York in 1884 for the declared
purpose of improving the public health by "prohibiting the manufacture of cigars and the preparation of tobacco in any form in tenement houses in certain cases." It will be noted that the measure did
not strike at the sweatshop system as such but only at one occupation
when carried on under this system. And even in the attainment of
this objective, the statute was, by any reasonable standard, a modest
enactment, for it prohibited the manufacture of cigars only on the
floors of tenements where those floors were also used as dwellings.
The application of the law was further limited by provisions defin-
ing tenements as buildings in which three or more families were
living, and declaring that only tenements in cities having more than
five hundred thousand inhabitants were within the meaning of the
legislation.

Peter Jacobs was arrested and ordered to stand trial for violation
of the law. A judge of the Supreme Court dismissed the writ of
habeas corpus for which the accused had applied, but the General
Term of the Supreme Court reversed this order. The state then carried the case to the Court of Appeals. The law, in its title, purported
to promote the public health. Its validity was challenged on several
grounds. Of these the contentions that the law arbitrarily deprived

persons of liberty and property and that it had no real relationship to the public health apparently were most pressed by counsel.[88]

The opinion of the court is one of the most extreme judicial statements of laissez faire ever made by an American tribunal; and, perhaps for this reason, *In re Jacobs* acquired in later years a certain preëminence in the world of citation. The opinion embodied a subtle blending of earlier decisions—both state and federal—with economic and sociological propositions, the result being the formulation of a rigid check on legislative power to regulate the economy. After having reviewed the provisions of the statute, Judge Robert Earl, speaking for a unanimous court, turned to the supposed consequences of the legislation: If the cigarmaker carries on his trade in certain tenement houses, he becomes a criminal "for doing that which it is perfectly lawful to do outside the two cities named."[89] (The court had already taken judicial notice of the fact that the law applied only to the cities of New York and Brooklyn.) He must abandon his trade which is the source of his livelihood or procure a room elsewhere or hire himself out "upon such terms as, under the fierce competition of trade and the inexorable laws of supply and demand" he can obtain from his employer.[90] He is denied freedom of choice because he may prefer to work independently and cannot. "In the unceasing struggle for success and existence which pervades all societies of men, he may be deprived of that which will enable him to maintain his hold, and to survive."[91] He may become a criminal through the act of another party if the latter should, by moving into the tenement, bring the cigarmaker's business within the purview of the statute.[92] Summarizing these hypothetical consequences, the court said:

It is, therefore, plain that this law interferes with the profitable and free use of his property by the owner or lessee of a tenement-house who is a cigarmaker, and trammels him in the application of his industry and the disposition of his labor, and thus, in a strictly legitimate sense, it arbitrarily deprives him of his property and some portion of his personal liberty.[93]

Judge Earl added that the constitutional guarantee of property due process could be invaded without a physical taking. According to him, the limitation protected not only title and possession but also the essential attributes of the thing possessed, that is, those attributes which rendered it valuable. The court relied on such cases as *Pumpelly v. Green Bay Co.* and *Wynehamer v. People* in reaching this conclusion.[94]

Having concluded its analysis of property rights, the court proceeded to examine the concept of liberty which was guaranteed by the same clause. Its analysis of liberty became, in later cases, one of its most important contributions to constitutional jurisprudence:

> So, too, one may be deprived of his liberty and his constitutional rights thereto violated without actual imprisonment or restraint of his person. Liberty, in its broad sense as understood in this country, means the right, not only of freedom from actual servitude, imprisonment or restraint, but the right of one to use his faculties in all lawful ways, to live and work where he will, to earn his livelihood in any lawful calling, and to pursue any lawful trade or avocation. All laws, therefore, which impair or trammel these rights, which limit one in the choice of a trade or profession, or confine him to work or live in a specified locality, or exclude him from his own house, or restrain his otherwise lawful movements (except as such laws may be passed in the exercise by the legislature of the police power, which will be noticed later), are infringements upon his fundamental rights of liberty which are under constitutional protection.[95]

In support of this proposition Judge Earl quoted from the concurring opinions of Justices Field and Bradley in *Butchers' Union v. Crescent City Co.,* from Bradley's circuit-court opinion in *Live Stock Ass'n v. Crescent City Co.* and from two New York cases—*Wynehamer v. People* and *Bertholf v. O'Reilly.*[96] All these quotations emphasized the economic interpretation of the constitutional term "liberty."

Judge Earl then directed his attention to the police power, which constituted the alleged justification for the legislation. Although he admitted that the power was very extensive, he pointed out that it was not above the state constitution, seemingly an incontrovertible principle. At this point he quoted from Cooley's *Constitutional Limitations* on the limits of the police power as applied to corporate charters:

> The limit in these cases must be this: the regulations must have reference to the comfort, safety, and welfare of society; they must not be in conflict with any of the provisions of the charter, and they must not, under pretense of regulation, take from the corporations any of the essential rights and privileges which the charter confers. In short, they must be police regulations, in fact, and not amendments of the charter in curtailment of the corporate franchise.[97]

In this case, of course, no corporate rights were involved and the quoted passage was irrelevant to the facts under consideration, but it sufficed for one purpose, that is, to distinguish between real and pretended exercises of the police power. *Watertown v. Mayo* (see pp. 39–40) and Field's dissent in the *Slaughter-House Cases* were also quoted in support of this view.

Having demonstrated that there were implied limits upon the police power, the court had next to discover which agency of government was to enforce these limitations. Judge Earl admitted that "generally it is for the legislature to determine what laws and regulations are needed to protect the public health and secure the public comfort and safety."[98] Legislative discretion, said the court, was not subject to judicial review where its measures were "calculated, intended, convenient, and appropriate to accomplish these ends." But the court added:

> Under the mere guise of police regulations, personal rights and private property cannot be arbitrarily invaded, and the determination of the legislature is not final or conclusive. If it passes an act ostensibly for the public health, and thereby destroys or takes away the property of a citizen, or interferes with his personal liberty, then it is for the courts to scrutinize the act and see whether it really relates to and is convenient and appropriate to promote the public health. It matters not that the legislature may in the title to the act, or in its body, declare that it is intended for the improvement of the public health. Such a declaration does not conclude the courts, and they must yet determine the fact declared and enforce the supreme law.[99]

Among the authorities cited with approval was the *Lake View* case from which was quoted a passage stating that the determination of the subjects of the police power was "clearly a judicial question." (See pp. 40–41.)

The court was prepared to take the final step and to answer the question: Is the statute a genuine exercise of the police power or is it merely an arbitrary enactment under the guise of that power? The court found that the law was in the latter category for a number of reasons. First, it did not deal with tenements as such but with the manufacture of tobacco. Tobacco, said the court, was widely used and its manufacture had never been hindered except for the purpose of raising revenue. Second, the manufacture of tobacco into cigars, so far as the court could ascertain, was not injurious to the health of those engaged therein, and it certainly did not impair the public health. Third, even if it were admitted that the manufacture of cigars injured persons engaged in that business, that would not constitute a ground for regarding the statute as a *public* health measure. Fourth, the law was not intended to protect the health of cigarmakers because they were permitted to continue their trade in any place except certain tenements. Fifth, the law was not intended to protect the health of persons dwelling outside the tenements because cigarmaking was permitted outside the tenements. Sixth, it was not intended to protect the health of tenement dwellers because if three or fewer families dwelt in such a place, the law was inapplicable. Moreover, the fact that the law, in its operation, was confined to only two cities indicated that in making the law the legislature did not have in mind the health of tenement-house occupants.[100]

The logical difficulties in these propositions stemmed from the court's willingness to confound and combine three different things: the intent of the legislature (as revealed by the language of the statute), the nature of the regulated business (as determined by the court), and the consequences which the court supposed would flow from enforcement of the law. The underlying fears which predicated this notorious opinion were candidly summarized by the court in a typical argument *ad horrendum:*

Under the guise of promoting the public health the legislature might as well have banished cigarmaking from all the cities of the State, or confined it to a single city or town, or have placed under a similar ban the trade of a baker, of a tailor, of a shoemaker, of a woodcarver, or of any other of the innocuous trades carried on by artisans in their own homes. The power would have been the same, and its exercise, so far as it concerns fundamental, constitutional rights, could have been justified by the same arguments. Such legislation may invade one class of rights to-day and another to-morrow, and if it can be sanctioned under the Constitution, while far removed in time we will not be far away in practical statesmanship from those ages when governmental prefects supervised the building of houses, the rearing of cattle, the sowing of seed, and the reaping of grain, and governmental ordinances regulated the movements and labor of artisans, the rate of wages, the price of food, the diet and clothing of the people, and a large range of other affairs long since in all civilized lands regarded as outside of governmental functions. Such governmental interferences disturb the normal adjustments of the social fabric, and usually derange the delicate and complicated machinery of industry and cause a score of ills while attempting the removal of one.[101]

The *Jacobs* case is one of the great landmarks in state constitutional history. Here, the most influential of state appellate courts had underwritten the principles of constitutional laissez faire. By combining the principle established in the *Watertown* and *Lake View* cases—that the courts may (in fact, must) distinguish between real and pretended exercises of the police power—with the principles of economic liberty enunciated by Bradley and Field in the *Slaughter-House Cases* and the *Crescent City* case and with the principle of substantive due process as stated in the *Wynehamer* and *Bertholf* cases, the court had made the tenets of laissez faire judicially enforceable safeguards against legislative innovation. The right to pursue a business was subsumed under two sacred guarantees, liberty and property. Moreover, the court served notice that no legislative chicanery might transpire under the guise of police regulations. The court had assumed the function of determining what served the public health and the public comfort. And the court would decide who the public was. Legislative discretion was not entirely destroyed, but the discretion was to be exercised at the pleasure of the court. Laissez faire had gained its most impressive victory.

That the New York Court of Appeals intended to perpetuate the principles of the *Jacobs* case was indicated six months later in *People v. Marx*.[102] In this case that court struck down a statute prohibiting the manufacture of butter substitutes. Here again a unanimous court, speaking through Judge Rapallo, found that the law was an arbitrary invasion of personal liberty under the mask of an exercise of the police power. The court observed that the purpose of the legislation was not to supplement existing provisions on fraud and deception but to prohibit absolutely the manufacture and sale of butter substitutes in order to protect dairy interests. Referring to the *Jacobs* case, the dissents in the *Slaughter-House Cases,* and Bradley's opinion in the circuit court, Judge Rapallo stated that the Fourteenth Amendment and the due-process clause of the state constitution guaranteed economic liberty. He also quoted from the *Bertholf* and *Jacobs* cases and concluded the opinion with a stern warning against the evils of class legislation. The *Marx* case added little to the *Jacobs* case, but it was an addition to the growing list of laissez faire precedents.

The Supreme Court of Illinois soon made it clear that the decisions of the New York tribunal were not to be isolated ones. Indeed, the solicitude of the Illinois court for property rights soon equaled, and perhaps surpassed, that of the New York Court of Appeals. After having acquired the dubious distinction, in 1884, of being the first state tribunal to recognize explicitly the liberty of contract doctrine, that same court was the first to apply this concept as a substantive limitation on legislative power. The case was *Millett v. People,*[103] decided in 1886.

Millett was arrested for failing to comply with a state law requiring the operators of coal mines to have installed track scales for the weighing of coal. The trial court, on a motion of the prosecutor, instructed the jury that contracts between the operators and miners which sought to avoid the weighing of coal should be regarded as invalid. The court refused, on the other hand, to instruct the jury to make a finding of not guilty if it appeared from the evidence that the mining company had contracts with the miners to compute wages at a box rate, rather than by weight. From this ruling counsel for Millett appealed.

A major part of the argument of counsel for the appellant was based upon quotations from and citations to Cooley's *Constitutional Limitations* and other works. The *Limitations* was quoted five times in the brief and Cooley's *Blackstone,* presumably the third edition, was cited once.[104] These quotations and citations were rather closely followed by the court in its unanimous opinion. Judge Scholfield, who wrote the opinion, noted, on the basis of Cooley's authority, that the terms "due process" and "law of the land" were synonymous, and he stated that they meant a "general public law, binding upon all members of the community, under all circumstances."[105] After this observation the judge quoted from the *Limitations* as follows:

> Every one has a right to demand that he be governed by general rules, and a special statute that singles his case out as one to be regulated by a different law from that which is applied in all similar cases, would not be legitimate legislation, but an arbitrary mandate, unrecognized in free government. Mr. Locke has said of those who make the laws: "They are to govern by promulgated, established laws, not to be varied in particular cases, but to have one rule for rich and poor—for the favorite at court and the countryman at plough." And this may justly be said to have become a maxim in the law by which may be tested the authority and binding force of legislative enactments.[106]

In addition, Judge Scholfield quoted Cooley's interdiction against class legislation (see p. 31), and summarized two cases in which such legislation was discussed. He proceeded:

> What is there in the condition or situation of the laborer in the mine to disqualify him from contracting in regard to the price of his labor, or in regard to the mode of ascertaining the price? And why should the owner of the mine, or the agent in control of the mine, not be allowed to contract in respect to matters as to which all other property owners and agents may contract? Undoubtedly, if these sections fall within the police power, they may be maintained on that ground; but it is quite obvious that they do not. Their requirements have no tendency to insure the personal safety of the miner, or to protect his property, or the property of others.[107]

Here again a state court had objected to a law directed against abuses practiced by the employer on the ground that, among other things, it restricted the abstract rights of employees. As for the police power, the court again invoked the distinction between real and pretended exercises of that power, a concept which was rapidly gaining judicial popularity.[108] After considering several other issues, the court concluded that the amendatory act nullifying contracts dispensing with the weighing of coal was unconstitutional.

Less than four months later the Supreme Court of Pennsylvania, speaking through Judge Gordon, delivered its opinion in *Godcharles v. Wigeman*.[109] The case was a rather curious one because neither counsel nor the court cited any of the applicable precedents or authorities which might have been used to dispose of the constitutional issue—the validity of the act of 1881 which prohibited the payment of wages, in merchandise or goods, to workers in mines and factories. It was contended by the attorney for the plaintiff in error that the law was contrary to Article III, section 7, of the state constitution. That provision declared:

> The General Assembly shall not pass any local or special law, regulating labor, trade, mining, or manufacturing, granting to any corporation, or individual, any special or exclusive privilege or immunity.[110]

In their written brief, counsel, after having made the general observation that "the text-books abound with definitions of general or public acts and of special or private acts," contented themselves with several innocuous quotations from Blackstone, Kent, Sedgwick, and Dwarris.[111] The court was even less explicit as to the authorities upon which its reasoning was based. Judge Gordon's entire statement concerning the constitutional issues was:

> The first, second, third, and fourth sections of the Act of June 29th, 1881, are utterly unconstitutional and void, inasmuch as by them an attempt has been made by the legislature to do what, in this country, cannot be done; that is, prevent persons who are *sui juris* from making their own contracts. The Act is an infringement alike of the right of the employer and the employee; more than this, it is an insulting attempt to put the laborer under legislative tutelage, which is not only degrading to his manhood, but subversive of his rights as a citizen of the United States.
> He may sell his labor for what he thinks best, whether money or goods, just as his employer may sell his iron or coal, and any and every law that proposes to prevent him from so doing is an infringement of his constitutional privileges, and consequently vicious and void.[112]

A close reading of the opinion fails to disclose what constitutional provision, if any, the court invoked to invalidate the legislation. Although, as Dr. Twiss suggested, the opinion may have been a paraphrase of the oft-quoted interdiction against class legislation appearing on page 393 of the *Constitutional Limitations,* there is no direct evidence to support this hypothesis.[113] In spite of the court's failure to cite any precedent in support of its sweeping assertions, the case became a leading authority for laissez faire constitutionalism and for the liberty of contract.

The decisions in the *Millett* and *Godcharles* cases, both of which were unanimous, were among the greatest victories registered by conservatives in the age of industrial enterprise. But before the end of the year in which these decisions were delivered, 1886, an even greater contribution to the cause of laissez faire constitutionalism was made.

Tiedeman's Limitations of Police Power and Laissez Faire as a Fully Developed Constitutional Dogma

In November, 1886, Christopher G. Tiedeman, a twenty-nine-year-old professor of law in the University of Missouri, published his *Limitations of Police Power*. This treatise far more clearly sustained and developed laissez faire constitutional principles than did that of Cooley, and it was second only to the work of the latter in the influence it was to exercise on bench and bar.

The early life and background of Tiedeman contrast markedly with Cooley's. He was born in Charleston, South Carolina, in 1857. His parents were prosperous and provided their prodigious son with an excellent education. Tiedeman received both the A.B. and A.M. degrees from the College of Charleston before he reached his nineteenth birthday. In 1877 he went to Germany where he spent nearly two years as a student, first at the University of Göttingen and later at the University of Leipzig. Upon his return to the United States in the autumn of 1878 Tiedeman enrolled in the Columbia Law School from which he received the LL.B. degree after one year of study.

Tiedeman's interests lay in the direction of legal scholarship, and he soon abandoned active practice which he had undertaken first in Charleston and later in St. Louis. In 1881 he joined the faculty of the University of Missouri Law School. He remained on the faculty for ten years, and during this time his reputation grew as a writer on legal subjects. The law school of the University of the City of New York offered him a professorship in 1891 and he accepted the position. Although he was successful as a teacher, his long-time desire to devote himself entirely to research and writing led him to resign six years later. For the next five years he pursued his literary projects, but in 1902 he accepted, with some reluctance, the position of dean in the law school of the University of Buffalo, a post that he held until his death in 1903.

Tiedeman never served as a judge, and as a practicing attorney he made no significant contributions to American law. Rather it was by his teaching and for his writings that he obtained renown. His influence as a teacher may not confidently be assessed, but it is probable that it was considerable, for books written by him on a wide variety of subjects—bills and notes, real property, commercial paper, sales, equity, jurisprudence, and municipal corporations—became standard texts in law schools throughout the country. But two of his treatises are largely responsible for his reputation as a leading writer on legal subjects. These were his *Limitations of Police Power* and a two-volume second edition of that work entitled *State and Federal Control of Persons and Property*.[114] These were works which became almost indispensable references for lawyers and judges in their attacks upon legislative power, and these were the works which admirably reinforced, and supplemented, Cooley's *Constitutional Limitations*.

In the preface to the first of these treatises Tiedeman expressed, with surpassing candor, the purpose of his work as follows:

> The principal object of the present work is to demonstate, by a detailed discussion of the constitutional limitations upon the police power in the United States, that under the written constitutions, Federal and State, democratic absolutism is impossible in this country, as long as the popular reverence for the constitutions, in their restrictions upon governmental activity, is nourished and sustained by a prompt avoidance by the courts of any violations of their provisions, in word or in spirit. The substantial rights of the minority are shown to be free from all lawful control or interference by the majority, except so far as such control or interference may be necessary to prevent injury to others in the enjoyment of their rights. The police power of the government is shown to be confined to the detailed enforcement of the legal maxim, *sic utere tuo, ut alienum non laedas.*
>
> If the author succeeds in any measure in his attempt to awaken the public mind to a full appreciation of the power of constitutional limitations to protect private rights against the radical experimentations of social reformers, he will feel that he has been amply requited for his labors in the cause of social order and personal liberty.[115]

This general bias pervades his whole constitutional philosophy, and undoubtedly it was this characteristic that made the work so valuable from the standpoint of the conservative lawyers and judges.

The underlying hypothesis made by Tiedeman was that the police power was the means whereby the legislature enforced the "fundamental rule of both the human and the natural law"—*sic utere tuo ut alienum non laedas.*[116] If this writer were satisfied that a law or regulation was in pursuance of this maxim, he regarded it as valid; otherwise he insisted upon its unconstitutionality. Like Cooley, Tiedeman rejected the notion that the courts could invalidate legislation because they regarded it as contrary to principles of natural right and of abstract justice.[117] But the force of this idea was almost wholly destroyed by his acceptance, apparently without reservation, of the doctrine of implied limitations on legislative power.[118] Thus, he said that the "unwritten law of the country is in the main against the exercise of the police power."[119]

Aside from his defense of these general propositions, Tiedeman's most influential contribution to constitutional law was made in his chapter entitled "Police Regulations of Trades and Professions." He strongly maintained that everyone had the right to pursue in a lawful manner any lawful calling. Although the state could prescribe reasonable regulations which served the public interest and welfare, its power was not an unlimited, arbitrary one. In discussing these guarantees, Tiedeman, in a rather curious manner, merged the due-process clause with the previously stated implied limitation—that the police power was limited to enforcement of the maxim, *sic utere tuo ut alienum non laedas*. As an abstract proposition this maxim is undoubtedly a sound one. It merely suggests that where the state or outside parties are unaffected by an individual's act, that act is not subject to regulation under the police power. But as an instrument of judicial review its implications are more far-reaching and controversial. The courts, in scrutinizing economic legislation, acquired the function of determining whether a prohibited act affected the public interest directly enough to warrant the legislature's action. Judicial judgment thus came to replace that of the legislature.

That Tiedeman himself was much inclined to restrict legislative discretion and to interpret the maxim strictly was indicated by his discussion of usury laws. He admitted that there could be no constitutional objection to statutes prescribing interest rates where no private contract was affected. He added, however:

But it is different when the legislature undertakes to prescribe what rate of interest the parties to a contract may agree upon. The rate of interest, like the price of merchandise, is determined ordinarily by the relation of supply and demand. *Free trade in money is as much a right as free trade in merchandise.* If the owner of the property in general has a natural right to ask whatever price he can get for his goods, the owner of money may exact whatever rate of interest the borrower may be willing to give. For interest is nothing more than the price asked for the use of money. No public reason can be urged for imposing this restriction upon the money lender, and the utter futility of such laws, in attempting to control the rate of interest, is, or should be, a convincing proof of their unreasonableness.[120]

Although the writer, in the same passage, admitted that such laws had long been acquiesced in, he did not think that that "precludes an inquiry into their constitutionality."[121] The tendency of Tiedeman to interpret strictly any public interest where private contracts were involved is manifest in the above statement. The individual's private acts must bear something more than a remote relationship to the public welfare if they are to be regulated. Thus, the writer distinguished between vice and trades making a business out of vice.[122] Only the latter might be the object of regulation. In discussing the prohibition of liquors, Tiedeman concluded that the prohibition of sale and manufacture, unless applicable only to minors, lunatics, and habitual drunkards or to the operation of drinking saloons, was unconstitutional. Admitting that there was an almost unbroken array of judicial opinions against his view, the writer asserted that "it is the duty of a constitutional jurist to press his views of constitutional law upon the attention of the legal world, even though they place him in opposition to the current of authority."[123]

Perhaps even more surprising to readers of the present day are the doubts which Tiedeman entertained on the constitutionality of laws prohibiting the sale of opium to all persons except qualified physicians and those having prescriptions for its purchase. Although the writer readily admitted that certain classes—and those mentioned by him closely corresponded to those lacking common-law capacities— could be denied the right of purchase, a legislative prohibition of this right to normal adults "would seem to be taking away the free will of those who are under the law confessedly capable of taking care of themselves."[124] This willingness on Tiedeman's part to oppose the current of authority and to insist upon his concept of public interest led him into extreme positions which the courts were unwilling to accept, but it also enhanced the creativeness and influence of his work in general.

Free trade, competition, and laissez faire were clearly the economic foundations of Tiedeman's constitutionalism. Even the protective tariff was condemned as unconstitutional by this writer.[125] Much of the force and prestige of his work undoubtedly derived from its logical consistency and rigor. When other authorities were lacking on a given proposition of laissez faire or when they were hostile to that proposition, the bench and bar might confidently refer to the works of Tiedeman for support. It was in this respect that he made his most notable contribution. Although Cooley may have anticipated the rise of laissez faire constitutionalism, Tiedeman most surely deserves credit for its crystallization into a fixed and pervading dogma.

With the publication of the *Limitations of Police Power,* the creative period of laissez faire constitutionalism in the states drew to a close. After 1886 the courts had at their disposal not only the works of Cooley and Tiedeman but also an impressive array of case law which might be applied as new cases arose. For the next twenty years laissez faire principles enjoyed unprecedented success. Moreover, during this period the United States Supreme Court gradually came to accept the principles of economic freedom and liberty of contract which the state courts were then applying.

The following chapter summarizes state applications of the liberty of contract in cases involving various kinds of legislation and analyzes developments in the federal courts.

3

Liberty of Contract: Application by State Tribunals and Acceptance by the Supreme Court of the United States

THE STATE COURTS exhibited great enthusiasm for the doctrines of laissez faire in the two decades following the decisions in the *Godcharles* and *Millett* cases and the publication of Tiedeman's *Limitations of Police Power*. A few courts, notably those of Rhode Island and Tennessee, held back; but, in general, state tribunals pursued the course previously laid out by the New York, Pennsylvania, and Illinois judiciaries. During this period the text writers, Cooley and Tiedeman, acquired tremendous prestige, and their works were widely quoted by lawyers and judges.

The Supreme Court of the United States continued to resist the new tendencies, but that resistance was enfeebled by a number of factors. Changes in personnel occurred. Pressures emanated from the state courts, from the bar, and from industrial property interests, generally. As a result, the Court eventually abandoned its attitude of self-restraint.

It is significant that the vast majority of statutes which the state courts struck down as contrary to the freedom of contract dealt with certain aspects of employer-employee relations.[1] Not only were relatively advanced kinds of legislation such as maximum-hours laws invalidated, but also declared void were such modest enactments as

[1] For notes to chap 3, see pp. 183–189.

those prohibiting the screening of coal before weighing, requiring the weekly payment of wages, and forbidding the maintenance of truck stores in company towns. These were the laws which, from the judicial viewpoint, infringed upon the liberty and equality of both the employer and the employee. They were the laws which, according to the judges, were enacted not in pursuance of the police power but under the mere guise of that power. And they were the laws which, upon the authority of Cooley, were said to be a species of class legislation prohibited in all constitutional governments. Such statutes stimulated cries of "paternalism" and "socialism," epithets which the judges frequently and uncritically repeated in their opinions.

The three sections which follow in this chapter analyze state judicial opinions in which the right to contract was the principal consideraiton. These opinions differ considerably in detail, but in all of them the liberty of contract principle emerges under one constitutional guise or another. In some of these cases the right to contract was derived from due process of law, in others from privileges and immunities, and in a few no specific constitutional provision at all was mentioned. The cases which are discussed were selected to serve three purposes: (1) to demonstrate something of the influence of Cooley and Tiedeman in cases involving the liberty of contract, (2) to indicate, in a general way, the spread of laissez faire principles into various state jurisdictions, and (3) to show what kinds of legislation were struck down as violative of the liberty of contract. This last purpose has dictated the general method of organization. Virtually all liberty of contract cases involved one of the following kinds of statutes: (a) those regulating the media and time of wage payments and the mode of computing wages, (b) those prohibiting discrimination by employers against union labor, and (c) those prescribing maximum hours of labor in certain occupations.

Laws Regulating the Media and Time of Wage Payments and the Methods of Computing Wages

It has already been noted (pp. 57–58) that one of the first liberty of contract cases, *Godcharles v. Wigeman,* resulted in a decision invalidating a Pennsylvania statute which prohibited the payment of wages in merchandise. Three years later, in 1889, the Court of Appeals of West Virginia struck down similar legislation in *State v. Goodwill*.[2] The statute involved in that case required those persons engaged in mining and manufacturing enterprises to pay their employees in lawful money of the United States or in paper redeemable at face value in that money.

Judge Snyder, the president of the court, delivered its unanimous opinion. Taking notice of the fact that the statute applied only to the manufacturing and the mining occupations, he observed that it did not cover wholesale merchants and railroad companies. The propriety or necessity of making the law applicable to these latter was "equally as great, if not greater" than it was to the former.[3] The rights of some employers were abridged while the rights of others in the employer class remained unimpaired. Citing Field's concurrence in the *Butchers' Union* case and Bradley's opinion in the *Live Stock Association* case, Snyder emphasized not due process of law but the privileges-and-immunities clause of the Fourteenth Amendment and the inherent-rights provision of the state constitution.

He then directed his attention to the evils of class legislation, the kind which violated the principle that "the rights of every individual must stand or fall by the same rule of law that governs every other member of the body politic under similar circumstances."[4] But it was not solely the partial character of the legislation which troubled the court. Judge Snyder, after analyzing in a general way the right of property, incorporated without citation into the court's opinion Adam Smith's statement that the right to work was derivable from the right to acquire and maintain property. And he added that this right to pursue a calling (along with those incidental rights arising therefrom) "constitutes the difference between freedom and slavery."[5] This, he said, was a principle which the Supreme Court of the United States had recognized in *Yick Wo v. Hopkins,*[6] the *Slaughter-House Cases,* and *Butchers' Union v. Crescent City Co.*

The laissez faire economic prejudices which the judges entertained were rather clearly enunciated in the following comment:

No one questions the position that, unless the government intervened to protect property and regulate trade, property would cease to exist, and trade would exist only as an engine of fraud; *but this does not authorize the government to do for its people what they can best do for themselves. The natural law of supply and demand is the best law of trade.*[7]

In keeping with this laissez faire position, the court emphasized that relations between the employer and the employee were especially free from legislative supervision. Referring to the *Munn* case (upon which the state's attorney had relied in his argument), Judge Snyder declared:

> But we are aware of no well-considered case in which a statute has been upheld which undertook to regulate the dealings between employer and employee, even in this class of occupations much less in cases that are not impressed with a public trust or duty.[8]

The court had not yet disposed of the argument that the law was an exercise of the police power. In that the previous discussion of liberty and property virtually answered this question, this feat did not prove difficult. The already familiar recitation that the police power was very broad and incapable of precise definition was followed by the equally familiar truism that the power was not above the constitution—a proposition abundantly supported by citations to Cooley, the *Jacobs* case, and *Mugler v. Kansas.*[9] As usual, the court paid its respects to legislative discretion, but it added that the judiciary had the duty of determining whether or not an act impairing the liberty and property rights of a citizen was a reasonable exercise of governmental power. It reviewed the *Godcharles* and *Millett* cases and concluded that the law was a "species of sumptuary legislation which has been universally condemned, as an attempt to degrade the intelligence, virtue, and manhood of the American laborer, and foist upon the people a paternal government of the most objectionable character, because it assumes that the employer is a knave, and the laborer an imbecile."[10] Such was the view taken by the highest tribunal of an American state with regard to an innocuous statute requiring that wages be paid in legal money of the United States or its equivalent. But on the same day that tribunal carried laissez faire principles even further.

The legislature of West Virginia had enacted a statute which forbade mining and manufacturing companies to sell their products at a higher rate of profit to their employees than was customarily realized on sales to other persons. The Supreme Court of Appeals reviewed this statute in *State v. Fire Creek Coal and Coke Co.*,[11] decided the same day that the court's opinion in the *Goodwill* case was delivered. The law was condemned by the court as a kind of class legislation, and primary reliance was placed upon the precedent established in *State v. Goodwill.*

The opinion in the *Fire Creek* case contains a number of laissez faire propositions. Thus, we are told that there are "many considerations for selling goods or supplies at less per cent of profit to one customer than to others," and the judges mentioned the character and promptness of the purchaser, the risk of loss, the time of payment, and the aggregate amount of purchases as considerations which could justifiably affect the per cent of profit which should accompany a particular sale.[12] The court stated:

> The statute is a Procrustean bed. . . . It excludes all freedom of trade. . . . It is an attempt to do for private citizens, under no physical or mental disabilities, what they can best do for themselves.[13]

The judges declared that they did not wish to give countenance to the idea that employers had the right to discriminate against employees when selling goods to them, and they added that no employee should buy his employer's products under such circumstances. The court had failed to grasp (or at least to mention) the obvious purpose of the legislation—to relieve the employee from discriminatory practices in which economic necessity forced him to acquiesce. Judge Snyder, who wrote the court's opinion in this case also, concluded that the law was an unjust and unreasonable interference with the rights of the employer and of the employee and that it placed upon both the "badge of slavery."[14]

Laissez faire principles were influential in many other state jurisdictions. In 1891 the Supreme Judicial Court of Massachusetts, a tribunal which had been noted for considerable caution in its exercise of the power of judicial review, indicated that it was not immune to the new ideological current. The case of *Commonwealth v. Perry*[15] involved the validity of a statute which forbade the owners and operators of textile mills to levy fines upon their employees and to withhold wages for imperfect workmanship. The court, over a vigorous dissent by Judge Holmes, held that the law was void, although the judges agreed that the statute might have been a valid exercise of the police power had it not abridged the freedom of contract. Judge Knowlton, speaking for the majority, invoked that clause in Article

I of the Massachusetts Declaration of Rights which guaranteed the inalienable right of "acquiring, possessing, and protecting property." From this right he derived the liberty to make contracts, and he cited the *Godcharles, Goodwill, Jacobs, Marx,* and *Millett* cases to support this view. In these cases, however, the right to contract had been associated more with "liberty" than with "property"; and the opinion in the *Perry* case represented something of an innovation: the liberty of contract had been based solely upon the right to acquire, possess, and protect property.

The Supreme Court of Illinois, in *Frorer v. People,*[16] gave additional evidence that it had not relinquished the preëminence it shared with the New York Court of Appeals as a bastion of laissez faire. The state legislature had enacted a measure which prohibited the owners and operators of mining and manufacturing enterprises to maintain truck stores for the purpose of supplying goods to their employees. Although this legislation differed in form from that invalidated in the *Godcharles* and *Goodwill* cases, its purpose was substantially the same. The company store was one of several devices whereby the individual workman was exploited by his employer. The law was designed to abolish these establishments and thereby to guarantee the laborer that his wages would be payable in lawful money.

The court found that the statute was objectionable for two reasons: (1) it violated the liberty of contract, and (2) it was partial in its operation. The judges admitted that the mining and manufacturing businesses, for some purposes, were subject to special laws applicable to them alone. But that was true only where laws regulated matters which differentiated those industries from all others. The court pointed out that truck stores could be, and were, operated in connection with any number of enterprises and that, consequently, the legislature could not single out the mining and manufacturing businesses and prohibit them from maintaining such establishments. The judges derived the right to make contracts from both liberty and property; and, as counsel for the operator had done, they quoted part of Cooley's much-used admonition against class legislation, appearing on page 393 of the *Limitations.*[17] Reverting to the question whether or not the law was class legislation, they observed that under exceptional circumstances a statute might affect some person or class of persons separately, but on the basis of another passage from page 393 of Cooley's work, they concluded that "distinctions in these respects should be based upon some reason which renders them important, like the want of capacity in infants and insane persons."[18] The court had almost, but not quite, made the common-law incapacities the criterion whereby the constitutionality of statutory classification was to be determined. Toward the end of the court's opinion the judges revealed their impatience with legislation which they regarded as favoring some particular class. They said:

> Those who are entitled to exercise the elective franchise are deemed equals before the law, and it is not admissible to arbitrarily brand, by statute, one class of them, without reference to and wholly irrespective of their actual good or bad behavior, as too unscrupulous, and the other class as too imbecile or timid and weak, to exercise that freedom in contracting which is allowed to all others.[19]

The tendency to regard the franchise as a magical wand whereby was conferred upon everyone economic as well as political equality was by no means peculiar to this case alone. It pervaded a large number of opinions, including those of the Supreme Court of the United States.[20]

Even in the 1890's, when laissez faire was at its zenith, corporate-property interests were not invariably upheld by the courts. There were cases in which the judiciary took a rather liberal view of economic legislation, but they were exceptional. The Court of Appeals of West Virginia adopted a more realistic attitude toward governmental regulation of the economy in *State v. Peel Splint Coal Co.*[21] than it had evidenced in either the *Goodwill* or the *Fire Creek* cases. The decision in this case was rendered by Judge Lucas in 1892. During the previous year the legislature had enacted two laws which regulated, in some measure, relations between the employer and the employee. The first required that coal be weighed before screening and the second prohibited the use of scrip (which was not made redeemable in lawful currency) to pay employees their wages. The outcome of the case turned on the constitutionality of these laws as applicable to corporations. Citing Tiedeman's *Limitations,* Judge Lucas declared that abstract principles of justice and of natural right could not be invoked by the courts to invalidate legislation.[22] He noted also that the bestowal of special privileges generally justified the imposition of special burdens, and he quoted Tiedeman on behalf of this proposition.[23] Corporations, said the court, were recipients of special privileges. Consequently, they were subject to special burdens. The court added, however, that it founded its conclusions not so much upon the idea that the business was affected with a public interest as upon still higher grounds—"that the public tranquility and the good and safety of society demand, where the number of employees is such that specific contracts with each laborer would be improbable, if not impossible, that in general contracts justice shall prevail as between operator and miner."[24] The court observed that the state frequently intervened on behalf of propertied interests to suppress strikes and labor conspiracies, and it added:

It is a fact worthy of consideration, and one of such historical notoriety that the court may recognize it judicially, that every disturbance of the peace of any magnitude in this State since the civil war has been evolved from the disturbed relations between powerful corporations and their servants or employees. . . . Collisions between the capitalist and the workingmen endanger the safety of the State, stay the wheels of commerce, discourage manufacturing enterprise, destroy public confidence, and at times throw an idle population upon the bosom of the community. Surely the hands of the legislature cannot be so restricted as to prohibit the passage of laws directly intended to prevent and forestall such collisions.[25]

The court made clear that its decision did not overrule the principle of the *Goodwill* case. Nevertheless, this decision was one of the few, since that delivered in the *Shaffer* case, to hold that corporations were of such a character that the police power might be invoked to regulate their right of contract. The *Shaffer* opinion, however, rested upon a somewhat narrower foundation—the reserved authority of the legislature to repeal and amend corporate charters—than did the opinion in the *Peel Splint* case. Both may be regarded as constituting the fountainhead of a new line of judicial decisions wherein the right of corporations to contract was regarded as subject to legislative restrictions.[26] Unfortunately the authority of the *Peel Splint* decision was partially undermined only a short time after the opinion had been delivered.

For reasons which are not made clear the Court of Appeals ordered a reargument of the case. Its first decision had been unanimous, but after the rehearing the court was evenly divided and the statutes involved were sustained only by virtue of this equal division. The opinions rendered by Judges Lucas and Holt in favor of upholding the validity of the legislation added little, if anything, to the original opinion of the court. But the vigorous dissenting opinion of Judge English was profuse with laissez faire propositions. In this opinion primary reliance was placed upon Cooley's *Constitutional Limitations* and Tiedeman's *Limitations of Police Power,* although a large amount of then recent case law favorable to the liberty of contract was also utilized.

Judge English began his dissenting opinion by virtually identifying corporations with natural persons. He was unable to discover any difference between the rights of either to make contracts. Cooley was quoted on the scope of the police power as exercisable with respect to corporations and on the limitations imposed upon such exercise.[27] Fixing his attention upon the due-process clause of the state constitution and the first section of the Fourteenth Amendment, Judge English asserted that the statute could be reconciled with neither. Unmined coal was the property of the mine owner, and the screening system, which the law sought to abolish, was a means whereby the value of mined coal might be ascertained and credited to the miner. He declared that the abolition of the screening system would penalize the experienced miner and would benefit the novice. Moreover, the wage level would be depressed.[28] Here again appeared the judicial practice of examining, according to the principles of the classical economists, the economic ramifications of a law and of relating these supposed ramifications to the more relevant issue of the law's constitutionality. Judge English asserted that there was no substantial difference between corporations engaged in the mining of coal and natural persons pursuing the same business. To prove that the police power was no more applicable to corporations than to natural persons, he quoted a passage from Tiedeman's work.[29] The law operated, said the judge, as a confiscation of property, which, as Tiedeman had said, a pretended exercise of the police power could never justify. The position taken by Judge English was more in keeping with judicial attitudes prevailing at that time than was the majority opinion. In later cases the court's decision was severely criticized, but it presaged the eventual decline of laissez faire principles, at least so far as they were guarantees of corporate privileges.

The Supreme Court of Missouri accepted the liberty of contract limitation on the police power in 1893 in another of the so-called scrip law cases. In *State v. Loomis*[30] a statute of this kind was alleged to be a violation both of the natural-rights and due-process clauses of the state constitution and of the equal-protection and due-process provisions of the Fourteenth Amendment. Applicable only to mining and manufacturing firms, the law was alleged to be a type of class legislation. In the course of its opinion the court accepted this argument and invalidated the law. The judges declared that due process was a prohibition against partial, arbitrary, and unequal laws and that the right to contract was secured by this provision. Classification for legislative purposes was constitutional provided that it rested upon some reasonable basis. Cooley's much-used statement on class legislation was quoted with approval in support of these propositions.[31] Following closely the reasoning of the West Virginia Court of Appeals in the *Goodwill* case, the Missouri court asserted that the law, being applicable only to manufacturing and mining firms, but not to agriculture and to the building and mercantile trades, discriminated against both the owners and the employees of the affected businesses. It denied to the former class the right to contract for labor payable in goods just as it denied to the latter, "though of full age" and competency, the right to sell labor "for meat and clothing as others may."[32] Although abuses by mine owners and manufacturers could be discovered, other groups were also guilty; and legislation could not legitimately single out such occupations for regulation of the kind contemplated here. Said the court:

[These sections of the statute] attempt to strike down one of the fundamental principles of constitutional government. If they can stand, it is difficult to see an end to such legislation, and the government becomes one of special privileges, instead of a compact "to promote the general welfare of the people." We place our conclusion on the broad ground that these sections of the statute are not "due process of law" within the meaning of the constitution.[33]

After reviewing the decisions in earlier cases where liberty of contract was sustained the court concluded its opinion with a rather startling observation: "The many adjudications upholding police regulations need not be noticed, for it cannot be claimed that the law in question is of that character."[34] This seemed to carry the court

to the ultimate of unreason. The legislature itself—a supposedly
coördinate branch of the state government—had, by passing the law,
claimed that it was a police regulation. But the court had insisted
that the provisions of the statute were so great an impairment of
liberty and property rights that no such claim could be made. In
earlier cases the judiciary had at least shown sufficient deference to
legislative judgment to apply the distinction between real and pretended exercises of the police power. Moreover, previous cases had
revealed some inclination on the part of the courts to accept limitations upon the right to contract provided that those limitations
flowed from valid exercises of legislative power. The opinion in the
Loomis case disclosed a change of emphasis. Having determined that
freedom of contract was restricted, the judges in effect refused to
consider the validity of that restriction. But even this case is not
illustrative of the extremes to which the courts went in their protection of the economic privileges and power which corporations
wielded. To the Supreme Court of Illinois must be accorded the
distinction of having delivered the opinion in which corporate rights
received their greatest latitude.

The legislature of Illinois was apparently undaunted by the unbroken line of laissez faire decisions delivered by the state supreme
court, for it enacted a law requiring corporations engaged in specified
businesses to pay their employees weekly. The validity of this legislation was challenged, and in the case of *Braceville Coal Co. v.
People*,[35] the court reviewed the law. Judge Shope, for a unanimous
court, invoked the due-process clause of the state constitution, a
provision which he interpreted as requiring that laws be general
and public in character and operation. Otherwise, he said, liberty
itself would cease to exist. After interpreting "liberty" in accordance
with the precepts of laissez faire, he associated liberty with property
by observing that labor was the source of all property. Therefore, the
right to work (economic liberty) was a part of the property right.
Judge Shope regarded the law as a type of class legislation and used
the frequently cited passage from page 393 of Cooley's *Constitutional Limitations;* and he referred to the same work at page 391
where Cooley had discussed some of the legitimate grounds for enacting laws which applied to only one class of persons.[36] After men-
tioning several liberty of contract cases, Judge Shope had only to

illustrate the discriminatory aspect of the legislation before him. He did so by enumerating some of the corporate enterprises not covered by the statute. Not only were the corporations to which the statute applied injuriously affected by the weekly payment law but the liberty of their employees was impaired also. The suggestion that the law constituted an amendment to corporate charters as contemplated under the reservation clause of the state constitution was unacceptable to the court because the constitution provided for the organization of corporations by general laws, a provision which the judges interpreted as prohibitive of any amendments except those made generally applicable to all corporations similarly situated. In conclusion the court declared:

> We need not extend this opinion by further discussion. The right to contract necessarily includes the right to fix the price at which labor will be performed and the mode and time of payment. Each is an essential element of the right to contract, and whosoever is restricted in either as the same is enjoyed by the community at large, is deprived of liberty and property.[87]

It is quite remarkable that a tribunal of justice could conclude, as here was done, that a law prescribing the frequency of wage payments was an invasion of any substantial property right. From a practical viewpoint what property right was impaired? Certainly not that of the corporations. They were merely required to pay their employees with stated regularity. Much less could the statute be termed an infringement of any property right belonging to the workers. It merely attempted to guarantee to that group that their property (in the form of wages already earned) be transmitted to them without unnecessary delay. Freedom of contract was responsible for this evident perversion of judicial realism—a perversion which but few courts and few judges were able and willing to avoid.

Most cases involving application of the liberty of contract arose in industrial states where serious economic and social conditions moved the legislatures to take action. But the courts of states in which there was very little industrialization had occasional opportunities to review economic legislation. These courts also displayed remarkable solicitude for laissez faire ideas. The Supreme Court of Kansas subscribed to the doctrines of laissez faire in *State v. Haun;*[38] and, in doing so, that tribunal grounded much of its argument upon citations to the works of the publicists, Cooley and Tiedeman. This case involved the constitutionality of a state law requiring the payment of wages in lawful money or in paper redeemable at face value. In its opinion the court quoted Cooley on the individual's right to be governed by general laws and on the invalidity of class legislation.[39] A passage from Tiedeman's *Limitations of Police Power* was inserted in the opinion to prove the unconstitutionality of laws which regulated the terms of hiring in private businesses.[40]

As has already been indicated in the footnotes, numerous other cases involving similar state statutes prescribing certain methods by which wages were to be computed and paid came before state tribunals in the period between 1886 and 1910. In most instances—not in all—these laws were invalidated because they impaired the freedom of contract. The relatively innocuous character of these measures apparently led a few courts to accept them, although these courts, in doing so, generally protested their allegiance to the principles of laissez faire. It was in the so-called yellow-dog contract cases—cases involving statutes which more directly challenged the established order and the power of corporations—that the courts displayed their greatest solicitude for laissez faire.

Statutes Prohibiting Discrimination Against Union Labor

Few types of legislation reflect the novel problems created by industrialization better than those which prohibited discrimination by employers against members of labor unions, and which proscribed and nullified the yellow-dog contracts. At the same time the judicial opinions in which these statutes were considered are among the foremost examples of laissez faire constitutionalism. Moreover, they illustrate the increasingly unrealistic attitude of the judges toward problems which industrialization had fostered. Legal abstractions such as the liberty of contract had given judicial philosophy a fictional foundation. Most judges dwelt in a world of their own.

The influence of Cooley and Tiedeman was most pronounced in these cases. Thus, in *State v. Julow*,[41] the Supreme Court of Missouri, which had already accepted the principles of laissez faire constitutionalism in the *Loomis* case, struck down a law which prohibited such contracts. Cooley's concepts of substantive due process and of class legislation contributed materially to this result.

The Supreme Court of Illinois also had occasion to consider legislation of this kind. The case of *Gillespie v. People*[42] involved a state law which prohibited employers from discharging their employees because of membership in trade unions. The court, true to past form, declared the law unconstitutional on the ground that it impaired the liberty of contract. And again freedom of contract was blended with Cooley's interdiction against partial and special laws in the court's opinion.

The most fully considered case which concerned the constitutionality of such laws was *State ex rel. Zillmer v. Kreutzberg*,[43] decided by the Supreme Court of Wisconsin. The statute which was challenged in that case closely resembled that struck down in *Gillespie v. People,* and the opinions in both cases were based upon much the same reasoning. The Wisconsin court quoted from and cited Cooley's works four times and referred to Tiedeman's *State and Federal Control of Persons and Property* seven times. Both Cooley's and Tiedeman's treatises were cited on behalf of the proposition that the property right encompassed all those rights which gave to the tangible object its value, including the right of making contracts with reference thereto.[44] And both writers were quoted to support the alleged right of the individual to accept or to refuse business relations with others.[45] Tiedeman was quoted, and his work cited, on the right of the employer to make contracts and to discriminate against union labor in doing so, and he was also quoted on the general limits of the police power.[46] Although a rather complete review of the case law was included in the opinion, the court had placed primary emphasis upon the text writers in reaching the conclusion that the law was invalid.

Similar evidence of the commanding influence of Cooley and Tiedeman in the state tribunals appears in *Coffeyville Vitrified Brick Co. v. Perry.*[47] In this case the Supreme Court of Kansas held void a statute endowing employees discharged from work because of their affiliation with labor unions with the right to obtain punitive damages by civil action against their former employers. Cooley and Tiedeman were quoted on the individual's right to accept and to refuse business relations with other parties;[48] and these quotations appear to have contributed more to the court's decision than did the case law which the court also utilized.

Thus, the courts refused to accept the fact that industrialization had wrought a change in employer-employee relations. Despite the rise of corporations and of trusts and monopolies, the liberty of the individual workman to contract was considered equal to that of his corporate employers. Perhaps in a legal and purely abstract sense it was; but, if so, the legal right had no roots in economic and social reality. Legislative efforts to encourage unionization and to equalize in fact through law the bargaining positions of the employee vis-à-vis his employer met with universal judicial condemnation. Here again liberty of contract had perverted judicial realism.

Maximum-Hours Laws

During the latter part of the nineteenth century, labor organizations emphasized three objectives, much as they do today—objectives which ran contrary to the immediate interests of the entrepreneur. First, they demanded the right to bargain collectively. A number of legislatures sought to meet this demand, at least partially, by prohibiting yellow-dog contracts and discrimination by employers against union labor. But these efforts were generally frustrated by hostile action emanating from the courts. Second, the unions demanded wage increases for workers. The legislatures were not so willing to comply with this demand, and progress along this line was generally made on the economic rather than on the political front. Even here, however, the courts by use of the injunction to restrain workmen and their leaders, frequently made effective economic pressure impossible. Third, labor unions demanded a reduction in working hours. Some state legislatures responded to this demand and enacted statutes which limited the hours of labor in certain occupations or for certain classes of persons.

Maximum-hours laws varied considerably in content and purpose. Some applied to child labor only, others to the labor of adult women, and a few to adults generally. But where child-labor laws were applicable to almost all kinds of business (except agriculture), those affecting adult women and adults in general were usually applicable only to those occupations regarded as especially deleterious to the health of those persons engaged therein. Maximum-hours legislation was also made applicable to certain occupations where the safety of the public, as distinguished from the safety of the individual worker, was endangered by excessively long working days. Thus, in a number of states, laws were passed which forbade transportation companies to keep motormen, gripmen, and conductors at work for more than eight or ten hours daily. These "public safety" measures generally received judicial approval as did those laws which regulated child labor. But the attitude of the courts toward maximum-hours laws for adult women was less predictable; and some statutes of this kind were invalidated. Where such legislation applied to adults in general, its fate, at the hands of the judges, was in even greater doubt. Liberty of contract was the principal constitutional concept which the judges considered when cases involving such laws came before them.

In 1890 the Supreme Court of California struck down an ordinance of the city of Los Angeles which prohibited private contractors working on municipal projects from contracting with their employees for more than eight hours of work each per day. The *per curiam* opinion, delivered in *Ex parte Kuback*,[49] was very brief, and liberty of contract was the only constitutional principle discussed. The brief of petitioner's counsel is interesting for the reliance placed upon citations to Cooley's work.

In attacking the ordinance, the petitioner stated four alternative grounds for invalidation: (1) the city council possessed no authority to pass the ordinance;[50] (2) the ordinance was void because it conflicted with general state laws;[51] (3) the ordinance was void because it conflicted with those provisions of the state constitution requiring that all laws of a general nature shall have a uniform operation and guaranteeing to the individual the rights of life, liberty, and property;[52] and (4) the ordinance conflicted with the privileges-and-immunities clauses of the Fourteenth Amendment and Article 4 of the Constitution of the United States. Counsel for petitioner cited appropriate passages in the *Constitutional Limitations* as authority for the first three propositions and concluded the brief with a quotation from that work. It was around this quotation that the court spun its opinion declaring the ordinance invalid:

The general rule undoubtedly is, that any person is at liberty to pursue any lawful calling, and to do so in his own way, not encroaching upon the rights of others. This general right cannot be taken away. It is not competent, therefore, to forbid any person or class of persons, whether citizens or resident aliens, offering their services in lawful business, or to subject others to penalties for employing them. But here, as elsewhere, it is proper to recognize distinctions that exist in the nature of things, and under some circumstances to inhibit employments to some one class by leaving them open to others. Some employments, for example, may be admissible for males and improper for females, and regulations in them would be open to no reasonable objection. The same is true of young children, whose employment in mines and manufactories is commonly, and ought always to be, regulated. And some employments in which integrity is of vital importance, it may be proper to treat as privileges merely, and to refuse the license to follow them to any who are not reputable.[53]

The above passage, fairly interpreted, scarcely justified the invalidation of the law. Actually, the court had, in its decision, gone well beyond the requirements of laissez faire orthodoxy and had stripped a governmental subdivision of part of its control over its employees. The ordinance might readily have been sustained had the court but assumed that it merely became a part of those contracts negotiated between the city and private companies. But the court refused to allow such an assumption; and, as a result, the city was accorded considerably less freedom in the making of contracts than was extended to private corporations and to individuals. Despite the abstract and practical difficulties evident in the *Kuback* opinion, it received widespread approval from other courts.[54] The decision did not augur well for the fate of legislation which prescribed the maximum hours of employment in private businesses. The case is interesting for another reason also. The court, in its opinion, failed to mention any specific constitutional provision in arriving at its decision. Could it otherwise have so cogently emphasized the assimilation of laissez faire, in general, and of liberty of contract, in particular, into the fabric of American constitutional law?

The first laissez faire opinion in which the judges passed on the constitutionality of maximum-hours legislation applicable to private employments was delivered in *Low v. Rees Printing Co.*[55] Decided by the Supreme Court of Nebraska in 1894, the case turned largely on the question whether or not the law was partial, that is, whether or not it was a kind of class legislation. Judge Ryan, speaking for a unanimous court, asserted:

For some reason, not necessary to consider, there has in modern times arisen a sentiment favorable to paternalism in matters of legislation. The outgrowth of this sentiment has been legislation for the regulation of the media of payment; the manner in which products shall be measured or weighed when compensation depends upon measure or weight; the hours of labor, and other kindred subjects. In each instance the statutory provision is necessarily a restriction of the right to regulate relations and duties by contract.[56]

This statement, by assumption, rejected the very grounds upon which any defense of the law as a legitimate police regulation had to rest. The reader is told, in effect, that it was not necessary to consider the reason for the new trend toward regulatory legislation. The net result, of course, was self-imposed judicial blindness to the economic and social changes wrought by industrialization.

The court's insensitiveness to the special problems of the industrial classes was further illustrated by its discussion of class legislation. The statute's exemption of farm and domestic labor from its provisions undermined, so far as the court was concerned, the validity of the argument "made in favor of the necessity that each day the excess over eight hours should be devoted to rest, recreation, and mental improvement,"[57] because, said the court, those persons not covered by the law generally worked longer hours than those to whom the law applied. In support of its general position the court relied upon a number of cases and quoted Cooley's well-known interdiction against class legislation.[58] The court made no new contribution to constitutional jurisprudence, but its opinion is significant because prevailing laissez faire principles were unhesitatingly applied to a new type of economic legislation.

The most far-reaching ramifications of the *Kuback* and *Low* cases materialized in *Ritchie v. People*,[59] a case in which the Supreme Court of Illinois struck down a law prohibiting the employment of women for more than eight hours daily in factories making wearing apparel. The brief filed by counsel for the plaintiff in error was replete with citations to the works of Cooley and Tiedeman and with references to the imposing amount of recently developed case law which served the cause of laissez faire.[60] In his opinion, Judge Magruder, who spoke for a unanimous court, placed more emphasis upon the case precedents and upon a passage from Tiedeman's work than upon the *Constitutional Limitations*. Perhaps this relative slight of Cooley can be attributed to a rather cogent remark made in the brief filed by the state's attorney. Referring to the previous liberty of contract decisions rendered by the Illinois tribunal, counsel for the people said:

> As in all these cases the decisions are largely based upon quotations from Judge Cooley's *Constitutional Limitations,* and as Judge Cooley says on page 745 of his *Constitutional Limitations* (already quoted herein), that "some employments for example may be admissible for males and improper for females, and regulations recognizing the impropriety and forbidding women to engage in them would be open to no reasonable objection"—it can hardly be possible that either Judge Cooley or the decisions of this court in those cases, are intended to be in conflict with our position in this argument. Indeed, Judge Cooley lays down the very rule we contend for himself.[61]

The fact that the court's principal authority for its earlier decisions had been rather cleverly turned against the cause of laissez faire was not to affect the outcome of the case, but it may have caused the court to search out other authorities for its decision. In his opinion Judge Magruder first showed that the statute was an abridgement of both the employer's and the employee's right to contract. This right, he asserted, was derived from the rights of liberty and property. It could be abridged only by due process of law. Although he was not "unmindful" that the right to contract was subject to limitations, he emphasized that these limitations must rest upon a reasonable basis. (It was not until 1910, however, that the Illinois court discovered a reasonable limitation upon this right.)[62] Judge Magruder held that the law was partial in its operation and void for that reason also. The act applied only to certain manufacturers; but, according to the court, even if it applied to manufacturers generally there would be no valid reason to exempt those engaged in the mercantile, the domestic, and the secretarial occupations from its provisions. The judiciary again gave evidence that it was unable to grasp the distinction between labor problems resulting from the factory system and labor problems as they existed in other pursuits—a distinction which was becoming increasingly obvious to the public. But Judge Magruder had yet another argument to hurl against the legislation. Adopting verbatim a statement appearing in Cooley's *Constitutional Limitations* (which he cited but did not quote), he declared that laws must, in order to be valid, not only be impartial but also be in accordance with those "ancient principles which shield private rights from arbitrary interference."[63]

Judge Magruder next turned to the contention that the law was an exercise of the police power. Approving the doctrine that the courts must distinguish between genuine and pretended exercises of the power, he asserted that there was nothing harmful in the manufacture of clothing and that it was not the nature of the things done, but the sex of the persons doing them which was the real basis for the legislation. But women, he said, also had the right to contract. Upon the basis of the *Slaughter-House Cases* he associated this right with the Fourteenth Amendment. Although the court's opinion contained a reference to that passage from Cooley's *Limitations* whereby the state's attorney sought to defend the constitutionality of the law,[64] it was passed by without comment; and the assertion was made that the occupation involved was not in itself harmful and that there was no reason which justified eight hours as the maximum limit for the employment of women in industry. Following a quotation from the *Jacobs* case to the effect that the police power could not be exercised to protect an individual from the consequences of his own acts was this passage from Tiedeman's *Limitations:*

> In so far as the employment of a certain class in a particular occupation may threaten or inflict damage upon the public or third persons, there can be no doubt as to the constitutionality of any statute which prohibits their prosecution of that trade. But it is questionable, except in the case of minors, whether the prohibition can rest upon the claim that the employment will prove hurtful to them. . . . There can be no more justification for the prohibition of the prosecution of certain callings by women, because the employment will prove hurtful to themselves, than it would be for the State to prohibit men from working in the manufacture of white lead because they are apt to contract lead poisoning, or to prohibit occupation in certain parts of iron smelting works, because the lives of the men so engaged are materially shortened.[65]

This quotation, embodying Tiedeman's principal thesis—that the police power was limited to the enforcement of the maxim, *sic utere tuo ut alienum non laedas*—was the most direct authority which the court found to sustain its position. Whenever Cooley's works and the case law failed to sustain extreme propositions of laissez faire, the courts and the lawyers could, with great confidence, refer to the *Limitations of Police Power* in which such principles were usually defended.

In a sense, the *Ritchie* case constituted the high point in the history of laissez faire constitutionalism in the state tribunals, but the decision there by no means marks the beginning of its decline. The courts clung tenaciously to a faith which a majority of the people and the legislatures were coming to doubt. Some state courts were, of course, far more senstive to the claims of laissez faire than were others. And in not a few instances certain tribunals were willing to go directly counter to the views of the United States Supreme Court. For example, in the case of *In re Morgan,*[66] decided by the Supreme Court of Colorado, an eight-hour law for men working in mines and smelters was declared unconstitutional although similar legislation had already received the assent of the United States Supreme Court in *Holden v. Hardy.*[67] The opinion in the *Morgan* case is profuse with citations to, and quotations from, the works of Cooley and Tiedeman. Both were quoted on the general limit of the police power—that is, to the enforcement of the maxim, *sic utere tuo ut alienum non laedas.*[68] Cooley's statement that the "maxims of Magna Charta and the common law are interpreters of constitutional grants of power" was used;[69] and Tiedeman was quoted in support of two propositions: (1) that laws were not to be enacted for the sole purpose of protecting an individual from injuries resulting from his own acts and (2) that laws regulating the terms of employment in private businesses were unconstitutional.[70] Four passages from Cooley's *Constitutional Limitations* and from his *Torts* were also quoted approvingly: (1) a statement condemning legislation which denied certain capacities to persons engaged in some specified trade or business;[71] (2) one alleging that, as a general rule, a person had the right to engage in a lawful calling in his own way, provided that others were not injured by his acts;[72] (3) a passage defending the right to labor and to sell that labor;[73] and (4) one defending the individual's right to control and use his property according to his own judgment.[74]

Decisions such as that rendered in the *Morgan* case and in any of the scores of liberty of contract cases which preceded it placed the United States Supreme Court under considerable pressure. It will be recalled that as of 1886 (when a state tribunal for the first time invalidated a law as contrary to the liberty of contract), the Supreme Court was not yet prepared to assume an active role in enforcing laissez faire dogmas upon the legislatures, although it was moving slowly and steadily in that direction. Its progress during the period when state courts were extremely active in supporting laissez faire principles must yet be noted.

Liberty of Contract Comes to the Supreme Court of the United States

The direct influence of the publicists upon the United States Supreme Court during the years after 1884, when the *Butchers' Union* case was decided, was far less pronounced than it had been in the state tribunals. Perhaps this was due to the fact that both the *Constitutional Limitations* and the *Limitations of Police Power* were primarily works in the field of state, as distinguished from federal, constitutional law. It is certain, however, that the laissez faire principles which Cooley and Tiedeman had formulated had a tremendous indirect bearing upon the outcome of litigation in the federal courts. That conservative attorneys constituted a channel through which the laissez faire ideology flowed upwards to the highest national tribunal has been decisively demonstrated by Benjamin Twiss in his *Lawyers and the Constitution*. But the fact remains that the Supreme Court failed to keep pace with the state judiciaries; and even after it had come to accept the principal elements of laissez faire, it did not go to the extremes exemplified by the opinions in such state cases as *Braceville Coal Co. v. People* and *Ex parte Kuback*. State judicial opinions were, of course, cited frequently by lawyers arguing before the Court. Although the Court in its liberty of contract opinions rarely mentioned the state cases as precedents for its position, one can be reasonably certain that the justices owed more to the state judges than they generally admitted.

Looking back to 1884, one finds that the Supreme Court of the United States was far removed from the goals set by conservative lawyers. But soon that tribunal began preparing the groundwork for liberty of contract, a groundwork which Field and Bradley had accepted much earlier. In *Mugler v. Kansas*[75] the Court adopted one of the concepts which had already played a significant role in the growth of laissez faire principles in the state jurisdictions. Although the Court, speaking through Justice Harlan, sustained the validity of the challenged statute (one prohibiting the manufacture and sale of alcoholic beverages), it adopted a position similar to that taken by the New York Court of Appeals in the *Jacobs* case. It admitted that the legislature was to decide whether or not the manufacture of liquor was injurious to the public welfare, but the practical effect of this assertion was materially undermined by the Court's insistence that there was a difference between pretended and real exercises of the police power. Courts, said Harlan, were bound not by form but by substance.[76] The Court was willing to concede, however, that the manufacture of liquor might be regarded as harmful. Consequently, the statute was sustained. Harlan's *dictum* that the courts must distinguish between form and substance was by no means a novel assertion; but as here applied, it constituted a contribution to laissez faire. This idea became the underlying justification for later decisions in which the Court was less moved by the supposed evils of the subject regulated and by the desirability of the particular regulation.

The Court had not yet accepted the principle that economic liberty was guaranteed by the Fourteenth Amendment. Although Justices Field and Bradley had consistently maintained this position, the Court itself refused to accept this interpretation of the amendment. Nevertheless, in *Powell v. Pennsylvania*[77] the Court, in one of its disconcerting offhand remarks, reversed its earlier position. Justice Harlan wrote an opinion upholding the validity of state legislation which prohibited the manufacture and sale of oleaginous substances designed to replace butter, but in the opinion he said:

The main proposition advanced by the defendant is that his enjoyment upon terms of equality with all others in similar circumstances of the privilege of pursuing an ordinary calling or trade, and of acquiring, holding, and selling property, is an essential part of his rights of liberty and property, as guaranteed by the Fourteenth Amendment. *The court assents to this general proposition as embodying a sound principle of constitutional law.* But it cannot adjudge that the defendant's rights of liberty and property, as thus defined, have been infringed by the statute of Pennsylvania, without holding that, although it may have been enacted in good faith for the objects expressed in its title, namely, to protect the public health and to prevent the adulteration of dairy products and fraud in the sale thereof, it has, in fact, no real or substantial relation to those objects.[78]

The full implications of the majority's acceptance of the very proposition explicitly rejected in the *Slaughter-House Cases* were made evident in a dissenting opinion by Justice Field. Using the two propositions which the Court had accepted in the *Mugler* and *Powell* cases—that the courts must distinguish between real and pretended exercises of police power and that freedom to choose and pursue a calling was guaranteed by the Fourteenth Amendment—Field concluded that the law was unconstitutional.[79] The differences between Justice Field and his colleagues were no longer differences in kind, but rather differences in degree. The majority was prepared, when the proper case arose, to strike down legislation which impaired economic liberty.

The more explicit principle of liberty of contract, which was derived from general propositions of economic liberty, possibly received the assent of the Court in *Hooper v. California*,[80] a case pertaining to the constitutionality of a law prohibiting any person from procuring for a resident of the state an insurance policy issued by a foreign corporation which had not complied with state law. Justice White, who wrote the majority opinion, declared:

> It is said that the right of a citizen to contract for insurance for himself is guaranteed by the Fourteenth Amendment, and that, therefore, he cannot be deprived by the State of the capacity to so contract through an agent. The Fourteenth Amendment, however, does not guarantee the citizen the right to make within his State, either directly or indirectly, a contract, the making whereof is constitutionally forbidden by the State.[81]

The language used by Justice White was, at best, rather ambiguous. But he may have meant that, under some circumstances, the state could not deprive the individual of the right to make contracts. Justice Harlan dissented, with Justices Brewer and Jackson concurring, and argued that the law was an unconstitutional encroachment upon the liberty of the person seeking the insurance policy as well as upon that of the agent who delivered the policy.

The freedom of contract received more explicit recognition in *Frisbie v. United States*,[82] decided shortly after the Court had delivered its opinion in the *Hooper* case. The case is an especially important one because it involved the liberty of contract as a restriction upon national, as distinguished from state, power. It concerned the constitutionality of a provision in the Pension Act of

1890 which prohibited any agent or attorney engaged in prosecuting a pension claim to demand or to accept a fee in excess of ten dollars. A unanimous Court, speaking through Justice Brewer, declared:

> A second objection insisted upon now as it was by demurrer to the indictment, is that the act under which the indictment was found is unconstitutional, because interfering with the price of labor and the freedom of contract. This objection also is untenable. *While it may be conceded that, generally speaking, among the inalienable rights of the citizen is that of the liberty of contract,* yet such liberty is not absolute and universal. It is within the undoubted power of government to restrain some individuals from all contracts, as well as all individuals from some contracts. It may deny to all the right to contract for the purchase or sale of lottery tickets; to the minor the right to assume any obligations, except for the necessaries of existence; to the common carrier the power to make any contract releasing himself from negligence, and, indeed, may restrain all engaged in any employment from any contract in the course of that employment which is against public policy. *The possession of this power by the government in no manner conflicts with the proposition that, generally speaking, every citizen has a right freely to contract for the price of his labor, services, or property.*[83]

Brewer's statement, on the surface, is a defense of governmental power. Nevertheless, liberty of contract had entered the federal Constitution through the back door. Presumably (although it is not so stated), it had been embodied in due process of the Fifth Amendment. That the Court emphasized, further on in its opinion, the great discretionary power of Congress in granting pensions indicated that in other fields it might not show the tolerance toward governmental impairment of the right to contract which it had exhibited in the *Frisbie* case.

The Court, for the first time in its history, struck down state legislation as violative of the right to contract in *Allgeyer v. Louisiana.*[84] The statute challenged in this case prohibited any person, firm, or corporation, on penalty of fine, to "fill up, sign, or issue in this State any certificate of insurance under an open marine policy" or to do "any act in this State to effect, for himself or for another, insurance on property, then in this State, in any marine insurance company which has not complied in all respects" with state law. In delivering the Court's unanimous opinion, Justice Peckham drew upon Bradley's concurring opinion in the *Butchers' Union* case and quoted approvingly that jurist's defense of the right to pursue a lawful calling. He also quoted from Harlan's opinion in *Powell v. Pennsylvania* where a majority of the Court had explicitly accepted, for the first time, an economic interpretation of the word "liberty" as used in the Fourteenth Amendment. Justice Peckham declared:

> In the privilege of pursuing an ordinary calling or trade and of acquiring, holding, and selling property must be embraced the right to make all proper contracts in relation thereto, and although it may be conceded that this right to contract in relation to persons or property or to do business within the jurisdiction of the State may be regulated and sometimes prohibited when the contracts or business conflict with the policy of the State as contained in its statutes, yet the power does not and cannot extend to prohibiting a citizen from making contracts of the nature involved in this case outside of the limits and jurisdiction of the State, and which are also to be performed outside of such jurisdiction.[85]

Had the Court's opinion been narrowly construed, it might have been regarded as inhibiting little more than *ultra vires* legislation. The Court, it seems, was especially concerned with that aspect of the law which restricted the citizen's right to make contracts outside the limits of the state. Proponents of laissez faire, including the justices of the Court, later overlooked this aspect of the *Allgeyer* case, however. For them it became a precedent against exercises of the police power which impaired the liberty of contract, even where the person and property regulated were clearly within the state's territorial jurisdiction.

In 1898 the Court decided the first of a series of cases raising the issue of freedom of contract in the field of employer-employee relations. *Holden v. Hardy*[86] concerned the validity of an eight-hour law for persons employed in underground mines and smelters. The Court, speaking through Justice Brown, again indicated its acceptance of the freedom of contract, which it said was comprehended in the general right to acquire property. It added, however, that the right to contract was subject to certain limitations which the state might impose in the exercise of its police power. Justice Brown indicated that this power had recently received expanded application because of an increase in the number of hazardous occupations. Work in mines and smelters, he thought, if pursued for excessive periods of time, might well prove deleterious to the health of the laborer. The opinion emphasized the discretion which the legislature possessed in enacting laws of this kind, but the Court's conviction that the regulated occupations were dangerous probably contributed more to the favorable reception of the law than did its endorsement of any abstract proposition sustaining legislative sovereignty. Unlike many state tribunals, the Court pointedly refused to accept the contention that the statute impaired rights of the employee as well as those of the employer. When *Holden v. Hardy* is compared with similar state cases, its principles appear unusually progressive. For a time, it seemed that this new set of principles would alter the course of judicial history, but this illusion was soon dispelled in *Lochner v. New York*.[87]

Decided in 1905, the *Lochner* case resulted in a decision holding unconstitutional a New York law limiting the employment of persons in bakeries to ten hours per day and sixty hours per week. In this case the implications of liberty of contract, as enunciated in the *Allgeyer* case, and of judicial distinctions between real and pretended exercises of the police power, as expounded in *Mugler v. Kansas*, bore fruit. Although the Court had at its disposal statistics which showed the relative unhealthfulness of the baker's occupation, it declared:

> There must be more than the mere fact of the possible existence of some small amount of unhealthiness to warrant legislative interference with liberty. It is unfortunately true that labor, even in any department, may possibly carry with it the seeds of unhealthiness. But are we all, on that account, at the mercy of legislative majorities?[88]

At another point Justice Peckham, who wrote the majority opinion, stated:

> Statutes of the nature of that under review, limiting the hours in which grown and intelligent men may labor to earn their living, are mere meddlesome interferences with the rights of the individual, and they are not saved from condemnation by the claim that they are passed in the exercise of the police power and upon the subject of the health of the individual whose rights are interfered with, unless there be some fair ground, reasonable in and of itself, to say that there is material danger to the public health or to the health of the employees, if the hours of labor are not curtailed.[89]

The above statement is strikingly similar to pronouncements made by a number of state judges. That this similarity was not a mere coincidence was indicated by the Court's later reference to several state cases including *Low v. Rees Printing Co.* and *Godcharles v. Wigeman.* The Supreme Court, like the state tribunals, had accepted the anomalous practice of permitting an employer to establish his defense on the ground that the statute under consideration impaired rights belonging to his employees. Moreover, the emphasis in the above passage upon the rights of "grown and intelligent men" indicates that the Court was applying the class legislation concept of Cooley, which in some state jurisdictions had become a proscription against virtually all legislative classifications not based upon the so-called natural, or common-law, incapacities. Although four of the justices disagreed with the majority and two of them, Harlan and Holmes, wrote vigorous dissenting opinions, the Court was to proceed still further before any retrenchment occurred.

As was indicated previously, the Court had come extremely close to writing liberty of contract into the Constitution as a limitation upon federal power in *Frisbie v. United States.* This step was eventually taken in *Adair v. United States,*[90] decided in 1908. Here the United States Supreme Court invalidated certain provisions of the act of 1898 whereby Congress had made it a crime for any employer (engaged as a carrier in interstate commerce) to do either of two things: (1) to discriminate against any employee because of the latter's membership in a labor union, and (2) to enter into contract with any employee or prospective employee preventing the latter from belonging to or joining such a union.

The Court, speaking through Justice Harlan, held that these provisions of the law were impairments of liberty and property rights guaranteed by the Fifth Amendment. It declined to consider whether or not the railroad corporation whose agent was indicted could claim the right to contract under the terms of that amendment. Rather it regarded the law as a restriction upon the right of the railroad's agent, Adair. Justice Harlan declared that it was the agent's right—"and that right inhered in his personal liberty and was also a right of property—to serve his employer as best he could, so long as he did nothing that was reasonably forbidden by law as injurious to the public interests."[91] After quoting a brief passage from Cooley's *Torts* in which that writer defended the right of the individual to accept or to refuse business relations with others,[92] Harlan reviewed the *Lochner* case and concluded that, although the Court was divided on the immediate issues, there had been no disagreement as to the existence of a liberty of contract which could not be unreasonably abridged. "The right of a person to sell his labor upon such terms as he deems proper is," said Harlan, "the same as the right of the purchaser to prescribe the conditions upon which he will accept such labor from the person offering to sell it."[93] Without considering the economic realities of the employee's status, the Court had assumed, as a basis for decision, the validity of the abstract proposition that the worker's right of contract equaled that of the employer—clearly an unsound principle when applied to relations between individual laborers and far-flung corporate enterprises.

The Court had one other question to decide: was the statute a valid exercise of the power of Congress to regulate interstate commerce? Justice Harlan, in answer, stated that membership in a labor union had no substantial relationship to interstate commerce, and that consequently, the statute was passed "under the guise of regulating interstate commerce." The Court thus sanctioned, as applicable to the powers of Congress, the distinction between real and pretended exercises of power which it had previously, in *Mugler v. Kansas,* accepted as a test of the constitutionality of police regulations.

With the *Adair* case laissez faire principles and especially the liberty of contract seemed to reach their zenith. The Court had not yet struck down a federal statute on the sole ground that it violated the freedom of contract, for in the *Adair* case the Court's restricted construction of the commerce power had contributed to the law's invalidation. During the next fifteen years it appeared that the Court would not take this final step in the expansion and application of laissez faire principles. Eventually, it did do so, but this development came some years later.

Between 1886 and 1910 the Supreme Court of the United States had capitulated before the pressures which the state courts, the lawyers, and conservative propertied interests had applied. Liberty of contract had been incorporated into the constitutional law of the nation and of the states. Not only was it a restraint upon exercises of the police power, it had come to be a serious limitation upon the powers of the central government also. But acceptance of laissez faire principles by the federal judiciary was, at best, belated. Already by

1900 some state courts had begun to retrench from the extreme positions which they had unhesitatingly assumed in the previous decade. Actually, the history of the origins and development of laissez faire principles, and especially of the liberty of contract, points up the fact that the Supreme Court, on social and economic issues, lagged behind not only the legislatures but also the state judiciaries. When the latter were boldly constructing the basis of laissez faire constitutionalism, the Supreme Court continued to speak in the language of the pre-Civil War era. When the state tribunals were applying these doctrines in a wide range of cases, the Court was feebly groping for the new principles. And, eventually, when the state tribunals began to abandon these principles, the Supreme Court began to apply them. After 1908 it appeared that the state and federal courts would proceed in concert and that laissez faire constitutional principles would undergo an eclipse in all jurisdictions. But again, appearances were misleading. In the state courts the decline of liberty of contract was real and, on the whole, permanent. In the Supreme Court the eclipse of the principle, if real, was only temporary.

The Decline and Resuscitation of the Liberty of Contract

The decline of the liberty of contract after 1900 was, for a time, almost imperceptible, but a careful analysis of state judicial decisions discloses that laissez faire principles no longer commanded the respect previously accorded to them.

The New York Court of Appeals, by a vote of four to three, sustained legislation limiting to ten hours the working day of bakers. Although this law was subsequently invalidated by the Supreme Court of the United States, the fact that the New York tribunal, long a major stronghold of laissez faire ideas, had accepted it was indicative of the new tendency of the time. In addition, several other state tribunals sustained statutes limiting the working hours of women in private establishments. In 1910 the Supreme Court of Illinois approved a ten-hour law for women, and the New York Court of Appeals sustained similar legislation in 1915.[94] Both of these tribunals, it will be recalled, had declared such measures unconstitutional only a few years earlier.

The abstract rigors of the liberty of contract gradually collapsed, or at least were tempered, as the result of efforts made by progressive and socially minded lawyers of the period. Louis Brandeis and a number of less-renowned attorneys pressed to the attention of the courts social and economic data which, when fairly construed, proved that the legislatures, even if they had acted unwisely, had not acted out of mere caprice in passing laws which regulated various aspects of the private economy. It was Brandeis who presented the principal brief in *Ritchie and Co. v. Wayman* where the Supreme Court of Illinois, in effect, overruled its infamous decision in *Ritchie v. People*. And it was Brandeis who presented the Supreme Court of the United States with sufficient economic facts that that tribunal unanimously sustained a ten-hour law for women in certain occupations.

During this period Professor Ernst Freund of the University of Chicago Law School published *The Police Power, Public Policy and Constitutional Rights*. This treatise was less original than were the works of Cooley and Tiedeman, but it exercised considerable influence upon the legal profession. In general, Freund presented a moderate defense of the police power, and his qualified acceptance of such dogmas as the liberty of contract was readily compatible with incipient trends in judicial attitudes.[95] Unlike the works of Cooley and Tiedeman, Freund's treatise did not become a standard citation in judicial opinions, but it was occasionally cited by attorneys in their written briefs and oral arguments before the courts. In *Ritchie and Co. v. Wayman*, for example, counsel for the state referred to the work six times, and the cited passages tended to prove that the law involved in that case was valid, a conclusion which the court reached in its opinion.[96] It is possible to say that Freund's treatise anticipated the moderation and partial eclipse of laissez faire principles much as the works of Cooley and Tiedeman, respectively, had portended their emergence and had declared their temporary triumph.

For a time it appeared that laissez faire dogmas, and especially the liberty of contract, would suffer similar desuetude in the federal courts. The United States Supreme Court had scarcely delivered its decision in the *Adair* case when it appeared to retreat somewhat from the extreme outposts of laissez faire. *Muller v. Oregon*[97] was the first of a series of cases in which the Court indicated that it would take judicial notice of economic and social data in reaching its conclusions. This practice could only, in the end, reduce the scope and alter the practical meaning of such abstract principles as the liberty of contract. (Probably it was the belated recognition of this effect which led Justice Sutherland, some years later, to raise questions as to the propriety of the Court's consideration of arguments drawn from statistical data.)[98]

The gains made by progessives in litigation before the Supreme Court during the fifteen years following the *Muller* case proved illusory, however. The Court, for a time, was content to sustain economic legislation which, from the standpoint of laissez faire enthusiasts, was of doubtful constitutionality. In doing so, the Court predicated its decisions upon the general right to contract, subject only to reasonable limitations; but during the Wilsonian era its conclusions more frequently emphasized the practical justice of the limitations imposed upon the right, rather than the abstract justice of the right itself.[99]

Contemporary writers were certain that laissez faire, as an element of American constitutional law, was dying; and it was Charles M. Hough who said in the annual lecture under the Frank Irvine Foundation in 1918:

> The direct appeal of property to due process has for the most part failed; and apparent successes have but taught legislators how to arrive at the same result in another way. The indirect appeal through liberty is still going on, for the American belief that every freeman can do what he likes, where and when he pleases, as long as it does not infringe the moral law as expressed in the usual criminal codes, dies very hard. But it is dying, and the courts, when invoked today under the due process clause, are doing little more than easing the patient's later days.[100]

The diagnosis was correct, but the prognosis proved premature. Only five years later the Supreme Court gave its decision in *Adkins v. Children's Hospital*.

With the decision in the *Adkins* case the apparent trend away from substantive due process, from liberty of contract, and from laissez faire was abruptly halted. In a very real sense the majority opinion delivered by Justice Sutherland (who was a former pupil of Cooley[101]) constitutes the high-water mark in the application of laissez faire principles by the Supreme Court. Here, the Court, for the first time, struck down federal legislation on the sole ground that the liberty of contract was impaired.

The *Adkins* case has already been mentioned as being a précis of past developments, but it was also the prelude to the Indian summer of laissez faire. This period of revival was relatively brief, and it ended as abruptly as it had begun. In *West Coast Hotel v. Parrish*,[102] decided in 1937, the Court delivered the first of a series of opinions which contributed materially to the disintegration of the laissez faire ideology. Nineteen years after his prediction was made, Judge Hough was proved correct. Economic liberty, as understood by a Cooley, a Tiedeman, or a Sutherland, disappeared as a principle of constitutional law which the judges would enforce upon the community. And its validity as a political dogma, although not entirely destroyed, was seriously impaired.

Liberty of contract during the age of industrialization had become a major weapon in the entrepreneur's struggle against governmental control. Made up of a number of elements—Cooley's interpretation of due process and his interdiction against class or partial legislation, Field's and Bradley's ideas of economic freedom and the meaning of property, and Tiedeman's principle of the implied limits of the police power—the liberty of contract doctrine was the constitutional sanction for economic and social ideas prevailing among propertied classes. An abstract principle, it derived much of its strength from the fact that it glossed over the real nature of employer-employee relations in an age when wealth and economic power were concentrated in the hands of a few. By its superficial appeal to "liberty" and "equality" (and these were the principal catchwords in judicial opinions where laissez faire principles were applied), it transmuted fundamental political and moral values of the American tradition into a justification for unbridled and irresponsible private economic power. Particularly applicable to cases involving relations between master and servant, it served the cause of corporate wealth admirably by seriously impairing legislative authority to cope with labor problems.

The era after the Civil War was one of the four creative periods in American constitutional history. The first had elapsed under Marshall and was one in which the Court had laid the groundwork for the growth and expansion-of national power. The second, under Taney, was characterized, in part, by the development of the police power of the states. The third, occurring between 1868 and 1937, was one in which governmental power, both state and national, was de-emphasized and restricted and in which private economic power was sanctified by resort to constitutional principles which had been developed and elaborated for that purpose. Finally, after 1937, came the fourth and contemporary period in which governmental power has been rapidly extended, either with the aid or with the acquiescence of the courts, into new areas of social and economic relations.

Viewed from the vantage point of today, the constitutional principles which characterized the third period stand out in bold contrast to those now accepted by most American jurists. In the age of industrialization virtually all those governmental powers by which the private economy is now regulated were subjected to rigorous judicial limitations. Paralleling the development and elaboration of limitations upon the police and commerce powers was the growth of restrictions upon the power to tax. Here again the publicists, and particularly Cooley, made important contributions to American constitutional law.

4
The Public Purpose Limitation on the Taxing Power: Origin and Early Development

HAD THE COURTS, the publicists, and the lawyers contented themselves with the discovery and application of limitations upon the police power alone, the victory of laissez faire constitutionalism, however impressive it might have been, would not have been complete. But the protagonists of the new constitutional order were, above all else, both energetic and thorough in their endeavors; and, through their efforts, the principles of laissez faire came to inhibit the exercise of other powers also. Like the police power, the power to tax was pregnant with dangers for the entrepreneur. By means of this power the state could regulate or even destroy his business. And by the expenditure of money raised by taxation, the state might seriously undermine his competitive position and reduce the area in which his initiative and enterprise could be applied. To check such menaces, principles restricting the taxing power were developed through the judicial process. Among the most effective was the requirement that taxes be levied for public purposes only. This restriction, innocuous though it was in the abstract, probably occasioned more judicial discussion of the ends and functions of government than did any other developed in the post-Civil War period. Although the validity of the principle as a guide for the determination of policy can scarcely occasion serious doubt or controversy, as an instrument of judicial review it was fraught with grave political and constitutional objections. It became another of those principles whereby legislative discretion in social and economic matters was controlled by judicial determination of the wisdom and policy of governmental measures; however, the courts invariably denied that such was the case.

The public purpose principle, in some respects, was more a limitation upon the powers to appropriate and to borrow money than upon the power to tax. In scores of public purpose cases no tax law was involved at all. Often the immediate question was whether or not a bond issue, authorized by the legislature, was to raise money for a public purpose. Other cases involved the constitutionality of legislative appropriations from the public treasury. In these cases, however, the courts, as a rule, assumed that the taxpayers would eventually be called upon to replenish the treasury or to pay the interest and principal on the bonded debt. Consequently, the taxing power and the public purpose doctrine were generally analyzed even in those cases where no tax law was under judicial scrutiny. A few cases actually raised questions as to the constitutionality of tax measures, but this occurred only in those instances where the tax law itself earmarked the funds to be raised thereby for a specific purpose. Public purpose was, then, something more than a restriction on the taxing power. Rather it was a vague standard whereby the courts tested the validity of the exercise of any fiscal power. For this reason it was a more stringent check upon legislative power than were those restrictions which applied to taxation alone.[1]

It has already been noted (p. 33) that the origins of substantive due process may be traced to the pre-Civil War period, but that this doctrine failed, at that time, to acquire the constitutional significance which it later was to possess. The public purpose restriction on the taxing power, which much later was encompassed in property due process, also had its origins in the decades preceding the Civil War, but it was not until after that conflict that it received the form, content, and orientation which were to make it an important tenet of laissez faire constitutionalism.

[1] For notes to chap. 4, see pp. 189–193.

Public Purpose before the Civil War

It is an ancient principle of political science that governmental powers should be exercised for public purposes only, and, as an abstract proposition, it is incontrovertible. In a preceding chapter (pp. 60–61) it was noted that the police power was restricted to the enforcement of the maxim, *sic utere tuo ut alienum non laedas.* This was but one way of saying that the police power was to be exercised for public, as distinguished from private, purposes. The same rule applied then, as it does now, to exercises of the power of eminent domain. By specific provision the federal Bill of Rights and virtually all state constitutions require that property taken in pursuance of this power be devoted to a public use. Although eminent domain was subject to this specific restriction, taxation was not. Consequently, if such a limitation on the taxing power were ever to be realized, the judiciary itself would bear the burden of discovery and elaboration.

The judicial history of public purpose is usually said to have begun with *Goddin v. Crump,*[2] a case decided by the Court of Appeals of Virginia in 1837. The date of the case is not without interest, for in that year occurred the panic which soon was to discredit state activity in the internal improvements field. Although this case involved municipal stock subscriptions to a private company which was engaged in making internal improvements, the dissenting opinion of Judge Brooke,[3] in which the public purpose concept was vaguely formulated, cannot be attributed to any general disillusionment with state-supported enterprise. Default and repudiation were near at hand, but that fact was rarely appreciated at the time. Later, after the tottering financial structure of many states had become evident to all, judicial opinions were to disclose concern with the wisdom of state-sponsored enterprises, but no such sentiment was revealed either by Judge Brooke or by the majority in the *Goddin* case.

The case involved the constitutionality of state laws permitting the city of Richmond to subscribe to the stock of a private company which had been previously authorized by the legislature to construct a transportation line between Richmond and the Ohio River. The laws enabled the city to issue bonds for the purpose of making the subscription and to levy taxes in order to pay interest and principal on the bonded debt. A majority of the city's voters had approved the stock subscription even before the legislature authorized it.

The majority judges held the laws constitutional on the ground that a majority of the city's voters, acting under legislative authorization, was better able to say what a local purpose was than were courts of justice. In his dissent Judge Brooke argued that the project was of state or national interest and not of merely local interest. Consequently, a municipal corporation, having no special interest in the project, could not be authorized to aid it by resort to the taxing power. Judge Brooke invoked several clauses of the state constitution, including the eminent-domain provision, to support his views, and he emphasized that these provisions were designed to check the tyranny of the majority as well as the tyranny of the one or of the few. One may search the dissent in vain for an explicit formulation of the public purpose doctrine. Still, the dissent is important in the development of that limitation. Judge Brooke, unlike his more traditionally minded colleagues, had urged that the judiciary could determine for itself the nature or character of the purpose and that upon the basis of this determination the judges could invalidate tax legislation. Although he admitted that the purpose was public, he denied that it was local. And he held, accordingly, that local taxes could not be levied for a general purpose, even though that purpose was public. The impact of these principles was not immediately felt, but before the Civil War a few other courts were to accept Brooke's ideas.

For sixteen years after the *Goddin* case, attorneys invariably failed in their efforts to make public purpose a means whereby the courts could control legislative discretion in fiscal matters. Thus, in *Thomas v. Leland,* the New York Court of Appeals explicitly rejected the contention that the public-use clause of the state constitution was a limitation on the taxing power. The court admitted that this power might be abused, but the judges denied that its exercise could be "judicially restrained so long as it is referable to the taxing power." Other tribunals also denied the applicability of the eminent-domain provision, usually in cases concerning the validity of legislation enabling municipalities to aid companies engaged in making internal improvements. At the half-century mark it appeared that the judges, if not the lawyers, had forgotten the principles set forth by Judge Brooke.[5]

Public purpose was not a dead constitutional theory, however. In 1853 the Supreme Court of Pennsylvania rendered its decision in *Sharpless v. Mayor of Philadelphia*,[6] and in this case Chief Justice Black formulated a classic defense of the public purpose principle. The character of the action itself was unusual, although not unprecedented, at that time. Sharpless and a number of other taxpayers of the city of Philadelphia filed a bill in equity whereby they sought to restrain the city and its officers from subscribing to the stock of certain railroad companies. The legislature had previously authorized the municipality to make the subscription.

The court sustained the validity of the laws and dismissed the bill by a vote of three to two. The dissenting judges filed no opinion, and one can only speculate as to their reasons for disagreeing with the majority. But the majority itself was divided on general principles. Judges Woodward and Knox relied upon the traditional view that the courts were bound to accept legislative judgment as to what was or was not a public purpose.[7] Chief Justice Black, however, was not satisfied with this rule; and, in a long opinion, he set forth his views. In the course of his opinion he said:

> This is, beyond all comparison, the most important cause that has ever been in this Court since the formation of the government. The fate of many most important public improvements hangs on our decision. If all municipal subscriptions are void, railroads, which are necessary to give the state those advantages to which everything else entitles her, must stand unfinished for years to come, and large sums, already expended on them, must be lost. Not less than fourteen millions of these stocks have been taken by boroughs, counties, and cities within this Commonwealth. They have uniformly been paid for, either with bonds handed over directly to the railroad companies, or else with the proceeds of similar bonds sold to individuals who advanced the money. It may well be supposed that a large amount of them are in the hands of innocent holders, who have paid for them in good faith. We cannot award the injunction asked for, without declaring that all such bonds are destitute of legal validity as so much blank parchment. Besides the deadly blow it would give to our improvements, and the disastrous effect of it on the private fortunes of many honest men, at home and abroad, it would seriously wound the credit and character of the state, and do much to lessen the influence of our institutions on the public mind of the world.[8]

These clearly were not judicial considerations, as the judge admitted further on in his opinion. Apparently he was unwilling that the courts should, in effect, repudiate financial obligations of the subdivisions of the state. Chief Justice Black saw an equally dismal alternative, however. Although Judge Brooke in the *Goddin* case had been unaware of the states' financial instability, which had been occasioned by aid to speculative and foolish enterprises, Black had not far to look for such evidence.[9] And, as a consequence, he placed himself upon the horns of a dilemma from which escape was difficult. After reviewing the evils of public aid to internal improvements, he concluded that "this plan of improving the country, if unchecked by this Court, will probably go on until it results in some startling calamity, to rouse the masses of the people."[10]

Judge Black's extended review of the woeful social and economic consequences which would flow from a decision (irrespective of what the decision was) was followed by a discussion of the constitutional aspects of the issue presented for determination. He denied that the law authorizing the subscription was in violation of the public-use and law-of-the-land clauses of the state constitution, and he added that a tax, if imposed in pursuance of a law not in conflict with the constitution, had to be borne by those upon whom it was imposed. In his discussion of the taxing power, Black emphasized the unrestricted character of that power, but this assertion (and it represented the traditional attitude of the courts) was qualified by the allegation that not everything which the legislature might call a tax was actually that. According to the judge, "a tax law must be considered valid, unless it be for a purpose, in which the community taxed had palpably no interest; where it is apparent that a burden is imposed for the benefit of others, and where it would be so pronounced at first blush."[11] Taxation, he said, had to be for a public purpose. If it failed to meet that test, it was mere legislative plunder, and unconstitutional "for all the reasons which forbid the legislature to usurp any other power not granted to them."[12]

One additional step had yet to be taken before a decision could be reached. The judge had to decide if financial aid to railroad companies served a public purpose. He noted that private companies received the aid; he did not, however, look upon that as the principal consideration. It was the ultimate aim of the aid, and not the character of the recipient, which determined the nature of the purpose. Railroads, even when privately owned, he regarded as public highways, and aid granted to them served a public purpose. From the power of the state to tax for such purposes was derived its authority to enable cities to do so. For these reasons the injunction was denied.

The Black opinion in the *Sharpless* case might be compared with Judge Comstock's opinion in *Wynehamer v. People*.[13] Both enunciated constitutional principles which were somewhat novel, and both anticipated the rise of laissez faire constitutionalism after the Civil War. It will be recalled, however, that the substantive interpretation of due process gained widespread acceptance only after it underwent considerable elaboration by the postwar publicists, particularly Cooley. The same may be said of the public purpose limitation on taxation. Even after the decision in the *Sharpless* case judges were unwilling to apply their notions of public purpose as a limitation on the taxing power. Although the courts were subjected to increasing pressure from the bar, most of them were reluctant to rely upon the *dicta* of Judge Black.

In 1861, on the eve of the war, a court for the first time applied the doctrine and invalidated a tax law, but the case was not to become an exceedingly important precedent for subsequent decisions. *Philadelphia Association v. Wood*[14] involved the validity of a special tax imposed upon foreign insurance corporations doing business in Philadelphia. The proceeds of the tax were to be turned over to the Philadelphia Association for the Relief of Disabled Firemen, a private corporation. The novelty of the legislation apparently shocked the court, and Chief Justice Lowrie delivered the unanimous opinion in which the law was invalidated. He regarded the statute as an attempt to transfer property from one private corporation to another. For this reason he held that it was a deprivation of property without due process of law. Although Chief Justice Black, some eight years before, had rejected the argument that the nature of the purpose depended upon the private or public character of the recipient, Judge Lowrie was seemingly troubled by the fact that the firemen's association was a private corporation, and it was that aspect of the case which he emphasized in reaching his conclusion.

One other exceptional case, decided during the Civil War, may also be noticed. In *State ex rel. Burlington R. R. Co. v. Wapello*

County[15] the Supreme Court of Iowa invalidated a law authorizing counties to subscribe to the stock of railroad companies. Although that tribunal had previously sustained similar legislation, it had been evident since 1859 that the judges were undergoing a change of heart.[16] In his opinion for a unanimous court Judge Lowe asserted:

> The supreme tribunals of some fourteen or fifteen States have expressed their opinions upon the exercise of this power by municipal corporations, without reaching, strange to say, conclusions that are satisfactory to inquiries and consciousness of the public heart. And hence the renewed agitation of the subject, which, doubtlessly, will continue to obtrude itself upon the courts of the country, year after year, until they have finally settled it upon principles of adjudication which are known to be of the class of those that are laid up among the fundamentals of the law, and which especially will leave the capital of private individuals where the railroad era, when it dawned upon the world, found it, namely, under the control and dominion of those who have it, to be employed in whatever field of industry and enterprise they themselves may judge best.[17]

Having thus attempted to clear the court of any obligation to follow established precedents, Judge Lowe proceeded to examine the issues presented in the case. In the first place, and contrary to earlier decisions of the Iowa court, he denied that the legislature had ever granted to counties the power to subscribe to the stock of railroad corporations. Had he chosen to confine his argument to this issue alone, the case would have been of only incidental and temporary significance; but Judge Lowe went much further and held that the legislature had no power to authorize such subscriptions. His principal objection to such a power was founded upon his conception of the purposes for which municipalities were created. He contrasted the purposes of railroad corporations with those of public corporations and concluded that aid to railroads was not a legitimate municipal function.[18] It was with some difficulty that he discovered a specific constitutional provision upon which to base his objections. In effect, he admitted that there was none because he invoked that provision of the state bill of rights which declared that "this enumeration of rights shall not be construed to impair or deny others, retained by the people." From this innocuous proposition he deduced the principle of implied limitations on legislative power.[19]

The opinion of the court in the *Wapello* case does not disclose whether or not the judges regarded aid to railroads as a public purpose.

It is fairly certain that the judges themselves were undecided on this question. Nevertheless, they made clear that such aid was not, and could not be made by statute, a municipal function. Some years elapsed before the Iowa tribunal passed upon the broader question.

Until a few years after the Civil War the prevailing judicial attitude in tax cases was that legislative purposes were public purposes. The *Philadelphia Firemen's Association* and the *Wapello* cases were exceptions to this general rule, but they indicated that a change was in the making. Throughout the war there were repeated efforts by a number of lawyers to make the public purpose principle a stringent check on legislative power. The war itself gave rise to a multitude of military bounty cases; and counsel, with little success, frequently argued that such bounties were void for want of a public character.[20] When, in 1868, Cooley published the first edition of his *Constitutional Limitations,* the public purpose doctrine had not yet acquired a firm constitutional status. After the publication of his work the principle became thoroughly respectable. Within a year Cooley's work had become a leading citation in those cases where fiscal measures were invalidated on the ground that they were not for a public purpose.

Years of Decision, 1868–1876

The restraints upon the police power which Cooley expounded in his *Constitutional Limitations* have already been analyzed. It will be recalled that his ideas in this area were enormously suggestive but that, in many respects, they were somewhat vague. As a consequence, many years elapsed in which the courts used much of their energies in the refinement of his principles and in the transmutation of them into laissez faire constitutional dogmas. Cooley's general ideas on taxation, however, did not require extensive judicial elaboration in order to make them effective guarantees of laissez faire. Although his discussion of some aspects of the public purpose maxim was superficially paradoxical, the general principle itself was clearly and explicitly formulated. On the whole, the courts had only to accept or reject his ideas as judicial inclination dictated.

Among the restrictions on the taxing power which Cooley accepted was the requirement that taxes be levied for public purposes only. At the time he wrote, no state constitution contained an explicit provision to this effect, and Cooley was too competent a lawyer to argue that the public-use limitation on the power of eminent domain—a limitation which appeared in almost all state constitutions—was intended to restrict the taxing power. But failure to discover a specific constitutional provision from which the public purpose doctrine was deducible did not frustrate his efforts to write that guarantee into state constitutional law. To gain his end he resorted to the concept of implied limitations on legislative power.

Citing Blackwell's *Tax Titles*[21] as his only direct authority, Cooley defined taxes as "burdens or charges imposed by the legislative power upon persons and property, to raise money for public purposes."[22] Had Cooley stopped at this point as Blackwell had done, the remark would have been of little significance, but he continued with the following statement:

Having thus indicated the extent of the taxing power, it is necessary to add that certain elements are essential in all taxation, and that it will not necessarily follow because the power is so vast, that everything which may be done under pretence of its exercise will leave the citizen without redress, notwithstanding there be no conflict with constitutional provisions. Everything that may be done under the name of taxation is not necessarily a tax; and it may happen that an oppressive burden imposed by the government, when it comes to be carefully scrutinized, will prove, instead of a tax, to be an unlawful confiscation of property, unwarranted by any principle of constitutional government.

In the first place, taxation having for its legitimate object the raising of money for public purposes and the proper needs of government, the exaction of moneys from the citizens for other purposes is not a proper exercise of this power, and must therefore be unauthorized.[23]

The sweeping application of the above passage to the taxing power of the states can be fully appreciated only if one recalls that all state constitutions contained at that time, as they do now, explicit provisions affirming the power of the legislatures to levy taxes. By resort to the distinction between real and pretended exercises of the taxing power, Cooley transmuted these provisions *affirming* the legislatures' powers of taxation (according to sound constitutional theory such provisions were not *grants* of power) into limitations upon those powers. Levies for public purposes were taxes, and those for private purposes were extortion. The former were valid, and the latter were void.

Cooley was willing to admit, in principle at least, that the courts could not intervene in every instance where they thought a public purpose was not served by a particular tax. The word "public," he emphasized, should not be interpreted in any narrow or restricted sense. Precisely what Cooley regarded as public purposes will be mentioned later, but he concluded that there were three degrees of possible usurpation by the legislature when it levied taxes. First, there were those which could be remedied only through the elective process. Second, there were usurpations which were of a doubtful character, and, relying upon the principle that judicial doubts were to be resolved in favor of the legislation, the writer concluded that in these instances the judiciary could afford no remedy.[24] Third, there were cases where "it is entirely possible for the legislature so clearly to exceed the bounds of due authority that we cannot doubt the right of the courts to interfere to check what can only be looked upon as ruthless extortion, provided that the nature of the case is such that judicial process can afford relief."[25] Cooley thus intimated that only in very exceptional cases were the courts to afford relief. But this counsel for the exercise of caution in these matters was frequently overlooked or deëmphasized by the courts. The latter were more interested in restricting legislative power than in imposing restrictions upon themselves. Even Cooley, when serving as a judge, did not follow his own recorded advice; for, in *People v. Salem,* he struck down legislation, which by any objective standard, could scarcely have been classified as clear usurpation.[26]

Cooley conceded that the legislature must, in the first instance, determine whether or not a certain purpose was public, and he also ascribed to that department the power to determine what purposes were municipal or local in character. Moreover, he emphasized that the legislature was not bound by any narrow rules in making such decisions. Thus, he said:

Certain expenditures are not only absolutely necessary to the continued existence of the government, but as a matter of policy it may sometimes be proper and wise to assume other burdens which rest entirely on considerations of honor, gratitude, or charity. The officers of government must be paid, the laws printed, roads constructed, and public buildings erected; but with a view to the general well-being of society, it may also be important that the children of the State should be educated, the poor kept from starvation, losses in the public service indemnified, and incentives held out to faithful and fearless discharge of duty in the future, by the payment of pensions to those who have been faithful public servants in the past. There will therefore be necessary expenditures, and expenditures which rest upon considerations of policy alone; and in regard to the one as much as to the other, the decision of that department to which alone questions of State policy are addressed must be accepted as conclusive.[27]

To support these views Cooley quoted several passages from early cases. But he added, on the authority of the *Sharpless* case, that there were cases where the courts could not legitimately decline to intervene on behalf of the individual taxpayer's rights. He appears to have doubted that the judiciary should ever "stay the collection of State taxes because an illegal demand was included in the levy."[28] On the other hand, he regarded as susceptible to judicial invalidation legislation where the state "ordered" a unit of local government to raise taxes for a private purpose. Cooley did not make clear whether he was using the word "order" interchangeably with the word "authorize." There were scarcely any cases, in later years, involving the power of the state to order municipalities to tax, but there were many in which the power of the state to authorize cities and counties to tax for allegedly private purposes was challenged.

Viewed as a whole, Cooley's ideas on public purposes were not altogether consistent. Perhaps the paradoxes which one meets in his discussion of the doctrine were due to his effort to reconcile the relatively new attitude of the legal profession toward the function of the courts in tax matters with the traditional view that in this area legislative discretion was so great that judicial interference was virtually precluded. Despite the discrepancies in Cooley's analysis and elaboration of the public purpose restriction, his ideas were warmly received by bench and bar. Long before his views on the police power received judicial approval, his ideas on public purpose had been incorporated into state constitutional law.

Four cases in which the public purpose doctrine was the primary consideration were decided in 1869 alone. The *Constitutional Limitations* was not cited in the first two of these cases, but it was an important citation in the third and fourth. After 1869 and prior to the liberalization of the public purpose requirement (which occurred in the first decades of the twentieth century), Cooley's treatise was cited in well over one-half of the public purpose cases.

The Supreme Court of Pennsylvania in *Hammett v. Philadelphia*[29] struck down state legislation and city ordinances in pursuance thereof which provided for the paving of a city street and the assessment of property abutting thereon for the cost of the improvement. The court found that the improvement did not especially benefit the property so as to permit it to be assessed for the cost of the improvement. Although a majority of the judges admitted that there was no constitutional provision which prohibited the tax, they regarded it as outright confiscation. And they derived this remarkable conclusion from the proposition that general taxes must be laid for general purposes and local taxes for local purposes.[30]

The second case decided in this year was of more enduring significance. The Supreme Court of Wisconsin in *Curtis v. Whipple*[31] invalidated a law authorizing the town of Jefferson to raise by taxation the sum of five thousand dollars to aid in the erection of buildings for the Jefferson Liberal Institute, a private school. In his opinion for the court Chief Justice Dixon emphasized that the town had no special rights in the corporation and that incidental benefits accruing to the community as the result of the school's establishment did not justify taxation on its behalf. He declared:

That there exists in the state no power to tax for such purposes, is a proposition too plain to admit of controversy. Such a power would be obviously incompatible with the genius and institutions of a free people; and the practice of all liberal governments, as well as all judicial authority, is against it. If we turn to the cases where taxation has been sustained as in pursuance of the power, we shall find in every one of them that there was some direct advantage accruing to the public from the outlay, either by its being the owner or part owner of the property or thing to be created or obtained with the money, or the party immediately interested in and benefited by the work to be performed, the same being matters of public concern; or because the proceeds of the tax were to be expended in defraying the legitimate expenses of government, and in promoting the peace, good order, and welfare of society.[32]

Judge Dixon was prepared to admit the validity of a tax for a purpose directly benefiting the public, even though such benefit be slight, but he thought that taxes for a purpose from which the public derived only incidental benefit were unconstitutional. According to him, the purpose of the tax under consideration was in the latter category.

The first public purpose case in which Cooley's views played an important part was *Hanson v. Vernon,*[33] decided by the Supreme Court of Iowa. The principal opinion in the case is particularly significant because it was rendered by Chief Justice John F. Dillon, who shared with Cooley preëminent influence as an expounder of the public purpose limitation. Both men were outstanding publicists, and both were highly esteemed judges. Cooley's *Constitutional Limitations* preceded Dillon's *Municipal Corporations*[34] by scarcely four years and Dillon's opinion in *Hanson v. Vernon* antedated Cooley's opinion in *People v. Salem* by only one.

Dillon's boyhood and youth, like Cooley's, were marked by hardship and poverty. In 1838, at the age of seven, he migrated from his birthplace in Montgomery County, New York, to Davenport, Iowa. Frontier conditions existed in that area at the time, and Dillon received only a meager formal education. As a youth he decided to become a physician, and he began his medical studies in an office in Davenport. Later he was graduated from the College of Physicians and Surgeons of Davenport, a medical department of the state university. Dillon's medical career was short-lived, however. Physical infirmity made it difficult for him to travel by horseback to treat his patients, and he gradually abandoned his practice while undertaking to prepare himself for a career as a lawyer. By borrowing books and studying them assiduously, he acquired sufficient knowledge to gain admission to the bar in 1852.

From that time on, Dillon's fortunes improved rapidly. Shortly after his admission to the bar he was elected prosecuting attorney, a post that he held until his election in 1858 as judge of the state's Seventh Judicial District. In 1862 he successfully aspired, on the Republican ticket, to membership on the state supreme court. Six years later he won reëlection, but he resigned a short time later when President Grant appointed him as United States judge for the Eighth Judicial Circuit.

Dillon served in this post for a period of ten years, and during that time the number of cases arising in his circuit increased tenfold. Attorneys came more and more to look to the federal courts to relieve their clients, and Dillon encouraged this trend by publishing in 1875 his *Removal of Causes from State Courts to Federal Courts.* By this time Dillon was among the best-known jurists in the country, and in 1879 he was offered a professorship in the Columbia University Law School. With great reluctance he accepted the position and finally terminated twenty-one years of continuous judicial service. At this time also he became solicitor for the Union Pacific Railroad. And it was this position that indicated the direction of his interests and activities during the remainder of his life. His private practice grew and prospered in New York, and within three years he resigned from the faculty at Columbia in order to devote all his energies to railroad and corporation affairs. For many years he argued more cases before the Supreme Court of the United States than any other attorney, and until his death in 1914 was regarded as the leading railroad lawyer in the country.

Although Dillon acquired an imposing reputation as a United States judge and lawyer, his principal contributions to American law were made when he was at the threshold of his career. In 1866, while still a justice of the Supreme Court of Iowa, he began the arduous task of examining the judicial reports of each of the states, as well as materials on English law, in order to obtain the information necessary for the writing of his *Municipal Corporations,* which he published six years later. And it was during his years on the Iowa bench that he delivered his highly controversial, but influential, opinion in the case of *Hanson v. Vernon.* Both contributions were important landmarks in the development of the public purpose doctrine.

The *Hanson* case pertained to the constitutionality of a state law authorizing counties and cities to levy taxes for the purpose of subsidizing private railroad corporations. Unlike the law invalidated in the *Wapello* case, the statute did not provide a means whereby the counties and municipalities might become stockholders in railroad corporations, a feature of the earlier law which the court had found objectionable. Chief Justice Dillon emphasized, however, that the act under consideration could not be distinguished from previous measures and, according to his view, the case was governed by the ruling in the *Wapello* case. Dillon admitted that courts of justice were not at liberty to strike down laws on the ground that they conflicted with judicial notions of natural rights and of sound public policy.[35] But he thought that there were four specific constitutional provisions which had to be examined by the court in determining the constitutionality of the challenged law: (1) the clause guaranteeing the right to acquire and possess property, (2) the due-process guarantee, (3) the public-use limitation on the power of eminent domain, and (4) the clause stating that the enumeration of rights shall not impair the existence of other rights belonging to the people.[36]

Chief Justice Dillon admitted that there were several powers whereby the legislature could constitutionally abridge the property rights of the citizen, and he mentioned the taxing power as one of these. He discovered, however, that the act under consideration was "not a valid or legitimate exercise of the taxing power."[37] He said:

> . . . though the money demanded of the citizen is called a *tax,* it is not such, but is, in fact, a coercive contribution in favor of private railway corporations, and violative, not only of the general spirit of the Constitution as to the sacredness of private property, but of that specific provision which declares *that no man shall be deprived of his property without due process of law* (Bill of Rights, § 9)—a provision which is adequate to protect the owner from being despoiled of his property by an unauthorized tax law or illegal tax.[38]

In support of this statement the writer cited Cooley's *Constitutional Limitations.*[39] It is extremely doubtful that Cooley had regarded taxation for so-called private purposes as a denial of due process of law; for in his brief discussion of due process, as applied to taxation, he emphasized only procedurally defective tax impositions as constituting a violation of that provision. Dillon, however, reënforced Cooley's doctrine of implied limitations on the taxing power by relating it to due process of law.

Much of the importance of the chief justice's opinion derived from his discussion and analysis of the nature of taxation. He defined taxes as "burdens or charges imposed by the legislature upon persons and property to raise money for public purposes, or to accomplish some governmental end."[40] In a footnote he quoted Cooley and other authorities to support this definition.[41] Dillon emphasized that taxes were a product of stringent necessity and stated that the severity of tax laws was tolerable only because the life of the state depended upon governmental revenue from that source. He added that the legislature was the final judge of the expediency of exercises of the taxing power and of the power of eminent domain. But the courts, he argued, were entitled to inquire into the nature of the use or purpose.[42]

Dillon thought that a law could be declared unconstitutional for either of two reasons. First, a statute might represent an effort to exercise a power not legislative in character. Second, it might contravene specific constitutional provisions. Having directed his attention to the tax under consideration, he concluded that it was void for both of these reasons because "it appropriates private property to private purposes it is not in the nature of a law, and, therefore, deprives the citizen of his property without due process of law."[43] His principal objection to the tax seems to have been based upon his analysis of the character of the recipient. Railroad corporations, he observed, were private corporations, organized for the profit of their investors. If they were public corporations, he contended, they would be subject to unlimited legislative supervision. By emphasizing the nature of the recipient rather than that of the purpose of the grant, Dillon avoided, to a large extent, the difficulties inherent in his position. His analysis of the character of the purpose was confined to two or three relatively brief passages in which he denied that railroads were common highways and that incidental benefits to the public justified taxation.

Dillon's opinion in *Hanson v. Vernon,* like the opinions in many of the liberty of contract cases, was not devoid of economic premises, although in this instance they were not made articulate until the closing paragraph of the opinion. He said:

> One of the counsel has drawn, in eloquent terms, a graphic picture of the disastrous effects, in retarding the growth and development of the State, of holding the act under consideration to be invalid. As such considerations have no place in the judicial determination of the question, except to superinduce greater care and more sedate deliberation, I dismiss them, with an expression of my disbelief in the dangers which are apprehended, of my skepticism in the healthfulness of an artificial growth caused by the unnatural stimulus of public taxation in favor of private enterprises, and of my firm conviction that any benefits resulting from a different holding would be dearly purchased at the expense of the fundamental rights of the citizen.[44]

Laissez faire ideas concerning the legitimate objects of taxation were thus written into the constitutional law of Iowa as restrictions upon legislative powers. Although the decision in *Hanson v. Vernon* was subsequently overruled,[45] the general principles upon which it was predicated were to enjoy many years of judicial application.

The legislature of Wisconsin enacted a law similar to that invalidated in the *Hanson* case; and shortly after the Iowa decision, the Supreme Court of Wisconsin, speaking through Chief Justice Dixon, considered the constitutionality of this law in *Whiting v. Sheboygan & Fond du Lac R. R. Co.*[46] Like Judge Dillon, Chief Justice Dixon listed Cooley as an authority for the conclusion reached by his court, but he relied primarily upon the case of *Curtis v. Whipple.* (See pp. 110.) The high court denied that railroads because they exercised the power of eminent domain, were to be looked upon as public corporations. It regarded the *Hanson* case and *Sweet v. Hulbert*[47] as the only direct precedents for cases of this kind, and although it admitted that for some purposes railroads were public in character, they were not so in the sense that taxes could be levied to subsidize their construction and operation. Chief Justice Dixon intimated that counties could be authorized to subscribe to the stock of railroads where the road was one "situated within or passing through the corporate limits of the municipality to be taxed, and so promoting the general prosperity and welfare of the people who are to pay the taxes."[48] In support of his statement concerning the limitations upon the power of the legislature to authorize municipalities to subscribe to railroad stock, he cited a paragraph in Cooley's *Constitutional Limitations.*[49] The opinion in the *Whiting* case did not have as wide an import as had Dillon's opinion, but it indicated that the public purpose principle was gaining widespread acceptance, and that, upon the basis of that principle, legislative activities, long acquiesced in, were to be subjected to increasing judicial scrutiny.

A rehearing was ordered in the case, and a new opinion was rendered by Chief Justice Dixon. To a large extent he covered much the same ground and repeated many of the arguments which had been utilized in the initial opinion. The court relied more heavily upon Cooley, however; and it came to grips with some additional issues. Thus, it was said that the door was open to taxation for all kinds of purposes if incidental public benefits justified the exercise of the taxing power.[50] In its discussion of public benefits the court confounded public use and public purpose; and, quoting Cooley's *Constitutional Limitations,* the majority judges declared that the public-use requirement was not satisfied, in a legal sense, by proof of incidental public benefits.[51] Concluding his opinion, Chief Justice Dixon remarked that there was a substantial difference between donations to railroads and subscriptions to railroad stock. The former were certainly void, and he intimated that the latter were of doubtful constitutionality when he said:

> Certainly the consequences of upholding such subscriptions have been most sad and disastrous to many cities, towns, and counties throughout the country; and it is obvious from the tenor of Judge Cooley's remarks, that the doctrine does not meet with his approbation. Const. Lim. 213, 214. Shall decisions thus doubted and questioned be held to justify or compel a further step in the same direction?[52]

Cooley himself was given an opportunity to apply and to elaborate in a specific case the principles which he had set down in his *Constitutional Limitations.* In *People ex rel. Detroit & Howell R. R. Co. v. Township Board of Salem,*[53] decided by the Supreme Court of Michigan in 1870, four separate opinions were delivered by the judges; but, of these, Cooley's opinion was most important in later adjudications. The case concerned the validity of a statute authorizing townships to pledge their credit to aid in the construction of railroads.

Cooley assumed, in his opinion, that the law, if valid, was referable to the taxing power. He admitted, as he had already done in the *Constitutional Limitations,* that the taxing power was very broad and that, because of this, some courts had fallen into the error of treating it as unlimited. But he denied, in the following passage from his opinion, that the taxing power was without limitation:

> It is conceded, nevertheless, that there are certain limitations upon this power, not prescribed in express terms by any constitutional provision, but inherent in the subject itself, which attend its exercise under all circumstances, and which are as inflexible and absolute in their restraints as if directly imposed in the most positive form of words.[54]

Judge Cooley listed three prerequisites for constitutional exercises of the taxing power—prerequisites which he had previously mentioned in the *Constitutional Limitations.* First, the purpose for which the money was raised had to be public.[55] Second, the tax was to be laid according to some rule of apportionment and not by mere caprice.[56] Third, when a tax was laid by a subdivision of the state, its purpose had to be both public and local.[57] The judge stated that these three principles were fundamentals of the law of taxation, and that taxation without reference to them was not taxation at all and was therefore void. Although the courts might find it unpleasant to pass upon the validity of tax laws challenged by aggrieved persons, it was, according to this view, their duty to do so.

Having directed his attention to the general question of what constituted a public purpose, Judge Cooley used language similar to that employed in the *Constitutional Limitations*. He thought that public purposes comprehended not only services which of necessity the state provided but also considerations of equity, gratitude, and charity. He added that where a general public purpose was to be subserved the state itself could lay taxes, or it could apportion taxes among its subdivisions. Although he appeared to doubt that a township should bear a tax burden for a purpose of the kind involved in this case, he placed his decision upon the broad ground that no public purpose, either general or local, was subserved by the challenged legislation. He declared:

> Primarily, therefore, the money when raised, is to benefit a private corporation; to add to its funds and improve its property; and the benefit to the public is to be secondary and incidental, like that which springs from the building of a grist-mill, the establishment of a factory, the opening of a public inn, or from any other private enterprise which accommodates a local want and tends to increase local values.[58]

Cooley admitted that railroads were, in some respects, public highways and, for that reason, subject to special legislative control. But he denied that they were public to a degree that the power of taxation might be invoked in order to aid them.

In his discussion of the nature of taxation the judge rather clearly disclosed the laissez faire economic principles upon which many of his constitutional theories were based:

> But when we examine the power of taxation with a view to ascertain the purpose for which burdens may be imposed upon the public, we perceive at once that necessity is not the governing consideration, and that in many cases it has little or nothing to do with the question presented. Certain objects must of necessity be provided for under this power, but in regard to innumerable other objects for which the State imposes taxes upon its citizens, the question always is one of mere policy, and if the taxes are imposed, it is not because it is absolutely necessary that those objects should be accomplished, but because on the whole it is deemed best by the public authorities

that they should be. On the other hand certain things of absolute necessity to civilized society the State is precluded, either by express constitutional provisions, or by necessary implication, from providing for at all; and they are left wholly to the fostering care of private enterprise and private liberality. . . . Certain professions and occupations in life are also essential, but we have no authority to employ the public moneys to induce persons to enter them. The necessity may be pressing, and to supply it may be, in a certain sense, to accomplish a "public purpose"; but it is not a purpose for which the power of taxation may be employed.[59]

Cooley thus denied that the question of public purpose was referable to the necessity of the object for which taxes were levied. In doing so, he made a notable contribution to the cause of laissez faire. As industrialization of the economy proceeded, as cities became larger and more congested, new needs arose; but, if necessity were not the measure of public purpose, how then could the state and local governments justify taxation where its object was to relieve these unprecedented necessities? Cooley had given minority interests (and they were usually propertied interests) an exceedingly powerful weapon with which they could beat back legislative attempts to extend the fiscal powers of government into new areas.

Cooley's laissez faire economic and social ideas were made even more articulate in another paragraph in his opinion:

By common consent also a large portion of the most urgent needs of society are relegated exclusively to the law of demand and supply. It is this in its natural operation, and without the interference of government, that gives us the proper proportion of tillers of the soil, artisans, manufacturers, merchants, and professional men, and that determines when and where they shall give to society the benefit of their particular services. However great the need in the direction of any particular calling, the interference of the government is not tolerated, because though it might be supplying a public want, it is considered as invading the domain that belongs exclusively to private inclination and enterprise.[60]

If the character of the purpose were not to be determined by its necessity or importance, then what standard was to be used by legislators and judges in distinguishing valid exercises of the taxing power from those which were invalid? Cooley answered that the term "public purpose" was a "term of classification, to distinguish the objects for which according to settled usage, the government is to provide, from those which, by the like usage, are left to private inclination, interest, or liberality."[61] By this standard the legitimate objects for which the government could tax were the traditional objects and only those. The area in which private enterprise currently operated was thus given constitutional status.

Cooley admitted that the state had once engaged in the transportation business, but he added that this was no longer the practice. He refused to accept the act as a bounty on the ground that the legislature had no power to spend money in order to establish private persons in business. Moreover, such enactments were void, he thought, because they discriminated between different occupations. Incidental public benefits did not make a purpose public, and provision for railroad facilities was not substantially different from making other facilities of a private nature available to a community. In his brief allusion to previous cases Cooley stated that they were either inapplicable or that they were decided under circumstances making careful analysis impossible.

Both Chief Justice Campbell and Justice Christiancy wrote separate concurring opinions, but these judges differed little, if at all, with Cooley. Their opinions were scarcely ever cited in later cases whereas Cooley's opinion was an extremely important source of constitutional propositions which the state courts, in subsequent cases, followed. Justice Graves, the fourth member of the court, wrote a forceful dissenting opinion in which he disagreed with every principle accepted by the majority except the general proposition that taxes were to be levied for public purposes only.[62]

The case of *People v. Salem* came as a climax to the rather belated judicial movement to arrest public financial aid, either direct or indirect, to railroad companies.[63] Three state supreme courts had come to accept the view that laws authorizing municipal and county aid to privately owned railroads were void.[64] The courts of Wisconsin and of Iowa were soon virtually to abandon this position, however,[65] and only in Michigan were such statutes declared void in later years.[66] A few individual judges continued to resist the overwhelming current of authority which sustained such aid, but their resistance proved futile. The Supreme Court of the United States consistently affirmed the constitutionality of taxation for such purposes, and the authority of that tribunal was sufficient to resolve any lingering doubts on the question.[67]

Superficially considered, the outcome of the judicial controversy over public aid to railroads appears to have represented a stunning setback to the ideas which Cooley and Dillon were advocating. It is true that on the immediate issue, the constitutionality of aid to railroad companies, these publicists had not carried the day. Their failure in this respect may be attributed largely to the fact that their efforts came too late—by 1870 most state tribunals had approved legislation of this kind. After that date a number of courts indicated that if the question were still an open one, they would be disposed to decide the case as Cooley and Dillon had done;[68] but these tribunals were not willing to overturn past precedents and to repudiate financial obligations which, in earlier decisions, had been declared valid and binding. The economic consequences of such judicial action would have been most grave. And but few judges were prepared, out of deference to abstract legal principles, to reach a conclusion from which these consequences would almost certainly flow. All things considered, it is remarkable that Cooley and Dillon were able to convince even individual judges of the correctness of the decisions given in the *Salem* and *Hanson* cases.

The failure of the Cooley-Dillon thesis that public aid could not be extended to railroads detracted very little from the over-all success of these two writers. The general principles enunciated by them in these cases were enormously influential. Cooley and Dillon had argued that taxes could be levied for public purposes only; they had urged that the courts were not bound by legislative judgment in these matters; and Cooley had maintained that custom and usage made up the criterion whereby the character of the purpose could be ascertained. These principles received almost universal approbation from the courts in later cases. And these principles had far greater effect upon the constitutional and political development of the country than did the outcome of the controversy over public aid to the railroads. Cooley and Dillon may have lost a battle, but they were winning a war.

After 1870 the public purpose maxim gained widespread judicial approval. In one state court after another it was accepted either explicitly or by implication. These cases served the proponents of laissez faire well in later adjudications, but they are more interesting as examples of the application of the public purpose restriction than as landmarks in its development and elaboration. For that reason analysis of them is deferred until the next chapter. The *Salem* case was not the last major contribution to the development of the public purpose doctrine, however. Cooley and Dillon had not been silenced, and Mr. Justice Miller had yet to speak.

In 1872 Dillon published his *Treatise on the Law of Municipal Corporations.* With the exceptions of Cooley's *Constitutional Limitations* and *Treatise on Taxation,* which appeared later (see pp. 125–127), Dillon's work was the most cited authority for the public purpose restriction. Actually, Dillon said nothing in the work which had not already been said before either by himself or by Cooley, but certain passages from his book became standard citations anyway. Only a few public purpose cases involved the validity of legislation whereby the states themselves attempted to obtain, by taxation, revenue for questionable objects. Most of the litigation in which the public purpose principle was an important consideration involved statutes authorizing cities and other governmental subdivisions to tax and to spend for certain purposes. Partly for this reason, the *Municipal Corporations,* dealing as it did with the powers and functions of cities, was widely quoted and cited in public purpose cases.

In the course of his discussion of the power of the states to enable cities to tax, Dillon declared:

... *taxes* (including, in the term, assessments) are burdens or charges imposed by the legislature, or under its authority, upon persons or property to raise money for *public,* as distinguished from *private, purposes,* or to accomplish some end or object *public in its nature.* There can be no legitimate taxation to raise money unless it be destined for the uses or benefit of the government or of some of its municipalities, or divisions invested with the power of auxiliary or local administration. A public use or purpose is of the essence of a tax. Theoretically, the tax-payer is compensated for the taxes he pays in the protection afforded to him and his property by the government which exacts the tax; but the substantial foundation of the power is political, civil, or governmental necessity, and taxes are largely, if not wholly, as Mr. Mill contends, sacrifices for the public good, "equality of sacrifice" being the rule dictated by justice.[89]

The above passage is one of the few in which Dillon mentioned the public purpose principle, and it was frequently cited by attorneys and judges in subsequent cases. Municipal activities were directly challenging the dogmas of laissez faire, but the courts and the lawyers were prepared to meet the challenge with a powerful weapon.

The Supreme Court of the United States was confronted with the rising tide of professional opinion to the effect that the public purpose maxim was judicially enforceable against state legislatures. When one recalls the belabored process whereby that tribunal came to accept the liberty of contract as a restraint upon exercises of the police power, the Court's relatively enthusiastic acceptance of the public purpose restriction is somewhat startling. Still, the latter limitation, unlike the liberty of contract, could be incorporated into American constitutional law without resort to the Fourteenth Amendment and without revolutionizing the Court's relations with the states.

In a number of the railroad-bond cases the Supreme Court had intimated that the public purpose limitation was a sound general principle, but in none of these cases was the principle interpreted in such a way that the statute involved was invalidated.[70] A majority of the Court always held that aid to railroads was a public purpose for which government bonds could be issued and taxes levied. The general proposition appeared to rest in a state of suspended animation, awaiting an occasion for vitalization and application. That opportunity presented itself in *Loan Association v. Topeka.*[71]

The case pertained to the constitutionality of a municipal-bond issue, authorized by the legislature of Kansas, to aid in the establishment of a privately owned bridge factory. Speaking through John Dillon (who had previously become a United States judge), the Circuit Court of the United States for the District of Kansas held that the bonds were devoid of legal obligation on the ground that the state legislature had no power to authorize the city to issue them.[72] The plaintiff sued out a writ of error, and the case went to the Supreme Court of the United States.

Justice Miller delivered the majority opinion holding that the bonds were void and without obligation, and this decision was based solely upon the Court's interpretation of the public purpose maxim. As was done in a number of state cases, Justice Miller assumed that the validity of a law authorizing a city to contract a debt for a certain purpose depended upon the validity of the purpose from the standpoint of taxation.[73] A major part of his opinion dealt with an analysis of the railroad-bond cases. He stated that the central issue in those cases was not the admissibility of the public purpose principle as a general maxim of constitutional law but rather whether or not that principle prohibited taxation for the purpose of raising money to be given or lent to private railroad companies. But the opinion of the Court was not based upon the railroad bond precedents alone. Justice Miller, in forceful language, declared:

The theory of our governments, State and National, is opposed to the deposit of unlimited power anywhere. The executive, the legislative, and the judicial branches of these governments are all of limited and defined powers.

There are limitations on such power which grow out of the essential nature of all free governments. Implied reservations of individual rights, without which the social compact could not exist, and which are respected by all governments entitled to the name. No court, for instance, would hesitate to declare void a statute which enacted that A. and B. who were husband and wife to each other should be so no longer, but that A. should thereafter be the husband of C., and B. the wife of D. Or which should enact that the homestead now owned by A. should no longer be his, but should henceforth be the property of B.[74]

This passage is reminiscent of the language employed by Justice Chase in *Calder v. Bull* (see p. 5), but to support his views Miller cited more recent authorities—the opinion of Chief Justice Dixon in the *Whiting* case, Cooley's *Constitutional Limitations*[75] and Dillon's *Municipal Corporations*.[76]

Miller's opinion continued with the declaration that taxation for private purposes was a form of robbery done under the color of legality. Quoting from Webster's dictionary and from Cooley's *Constitutional Limitations,* he concluded that the idea of a public purpose or use inhered in the very nature of a tax. But it was with respect to the functions of the legislature and of the judiciary in ascertaining the nature of a given purpose that Miller made his most interesting observation. He said:

It is undoubtedly the duty of the legislature which imposes or authorizes municipalities to impose a tax to see that it is not to be used for purposes of private interest instead of a public use, and the courts can only be justified in interposing when a violation of this principle is clear and the reason for interference cogent. And in deciding whether, in the given case, the object for which the taxes are assessed falls upon the one side or the other of this line, they must be governed mainly by the course and usage of the government, the objects for which taxes have been customarily and by long course of legislation levied, what objects or purposes have been considered necessary to the support and for the proper use of the government, whether

State or municipal. Whatever lawfully pertains to this and is sanctioned by time and the acquiescence of the people may well be held to belong to the public use, and proper for the maintenance of good government, though this may not be the only criterion of rightful taxation.[77]

The standard of measurement which Miller set forth in the above statement is similar to that which Cooley had formulated in the *Salem* case, but that precedent was not cited by the Court in this connection. Although Justice Miller indicated that the custom and usage criterion was not the only standard whereby the nature of the object might be determined, his emphasis upon past practices tended to make legislative innovation the object of judicial suspicion. The burden of proof borne by the champions of laissez faire was thus materially lightened.

The majority judges denied, upon the authority of several state precedents, that incidental public benefits justified taxation. They admitted that such benefits would probably accrue to a community which induced, by means of subsidies, private persons to establish businesses therein. But the benefits would not be direct, and subsidies of that kind were therefore void. Miller observed that "no line can be drawn in favor of the manufacturer which would not open the coffers of the public treasury to the importunities of two-thirds of the business men of the city or town."[78] The Supreme Court thus accepted, without allusion to any specific constitutional provision, the doctrine of public purpose.[79] Cooley's defense of implied limitations on the taxing power had been formally vindicated by the nation's highest tribunal.

It is perhaps significant that the senior justice, Nathan Clifford, was the lone dissenter in the *Topeka* case. In an opinion recalling those of the judicial era when legislative power was virtually identified with the sovereignty of the states, he declared that the judiciary possessed no power to invalidate laws because they were deemed unwise or contrary to the general latent spirit of the Constitution. He argued:

Vague apprehensions seem to be entertained that unless such a power is claimed and exercised inequitable consequences may result from unnecessary taxation, but in my judgment there is much more to be dreaded from judicial decisions which may have the effect to sanction the fraudulent repudiation of honest debts, than from any statutes passed by the State to enable municipal corporations to meet and discharge their just pecuniary obligations.[80]

Justice Clifford's brief dissent had firmer roots in past practice than had the opinion of the majority, but it passed virtually unheeded by bench and bar. On the other hand, the majority opinion was a response to the insistent demands of the proponents of laissez faire constitutional principles; and, for that reason, it became a leading precedent in later cases.

As of 1874 the advocates of the public purpose maxim as a judicially enforceable requirement for constitutional exercises of the taxing power had at their disposal an impressive array of authorities supporting their position. Cooley's *Constitutional Limitations,* Dillon's *Municipal Corporations,* and Miller's opinion in the *Topeka* case were basic documents upon which they repeatedly relied for support. In addition, the case law of the states provided these tribunals with valuable citations. But one other basic contribution to the early development of laissez faire restrictions upon the taxing power must yet be noticed. Two years after the decision in the *Topeka* case, Cooley published his immensely popular *A Treatise on the Law of Taxation,*[81] which, together with his *Constitutional Limitations* and his *Torts,* accounts for the esteem which his profession accorded him.

The work contains no innovation on the general principle of public purpose as set forth by him in the *Constitutional Limitations.* A minute comparison of the two works may disclose possible changes of emphasis, but Cooley's language is elusive and one cannot be sure that these changes represent anything more than modifications in style and expression. If any change did occur in the eight years intervening between the publication of the two works, it was in the direction of reducing the rather wide area of legislative discretion which the language of the *Constitutional Limitations* seemed to allow. In both works, however, Cooley maintained that a presumption always existed in favor of the law, a contention which the courts honored as much in its breach as in its observance.

The influence of the treatise in public purpose litigation derived from its exhaustive treatment of the subject. In the *Constitutional Limitations* and in Dillon's *Municipal Corporations* only a few paragraphs discussed the subject, but the *Treatise on Taxation* contains, in addition to a few scattered passages, a chapter entitled "The Purposes for Which Taxes May Be Laid."[82] There Cooley discussed more fully than had been done previously the objects for which taxes could be levied and money expended. The writer classified the objects for which the legislatures had attempted to lay taxes as follows: (1) religious instruction, (2) secular instruction, (3) public charity, (4) private business enterprises, (5) moral obligations, (6) amusements and celebrations, (7) highways and roads, (8) municipal water and light works, (9) military bounties, (10) public health, (11) protection against calamities, and (12) payment of public debt.[83]

Cooley regarded some of these objects as unquestionably public in nature. Without hesitation, he placed public charity, the fulfillment of moral obligations, municipal water and light works, military bounties, preservation of the public health (through provision for drainage and protection against overflow), and payment of the public debt in this category.[84] No serious objections to the public character of these purposes could be adduced or entertained.

According to his view, certain other objects were of a more doubtful nature. Under most circumstances they could be regarded as public purposes, but there were important exceptions to this general rule. Thus Cooley defended the power of the legislature to lay taxes for the support of secular education, but he insisted that such support be confined to public schools.[85] The state had no power to subsidize privately controlled educational institutions even though they were engaged in secular instruction. With respect to amusements and celebrations, he observed that "to furnish amusements to its citizens is not one of the functions of government."[86] Nevertheless, he approved, even lauded, the establishment of public parks through the expenditure of public money. While maintaining that the state could legitimately engage in the construction of highways, roads, canals, and railroads, he intimated some continuing doubt as to its power to aid private companies organized for those purposes.[87] As to the constitutionality of taxes laid for the purpose of protecting the community against disaster, he declared that "if the danger is sufficiently great and extensive to make the threatened calamity a matter of general concern, the purpose is public; if not, it will not justify taxation."[88]

Only two purposes which Cooley discussed were regarded by him as clearly private in character. Although admitting that it had once been the business of government to provide for and to support religious instruction, he asserted that this was no longer true and that many state constitutions, by express provision, forbade the practice.[89] He was even more emphatic in denying that aid to private business enterprises was a public purpose justifying subsidies or loans by the government. Articulating one of the economic ideas underlying his legal principles, Cooley declared that "enlightened states leave every man to depend for his success and prosperity in business on his own exertions, in the belief that by doing so his own industry will be more certainly enlisted, and his prosperity and happiness more likely to be secured."[90]

During the eight years which elapsed between the publication of the *Constitutional Limitations* and the appearance of the *Treatise on Taxation* all basic authorities which the courts utilized in applying the public purpose limitation had become available. Cooley, in his first work, had brought together the scattered and rather flimsy precedents of the pre-Civil War period and had derived from them a reasonably coherent doctrine. Dillon, both as judge and as text writer, had added the weight of his authority to the cause; and the Supreme Court of the United States had approved the fundamental principle for which these men had contended. Finally, in 1876, Cooley had presented his profession with the first comprehensive analysis of the public purpose limitation on legislative power. For approximately forty years these were the principal materials upon which bench and bar relied in their efforts to make the taxing power compatible with principles of laissez faire.[91]

Discussion of the public purpose maxim as an important element in laissez faire constitutionalism would be neither complete nor meaningful, however, without reference to judicial applications of the principle in specific cases. It was in the opinions that the judges disclosed, often with startling candor, the economic and social predilections from which the maxim was derived and which ensured its continued vitality. Moreover, it is from the cases that one may gather something of the enormous influence which Cooley and Dillon enjoyed during the period.

5 *The Application and Decline of the Public Purpose Maxim*

MORE THAN ONE HUNDRED opinions involving discussion of the public purpose maxim as a restriction upon governmental fiscal powers were delivered by the state and federal courts between 1870 and 1910—those years roughly marking off the period in which the principle was most frequently utilized by bench and bar.[1] A considerable number of these had but little constitutional or social significance, and some represented minor setbacks to the cause of laissez faire. But, on the whole, the proponents of the new constitutional order gained impressive victories in these opinions. The influence which Cooley and Dillon, two of the foremost spokesmen for laissez faire principles, were currently exercising upon the members of their profession is evidenced by the reliance which the courts placed upon their works in well over 50 per cent of these opinions.

The cases which are analyzed in this chapter were selected with two ends in view: (1) to show how and to what extent the treatises and judicial opinions of these publicists were used by the courts and (2) to illustrate the objects for which the courts refused to permit the taxing and spending powers to be exercised. These objects, with a few unimportant exceptions, fall into one of three categories: financial assistance to private business enterprises, financial aid to individuals and to private noncommercial associations, and establishment of state or municipal enterprises. Under certain circumstances these objects were regarded by the judiciary as legitimate bases for the

---

[1] For notes to chap. 5, see pp. 193–198.

exercise of the taxing and spending powers, but the subtle, and often quite meaningless, distinctions in which the courts indulged when cases arose involving taxation and expenditures for such purposes may be appreciated only by reference to the opinions themselves.

Aid to Private Business Enterprises

It will be recalled from the preceding chapter that many public purpose cases decided before the Civil War were the products of legislative attempts to extend financial assistance to private business enterprises. Generally, these enterprises were engaged in making internal improvements, an activity long considered a matter of public concern. For that reason, the courts, often with misgivings, usually sustained the constitutionality of taxation and appropriations for these objects. But considerable resistance to this kind of aid soon developed. A number of individual judges and three state supreme courts refused to tolerate the expenditure of public money for the purpose of aiding private railroad companies. (See pp. 111–120.) Eventually, this resistance was overwhelmed, and, by the early 1870's, it had become reasonably clear that railroad companies were the only important private businesses which the state and its subdivisions could subsidize.

In 1871 the Supreme Judicial Court of Maine was called upon, by the legislature of that state, to answer two important questions. Only the first of these questions is relevant to the subject here, and the second is considered in a subsequent section.[2] The first question propounded was as follows: "Has the legislature authority under the constitution to pass laws enabling towns, by gifts of money or loans of bonds, to assist individuals or corporations to establish or carry on manufacturing of various kinds, within or without the limits of said towns?"[3] Five separate opinions were prepared by members of the court, but there was general agreement that the question should be answered in the negative. The principal opinion, rendered by Chief Justice Appleton and supported by two associate justices, reveals the economic theories underlying the constitutional principles which the judges applied. After resorting to the increasingly popular doctrine of implied limitations on the taxing power, Appleton noted that manufacturers, like those engaged in other pursuits, were interested primarily in realizing profits. Then, in language which would have done credit to Adam Smith, he declared:

Capital naturally gravitates to the best investment. If a particular place or a special kind of manufacture promises large returns, the capitalist will be little likely to hesitate in selecting the place and in determining upon the manufacture. But whatever is done, whether by the individual or the corporation, it is done with the same hope and expectation with which the farmer plows his fields and sows his grain—the anticipated returns.[4]

Having made this observation, the judge pointed out that a particular business either operated at a profit or at a loss. If it returned a profit, no public purpose was realized by spending money to increase that profit. And if it operated at a loss, no public purpose was fulfilled by requiring the taxpayer to make up for that loss.

Chief Justice Appleton admitted that communities were benefited by "every description of well-directed labor," including manufacturing.[5] But, in language strikingly similar to that employed by Cooley in the *Salem* case, he emphasized that the state had no power to discriminate in favor of any one type of employment.[6] Appleton did not choose, however, to rest his decision upon the doctrine of implied limitations and upon economic considerations alone. Three constitutional provisions were invoked to justify the holding. In the first place, he mentioned the public-use clause of the constitution and argued that it was intended to protect the individual against "private rapacity."[7] He added that the constitution guaranteed the rights of acquiring and possessing property and that this provision would be of little import if the legislature possessed the power to authorize the majority to transfer, by means of taxation, property from one person to another. The third constitutional provision which the judge regarded as applicable was the law-of-the-land clause. In language which may have been based in part upon a passage from Chief Justice Dillon's opinion in *Hanson v. Vernon,* he remarked:

The constitution provides, that no person shall "be deprived of his life, liberty, property, or privileges, but by judgment of his peers or the law of the land." Property taken by taxation is not taken by the judgment of our peers. A statute in direct violation of the primary principles of justice is not "the law of the land" within the meaning of the constitution. Every citizen holds life, liberty, and property by the law and under its protection. Every enactment is not of itself and necessarily a law or the law of the land. Such

is not a statute passed for the very purpose of working a wrong and in violation of the constitution. To declare it to be so would render this part of the
constitution nugatory and nonsensical.[8]

Upon the basis of these considerations, Chief Justice Appleton concluded that the question raised by the legislature had to be answered
in the negative.

Apparently the state legislature was not much impressed by the
court's advice. Scarcely two weeks after the delivery of the opinion,
it ratified an ordinance of the town of Jay whereby the town agreed
to lend its credit, up to ten thousand dollars, to certain persons in
order to induce them to erect within the town a steam sawmill, a
gristmill, and a box factory and to operate same for a period of not
less than ten years. Several taxpayers of the town challenged the
validity of the law and of the ordinance, and these measures were
reviewed by the Supreme Judicial Court in *Allen v. Inhabitants of
Jay.*[9]

The court, speaking through Chief Justice Appleton, struck down
the ordinance and the statute purporting to validate it on the ground
that the object of the proposed loan was private in character. The
chief justice pointed out, on the authority of Dillon's opinion in
Hanson v. Vernon and the definitions given by other judges, that
taxes could be laid for public purposes only. Although no tax law
was involved in the litigation, the public purpose principle was
thought to be applicable because, as the judges reasoned, the money
for the loan would ultimately come from the pockets of the taxpayers of the community. Just as he had done in his advisory opinion
of the preceding year, Appleton invoked, together with the doctrine
of implied limitations on legislative power, the public-use and the
law-of-the-land clauses of the state constitution.

Appleton's opinion has many passages which give evidence of the
economic theories which he and his colleagues entertained. Thus, he
said that the owners of capital seek the best investment and that
those who have, by industry and economy, acquired capital are the
best judges of where it should be invested.[10] He added that no loan
of the kind contemplated in the ordinance would be necessary if
private investors regarded the project as one promising financial
reward. And he emphasized that the promotion of losing enterprises
was not a public purpose for which money could be raised by taxa-

tion. In his discussion of the loan Judge Appleton expressed some of the judicial fears which legislation of this kind was likely to stimulate:

If the loan be made to one or more for a particular object, it is favoritism. It is discrimination in favor of the particular individual, and a particular industry, thereby aided, and is one adverse to and against all individuals, all industries not thus aided.

If it is to be loaned to all, then it is practically a division of property under the name of a loan. *It is communism incipient, if not perfected.*[11]

The Supreme Court of Maine thus declared that public loans to private enterprises were in the same category as subsidies of that kind. Both types of assistance were unconstitutional for want of a public purpose. Had the court been disposed to do so, it could have found ample grounds for sustaining the law and the ordinance without creating any doubts as to its complete acceptance of the public purpose maxim. For many years it had been the practice of American governments, both local and state, to permit the power of eminent domain to be exercised for the purpose of establishing privately owned sawmills and gristmills. The courts, in the past, had almost always said that the public-use requirement for exercises of this power was not violated by such legislation. In the *Allen* case, however, the court, when it invoked the public-use clause as a basis for its holding, carefully avoided reference to this line of precedents as well as to those sustaining the constitutionality of railroad aid.

The efforts of local governments to aid manufacturing enterprises and to encourage industrialization received another staggering blow from the Supreme Court of Maine during the following year. In 1870 the town of Brewer had voted to exempt from taxation, for a period of ten years, all manufacturing enterprises thereafter established within its limits. Shortly after this vote was taken, the Brewer Brick Company was organized and began operations in the town. Local officials, in accordance with the town vote, exempted the company from taxation in 1871, but the following year these officials, possibly out of deference to the court's decisions and *dicta* in the *Allen* case, refused to allow the exemption and proceeded to collect taxes on the assessed valuation of the company's property. The company paid the tax but subsequently instituted proceedings against the town to recover the amount paid. The Supreme Court of Maine was given the opportunity to determine the validity of the tax-exemption ordinance in *Brewer Brick Co. v. Inhabitants of Brewer.*[12]

Chief Justice Appleton wrote the opinion for a unanimous court. Upon the basis of the public purpose maxim, he declared that the vote was invalid and that state legislation, passed in 1864, permitting the towns to grant such exemptions was unconstitutional. In support of the public purpose restriction, he quoted from Dillon's opinions in *Hanson v. Vernon*[13] and *Commercial National Bank v. Iola* and from Cooley's *Constitutional Limitations*.[14] Judge Appleton observed that it was settled that outright gifts to private business enterprises could not be made by the public; and he reasoned that a tax-exemption was in effect a subsidy and, for that reason void, unless the exemption was made for some public purpose. Moreover, he contended that the exemption of one business from the payment of taxes undermined the competitive position of businesses not so favored. He added:

One manufacturer is taxed for his own estate and for that which is exempted, to relieve his competing neighbor, and to enable the latter to undersell him in the common market;—and that is precisely the relation these plaintiffs bear to their competing brick makers;—a grosser inequality is hardly conceivable![15]

In conclusion, Appleton declared that the exemption would serve one of two purposes—either it would increase the profits of the one at the expense of many, or it would support the operation of a losing business. And these supposed alternative results made the exemption "either unnecessary or unwise."[16] The courts of the time were not reluctant to invalidate legislation because they regarded it as unnecessary or unwise, but it is seldom that one finds them clearly stating those reasons, as was done in this case.

Aside from the shadowy precedent established in the case of *Weeks v. Milwaukee*,[17] the *Brewer* case was the first in which a tax exemption was invalidated on the ground that it was, in effect, a gift for a private purpose. Formerly, the courts had been content to test such exemptions upon the basis of uniformity clauses in state constitutions and municipal charters. To some extent, the court relied on such provisions in the *Brewer* case, but it placed greater emphasis upon the public purpose maxim in reaching its conclusions.

The principles which were applied in the *Allen* and *Brewer* cases received the enthusiastic endorsement of the Supreme Court of the United States in 1874. As a result of the decision in *Loan Association v. Topeka,*[18] it became a settled proposition of American constitutional law that aid to private business enterprises (railroads, of course, excepted) was not a public purpose for which the state legislatures could exercise their taxing and spending powers. Some forty cases involving aid to private businesses (other than railroads) came before state supreme courts and federal courts between 1870 and 1910. In all but one of these, the judiciary ruled against the constitutionality of the aid on the ground that it was not for a public purpose.[19] The courts, as a rule, were satisfied that public financial assistance could not be extended to businesses which were privately owned and operated; and the judges, in their opinions, paid but little attention to the specific kinds of businesses involved in these cases. Thus, they invalidated measures granting either loans or subsidies to a lumber company,[20] to a wool manufacturer,[21] to a corporation engaged in mining and manufacturing iron,[22] to a stave mill,[23] to producers and manufacturers of sugar,[24] and to a company making boxes.[25] And in most opinions delivered in this general category of cases the debt which the bench owed to Cooley and Dillon is evidenced by direct citations to their works and opinions.

During the same period the public purpose maxim was applied in cases involving other kinds of legislation. In these cases there was somewhat less harmony among the judges and among the courts than there was in those cases pertaining to the constitutionality of subsidies to private businesses. Nevertheless, the decisions established effective barriers against other kinds of "paternalism" and "socialism."

Aid to Individuals and Private Associations

Not even charitable and relief measures enacted by the legislatures were safe at the hands of the judges as they interpreted and applied the public purpose maxim. The judiciary had discovered an effective weapon—one which might be used whenever considerations of public charity appeared to challenge the tenets of laissez faire. The orientation of the public purpose principle so as to make it a standard whereby public charity, as provided for by the legislature, might undergo judicial scrutiny had been anticipated in *Philadelphia Association v. Wood,* but it was not fully realized until after 1870.

In 1872 a great fire swept through a large section of Boston. As a result, many persons were made homeless, and a number of business establishments were destroyed. Shortly after the disaster occurred, the state legislature passed a law authorizing the city to issue bonds, in an amount not exceeding $20,000,000, the proceeds from which were to be used for the rehabilitation of the devastated area. The statute provided for the creation of a special commission endowed with authority to make loans, properly secured by mortgages, to owners of land upon which the buildings had been burned. The recipients of these loans were required to use the money for the purpose of reconstructing buildings which the fire had destroyed.

A taxpayers' suit was instituted to enjoin the city from issuing the bonds, and in the case of *Lowell v. Boston*[26] the Supreme Judicial Court of Massachusetts was asked to review the law and to pass upon its validity. Judge Wells, speaking for a unanimous court, delivered an opinion holding the statute unconstitutional. In the second paragraph of his opinion he assumed that the question of the validity of the bonds was referable to the taxing power on the ground that only by taxation could the interest and principal on the bonded indebtedness be paid by the city. Moreover, he maintained that there was no question of municipal authority involved in the case. Rather it was a question of legislative power. In his discussion of the character of the taxing power he declared:

The power to levy taxes is founded on the right, duty, and responsibility to maintain and administer all the governmental functions of the State, and to provide for the public welfare. To justify any exercise of the power requires that the expenditure which it is intended to meet shall be for some public service, or some object which concerns the public welfare. The promotion of the interests of individuals, either in respect of property or business, although it may result incidentally in the advancement of the public welfare, is, in its essential character, a private and not a public object. However certain and great the resulting good to the general public, it does not, by reason of its comparative importance, cease to be incidental.[27]

Judge Wells invoked a number of specific constitutional provisions to support this view, but, at best, they were of doubtful applicability.[28] Although he admitted that there was a distinction between the power of eminent domain and that of taxation, he thought that they were identical as to their source (governmental necessity) and their ends (public service and public use).

Most of the opinion consists of a review of precedents affirming the authority of the legislature to invoke either the power of eminent domain or the taxing power on behalf of private persons. Judge Wells admitted that there were many such cases but insisted that they could be distinguished as exceptions to the general rule. Thus, he justified milldam acts, aid to private aqueduct companies and to railroads, and the regulation of the right of flowage. Turning to that clause of the state constitution which empowered the legislature to make reasonable laws and ordinances for "the good and welfare of the Commonwealth," he observed that it was a much broader ground for the exercise of legislative power than were "public use" and "public service," but he added that the former merely expressed the ultimate purpose of any exercise of legislative power whereas the latter specified that there must be "a direct relation between the object of an appropriation and the public enjoyment."[29] Citing Cooley's *Constitutional Limitations,* he pointed out that the public use or service intended might practically affect only a small number of the inhabitants of the state and that "the essential point is, that it affects them as a community, and not merely as individuals."[30]

Judge Wells found that there was no public use or public service declared in the fire-loan law, and he thought that none could be inferred from its language. He maintained that the expressed purpose of the statute—to stimulate rebuilding on land swept by the fire— was a way of stating collectively the general result as a single object of attainment, and he added:

. . . but the fund raised is intended to be appropriated distributively, by separate loans to numerous individuals, each one of which will be independent of any relation to the others, or to any general purpose, except that of aiding individual enterprise in matters of private business.[31]

He reiterated that such purposes were private in character and that the magnitude of the calamity, although a matter of legislative concern, was not relevant to the question of the constitutionality of the statute. In conclusion, the judge invoked *Allen v. Jay* as a precedent for the court's decision.

The *Lowell* case represents a remarkable application of the public purpose principle as discovered by the court in certain constitutional provisions which gained judicial attention only by their indefinite language. The *Lowell* case was not an exceptional one. Some eleven years later, the Supreme Court of South Carolina struck down a law whereby the legislature of that state attempted to ratify a bond issue of the city of Charleston. The bonds were issued for the purpose of obtaining money to be lent to persons whose property was destroyed by a fire which had devastated the city. In *Feldman & Co. v. City Council of Charleston*[32] the court, speaking through Judge McIver, declared that taxation implied a public purpose. Cooley's *Constitutional Limitations* and several recently decided cases served as authorities for this principle.[33] The court invoked, to support the public purpose maxim, a constitutional provision which declared that "the enumeration of rights in this Constitution shall not be construed to impair or deny others retained by the people, and all powers not herein delegated remain with the people."[34] Quoting from Dillon's *Municipal Corporations,* the court argued that incidental public benefits alone could not justify taxation.[35] The court found that, at best, the public benefits derived from this statute were incidental and that, consequently, the law was void.

The judiciary thus arrested legislative relief to devastated urban communities. And that branch of the government soon indicated that it would play no favorites in matters of this kind. In 1874 a large area in the state of Kansas was visited by a drought, which destroyed crops and rendered the farmers of that area virtually destitute. The state legislature enacted a law which authorized townships to issue bonds for relief purposes or, more specifically, for the purpose of lending seed and feed grain, as well as other provisions, to needy farmers. The recipients of the aid were required to execute notes promising to repay the loan with 10 per cent interest; and these notes, by statutory provision, were made liens upon the recipients' properties. Certain taxpayers of Osawkee Township sought to enjoin the enforcement of the statute, and the Supreme Court of Kansas considered the validity of the bonds and the law authorizing them in *State ex rel. Griffith v. Osawkee Township.*[36]

Judge Brewer delivered the court's unanimous opinion, in which he declared that two propositions were settled. He maintained that taxes could be levied only for public purposes and that the validity of municipal bonds, to be paid for by taxation, turned upon whether or not they were issued for a public purpose. He admitted that "the

relief of the poor, the care of those who are unable to care for themselves, is among the unquestionable objects of public duty," but he
thought that the word "poor" must be interpreted carefully.[37] In its
popular sense, he said, it meant the opposite of rich and was thus
applicable to multitudes of ordinary people who were self-support-
ing. Judge Brewer added that the word was also used to describe
those who were absolutely destitute and, for that reason, objects of
public charity. And he observed that only in this latter sense was the
term used when it was said that aid to the poor was a public duty.
Explaining his view further, he stated:

> We have no thought of asserting that because a man is not rich, or even
> because he has nothing but the proceeds of his daily labor, therefore taxation
> may be upheld in his behalf. Such taxation would be simply an attempt on
> the part of the state to equalize the property of its citizens. Something more
> than poverty, in that sense of the term, is essential to charge the state with
> the duty of support. It is, strictly speaking, the pauper, and not the poor
> man, who has claims on public charity. It is not one who is in want merely,
> but one who, being in want, is unable to prevent or remove such want. There
> is the idea of helplessness as well as of destitution.[38]

Common-law standards as to the legitimate objects of public charity
were thus incorporated, by judicial interpretation of the public purpose restriction, into the constitutional law of Kansas.

Brewer then directed his attention to the purpose of the act, which
he said was to provide the destitute with provisions and grain, the
latter to be used either as seed during the planting season or as feed
for livestock. He observed that the act was not designed to aid the
helpless and dependent but that it was an attempt to enable farmers
to "pursue with better prospects of success their ordinary avoca-
tions."[39] From the constitutional standpoint the statute, he contended,
could not be differentiated from legislation purporting to supply the
farmer with livestock or with tools and machinery. Judge Brewer
and his colleagues were apparently somewhat troubled, however, by
one argument made in support of the law. Counsel had urged that
if the legislature was empowered to tax the people for the purpose of
relieving want, it could authorize taxation to prevent it—the prospect
being that if the farmers did not receive seed grain and feed for their
animals, they would be reduced to outright poverty during the following winter. The judges admitted that this argument had great

force and added that if they had only their personal sentiments to consult, they would accept it. But the court declared that such a principle was fraught with great danger.

Let the doorways of taxation be opened, not merely to the relief of present and actual distress, but in anticipation of and to guard against future want, and who can declare the result? How certain must be the expectation of want? How nigh its approach? What efforts must the individual make to ward it off? May he do nothing, and demand that the public make provision to guard against the possibility of future suffering? Must widespread and general calamity precede the granting of such anticipatory relief, or is it enough that individual misfortune or indolence render probable the approach of want? The mere mention of these questions suggests the dangers which would follow the adoption of this as a rule of public conduct.[40]

For a court of justice, these questions were undoubtedly difficult, but only because they were eminently suited to legislative, rather than to judicial, judgment. But the court did not rest its case against such legislation on these hypothetical arguments alone. It found that the statute failed to make any direct appropriation to relieve future want and that the law merely provided a form of assistance which was indirect and contingent upon the successful operation of the farmer's business during the ensuing year. And, citing the *Topeka, Allen,* and *Lowell* cases, the court declared that indirect benefit to the community was not a purpose for which the taxing power could be exercised.

The opinion in the *Osawkee* case was widely cited by lawyers and judges in other jurisdictions. That it was in keeping with laissez faire notions prevailing among the propertied classes is indicated by the fact that it was subject to but little professional criticism. It is true that the Supreme Court of North Dakota refused to follow the precedent in *State v. Nelson County;*[41] but, on the other hand, a more influential tribunal, the Supreme Court of Minnesota, regarded the *Osawkee* case as a reasonably sound precedent in *Deering Co. v. Peterson.*[42] The Minnesota court, like the Supreme Court of Kansas, indicated that public charity could be extended only to paupers, but it implied that the prevention of pauperism was a purpose for which money could be expended—a principle which the Kansas tribunal had rejected.

The fire-loan and seed-loan statutes were unusual enactments which resulted from exceptional conditions. Possibly the novelty of such legislation influenced the courts to treat it with pronounced hostility. But there were other statutes involving considerations of public charity, which were of a less exceptional character, and some of these fared no better at the hands of the courts. Among these were laws authorizing the treatment of habitual drunkards in private institutions at public expense. The Supreme Court of Maryland had sustained such a law in 1895,[43] but the Supreme Court of Wisconsin refused to approve such legislation in *Keeley Institute v. Milwaukee County*, a case decided in 1897.[44] In his opinion for the court, Chief Justice Cassoday declared, with quotations from Cooley and Tiedeman to support his views, that such a law was not a valid exercise of the police power.[45] Although he admitted that the state might prescribe laws for reclaiming drunkards "by public authority," he maintained that their treatment in private institutions was not an object for which public money could be expended.[46] The court had fallen into the common error of confounding the nature of the purpose with the character of the immediate recipient, and, in doing so, it established a judicial check not only upon the objects of public charity but also upon the means whereby the charity might be extended.

Chief Justice Cassoday did not rest his objections to the law upon the mere fact that it provided for treatment by private institutions. He argued that the state could aid only those persons who were, in a legal sense, paupers; and he added that the legislature had no power to compel counties to pay for the medicine and board of persons suffering from noncontagious maladies. The remainder of the opinion reviewed several public purpose cases.

Six years later, the Wisconsin courts reaffirmed the principles of the *Keeley* case. In *State ex rel. Garrett v. Froehlich*[47] that tribunal, again with Chief Justice Cassoday as its spokesman, invalidated a law appropriating a certain sum of money to be distributed *pro rata* to the innocent holders of orders issued under the statute declared unconstitutional in the *Keeley* case. The judge had no difficulty in discovering reasons for declaring the law unconstitutional. Citing and reviewing the earlier decision, he pointed out that it was controlling in this case. He noted that counsel for the relator had, in order to find a justification for the law, argued that the public purpose maxim was not a sound principle of constitutional law. In reply, Cassoday quoted from Cooley's *Constitutional Limitations* and *Treatise on Taxation* and from Dillon's *Municipal Corporations.*[48] Concluding his argument, he held that orders upon the county treasury held by innocent purchasers and issued under an unconstitutional statute were devoid of all legal obligation. The purpose of the original appropriation was private, and, in his view, the purpose of this appropriation was quite the same.

Public charity, as related to public educational policy, was also due for a setback in the courts. And again it was the public purpose maxim upon which the judiciary relied in reaching its decision. In *State ex rel. Garth v. Switzler,*[49] the Supreme Court of Missouri was called upon to determine the validity of a collateral succession tax, passed by the legislature of that state in 1895 and amended in 1897. It was stipulated that three-fourths of the money obtained from this tax was to be turned over to the counties and that proceeds from the funds were to be used to provide scholarships for needy and worthy students who wished to attend the state university. Applicants for such assistance were required to take examinations, and those persons having the highest score were granted scholarships.

The court, speaking through Chief Justice Gantt, declared the law unconstitutional on the ground that it violated section 3 of Article X of the state constitution—that provision declaring that "taxes may be levied and collected for public purposes only."[50] At the outset, Judge Gantt observed that "this provision of our Constitution accords with the definition of a tax as expounded by the courts and law-writers of this country."[51] Quoting from Cooley's *Constitutional Limitations* and from several cases, he showed, to his satisfaction, that taxation, by its very nature, implied a public purpose. The judge was prepared to admit, however, that it was not easy to draw a clear line between public and private purposes; but, invoking the authority of the *Topeka* and *Salem* cases, he stated that the courts were guided by custom and usage in making the distinction.

The court apparently feared that the law would segregate a privileged group of persons from the great mass of the community or, in other words, that it was a kind of class legislation. Judge Gantt's long comment on the evils of paternalism is particularly significant as a statement of the social and political ideas which lay behind the court's decision. He said:

> Paternalism, whether State or Federal, as the derivation of the term implies, is an assumption by the government of a quasi-fatherly relation to the citizen and his family, involving excessive governmental regulation of the private affairs and business methods and interests of the people, upon the theory that the people are incapable of managing their own affairs, and is pernicious in its tendencies. In a word it minimizes the citizen and maximizes the government. Our Federal and State governments are founded upon a principle wholly antagonistic to such a doctrine. Our fathers believed the people of these free and independent States were capable of self-government; a system in which the people are the sovereigns and the government their creature to carry out their commands. Such a government is founded on the willingness and the right of the people to take care of their own affairs and an indisposition on their part to look to the government for everything. The citizen is the unit. It is his province to support the government, and not the government's to support him. Under self-government we have advanced in all the elements of a great people more rapidly than any nation that has ever existed upon the earth, and there is greater need now than ever before in our history of adhering to it. Paternalism is a plant that should receive no nourishment upon the soil of Missouri.[52]

The judge remarked that, true to this theory of governmental functions, the framers of the state constitution had jealously limited the power of taxation. In his view, taxation for the purpose of providing scholarships was no more justified than was taxation for the purpose of providing school children with clothing.

Turning to the powers and duties of the state with respect to public education, Judge Gantt argued that although the state could endow a public university, it could not endow private scholars. He added that it was against the constitution and "sound public policy" to stifle individual effort and ambition. Concluding that part of the opinion dealing with the public purpose requirement, he observed that the beneficiaries of the act were not, in any legal sense, paupers, and he quoted a passage from Cooley's *Treatise on Taxation* to the effect that taxes for educational purposes were valid only if the privilege were open to all on terms of practical equality.[53] The court's expressed distaste for paternalism, its condemnation of class legislation, its insistence upon the benefits of private initiative, and its distrust of legislative innovation—these were the substantial factors behind the decision, and they were the ones which made "public purpose" a shield of laissez faire. But it was not the Supreme Court of Missouri which extended the public purpose maxim to its outermost limits in public charity cases. That dubious distinction may be ascribed, with better reason, to the Supreme Court of Ohio.

The legislature of Ohio, in 1904, passed an act providing that every male blind person over the age of twenty-one and every female blind person over the age of eighteen who met certain residence requirements and who had no property or other means of support should be entitled to a quarterly payment of twenty-five dollars from the treasury of the county wherein he or she resided. The law declared that these persons did not forfeit their rights to these payments by removal to institutions for the blind not maintained by the state or the county. The Supreme Court of Ohio reviewed this statute in *Auditor of Lucas County v. State ex rel. Boyles*,[54] and Judge Summers delivered the court's unanimous opinion. At the outset, he admitted that the state could provide for the care of its dependent classes, and he listed in detail the institutions which the state operated for this purpose. He added, however, that "it does not follow that it would be either wise or constitutional to select out a class, having some particular physical infirmity, and then confer a bounty upon individuals of that class."[55] If this could be done, then the legislature could extend such aid to other classes of persons having some physical infirmity. The judge remarked, that this being so, "why may not all property be distributed by the state?"[56]

In his review of relevant constitutional provisions, Judge Summers observed that the taxing power, as vested in the legislature, could be exercised only for state purposes. Among the authorities cited at this point was Cooley's *Constitutional Limitations*.[57] The general limits of the taxing power having thus been established, the court had only to determine whether or not the statute fell within those limits. Summers stated that there was no fixed rule by which the judiciary could distinguish private from public purposes, but he implied that the custom and usage criterion, which the United States Supreme Court had accepted in the *Topeka* case, was a reasonably good standard whereby the character of a purpose could be discovered. And he added:

If that rule is applied here, it must be said that the act under consideration is without precedent in this state and that no provision is made in the act to insure the application of the money to the support of the individual, or to prevent him from becoming a public charge, or in any manner to control its use by him. The act does not direct that the payments shall continue during the lifetime of the beneficiary, nor does it limit the time, nor provide that payments shall cease with the needs of the donee, or provide for any subsequent inquiry. It is an indeterminate gratuitous annuity, a gift pure and simple, and, being so, the Legislature is without authority to make it from the public funds.[58]

The court, through Judge Summers, concluded its opinion by rejecting one last argument made by supporters of the law—that it would prevent the blind from becoming public charges. Invoking the rule enunciated in the *Topeka* case and citing, among others, the *Keeley* and *Switzler* cases, the court held that incidental public benefit (and it apparently regarded the prevention of pauperism among the blind as benefiting the public only indirectly) did not suffice to sustain an exercise of the taxing power.

There are other cases in which the judiciary seriously impaired legislative power to provide for the care of the needy, for the relief of disaster-stricken communities, and for the educational and cultural advancement of the citizen.[59] But the principles established and utilized in those cases do not differ materially from those laid down in the opinions mentioned above. There is another class of cases, however, in which the courts struck not so much at the "paternalistic" tendencies of the age, but at those which the judges regarded as either "socialistic" or "communistic." In these cases also, laissez faire economic and political tenets were accorded constitutional status.

Municipal and State Enterprises

The industrialization of the economy which occurred in the post-Appomattox period created unprecedented problems for the several levels of American government. The political branches of the national and state governments were, as the result of popular pressure, prepared to legislate against some practices of private business; but they rarely went so far as to undertake the ownership and operation of such enterprises. On the other hand, municipal governments rather frequently attempted to provide directly some services which previously had been regarded as objects of private initiative. Certain of these municipal enterprises received universal judicial approbation, and their constitutionality was rarely questioned save by lawyers who had cases to win and clients to satisfy. Municipal water and light works were in this category. There were other municipal activities which evoked greater protest, however; and, in a number of cases, the courts refused to tolerate them on the ground that they did not serve a public purpose. Eventually, the attitude of the judiciary softened somewhat, but in the heyday of laissez faire, 1870–1910, the efforts of municipalities to provide directly for the needs of their inhabitants were not infrequently frustrated.

In 1870 the legislature of Maine directed the supreme court of that state to advise it as to whether or not it had the power to enable towns and cities to establish and operate manufacturing establishments.[60] Chief Justice Appleton wrote the principal opinion, in which the judges advised the legislature that it had no such power. The core of his argument was presented in one succinct paragraph:

> The entering into contract is a consensual act. The formation of a partnership is a contract. The consent of the partners is necessary thereto. The legislature could not, by any statute, compel individuals without their consent to be partners and to assume the liabilities of partnership, and give the control of the funds to those who do not, and take it from those who do furnish the capital. But giving the town authority to establish manufactories is thus coercing a partnership. It is despotically taking the control of capital from its owners and transferring it to others. It is enabling the majority of a town to incur unlimited indebtedness. If the towns can embark in manufacturing, they can create a partnership, by which all the property of the inhabitants is pledged to meet the contingencies of business. If they can embark in manufacturing, why not in mercantile pursuits of any and every description? What conceivable limits are there to the spirit of reckless speculation, especially when those without means may have the power to dispose of and control the estates of those who have?[61]

With rare candor, Appleton added that "the less the State interferes with industry, the less it directs and selects the channels of enterprise, the better."[62] The advice which the court gave to the legislature might well have been expected. At that time, the suggestion that municipalities should enter the manufacturing field was, without question, a radical one, which not only conservatives but also many liberals opposed. It was in later cases involving the constitutionality of less pretentious projects that the courts proved their surpassing devotion to the tenets of laissez faire.

South Carolina was one of the few states which undertook, during the nineteenth century, the ownership and operation of a commercial business. In 1892 the legislature of that state passed a dispensary act providing for the establishment and operation of state liquor stores. Certain taxpayers of a county in which such a store was to be located sought an injunction to restrain officials from carrying out the law. The state supreme court passed upon the constitutionality of the law in the case of *McCullough v. Brown*.[63] The court, in its opinion, did not come fully to grips with the question whether or not such an enterprise was sustainable as a public purpose for which taxes could be levied and money appropriated. However, in the final paragraph of the majority opinion, Chief Justice McIver asserted that the "real object of the action is to prevent certain persons from engaging in a business involving the use of public funds derived from taxation under an act of the legislature claimed to be unconstitutional."[64] Apparently, the state's attorney had emphasized, in his argument, that the law was a valid exercise of the police power, for the majority opinion largely discussed that question. The majority denied that the establishment of such stores was a constitutional exercise of the police power on the ground that these enterprises were to be operated at a profit. According to the court, the statute was "simply an act to increase the revenue of the State and its subordinate governmental agencies."[65]

McIver considered other objections to the law, also. Among these was the argument that the state had no authority to establish a trading enterprise. In discussing this contention, he admitted that there was no express constitutional provision whereby such action was prohibited; but he added that, by implication, legislative power was confined to the enactment of laws necessary to the "formation of civil government."[66] He invoked, as he had done in the *Feldman* case, the theory of implied limitations on legislative power, a theory which he derived from the state constitutional provision declaring that "the enumeration of rights in this Constitution shall not be construed to impair or deny others retained by the people, and all powers not herein delegated remain with the people."[67] The judge cited the *Topeka, Feldman, Lowell,* and *Allen* cases to prove that the taxing power was limited by the nature of civil government. Upon the basis of this principle, he maintained that "any act of the legislature which is designed to or has the effect of embarking the State in any trade which involves the purchase and sale of any article of commerce for profit, is outside and altogether beyond the legislative power conferred upon the General Assembly."[68] In conclusion, he cited a passage in Cooley's *Taxation* as establishing the right of an aggrieved taxpayer to seek an injunction restraining officials from spending public funds to carry out the mandate of an unconstitutional statute.[69]

The majority, made up of Chief Justice McIver and Judge Mc-Gowan, had, in effect, argued as follows:

(1) Public money may be spent in pursuance of an exercise of legislative power.

(2) Legislative power, however, is limited both by express constitutional provisions and by implication.

(3) A commercial undertaking by a state, where profits are realized, is not one of the purposes for which civil government was established; therefore, the legislature is not empowered to spend public money for the purpose of engaging in such enterprises.

Judge Pope, the third member of the court, wrote a cogent dissenting opinion in which he argued that the statute was a valid exercise of the police power.

The principles enunciated by Judge Pope in his dissent were soon accepted by a majority of the court. Six months after the opinion in *McCullough v. Brown,* the court handed down its decision in *State ex rel. George v. Aiken,*[70] where it sustained a statute practically identical with that struck down in the earlier case. During the interval between the decisions in these cases, the court's membership had changed. Judge McGowan had been replaced by Judge Gary, and the latter joined with Judge Pope to constitute a new majority. Judge Gary, in his opinion for the court, argued that the dispensary law was a valid exercise of the police power. He emphasized, however, that the statute could not be sustained if the court found that its purpose was to embark the state in a commercial enterprise.[71] But he insisted that the object of the legislature in enacting the law was primarily to control the liquor trade and that the law was, for that reason, a valid exercise of the police power. Chief Justice McIver dissented and restated the views which he had expressed in the

McCullough case. The differences between Judges Gary and Pope, on the one hand, and Chief Justice McIver, on the other, were differences in degree. Both sides agreed that the state could not engage in business for the purpose of realizing profits. The majority had looked upon the statute as a police regulation whereby the state incidentally engaged in business. Chief Justice McIver denied that the principal object of the legislation was to regulate the sale of liquor and contended that the primary motive of the legislature was to establish the state in a profitable business. The differences between the majority and the minority with respect to the constitutionality of the law may be attributed very largely to their diverse interpretations of legislative intent.

Had the judiciary been content to strike down, as violative of the public purpose requirement, only those statutes whereby the states and, as was more often the case, the municipalities attempted to engage in manufacturing and mercantile activities for profit, no very substantial impairment of legislative power would have resulted. But the courts went much further and in numerous instances invalidated attempts by municipalities to provide goods and services which were of general importance, if not of absolute necessity, to the community. In 1892 the House of Representatives of Massachusetts presented the supreme court of that state with three questions upon which the counsel of the judges was sought:

(1) Is it within the constitutional power of the legislature to enact a law conferring upon a city or town the power to purchase coal and wood as fuel, in excess of its ordinary requirements, for the purpose of selling such excess to its own citizens?

(2) Is it within the constitutional power of the legislature to authorize cities and towns, for the purpose of sale, to purchase coal and wood for fuel?

(3) Is it within the constitutional power of the legislature to authorize cities and towns to establish and maintain municipal fuel yards?[72]

Only two years before the submission of these questions the court had advised the legislature that it could authorize towns to manufacture gas for lighting purposes.[73] But the judges found that there was a difference, in a constitutional sense, between municipal light plants and municipal fuel yards.

Five judges joined in an opinion in which all three questions were answered in the negative. In the course of their opinion, they declared:

Constitutional questions concerning the power of taxation necessarily are largely historical questions. The Constitution must be interpreted as any other instrument with reference to the circumstances under which it was framed and adopted. . . . We know of nothing in the history of the adoption of the Constitution that gives any countenance to the theory that the buying and selling of such articles as coal and wood for the use of the inhabitants was regarded at that time as one of the ordinary functions of the government which was to be established. There are nowhere in the Constitution any provisions which tend to show that the government was established for the purpose of carrying on the buying and selling of such merchandise as at the time when the Constitution was adopted was usually bought and sold by individuals, and with which individuals were able to supply the community, no matter how essential the business might be to the welfare of the inhabitants. The object of the Constitution was to protect individuals in their rights to carry on the customary business of life, rather than to authorize the Commonwealth or the "towns, parishes, precincts, and other bodies politic" to undertake what had usually been left to the private enterprise of individuals.[74]

This was merely a more recent variant of the "custom and usage" criterion which Cooley had devised in the *Salem* case and to which Miller had given his qualified assent in the *Topeka* case.

Judge Holmes wrote a cogent dissenting opinion in which he argued that a public purpose was involved whenever taxes were laid to enable a public body to offer to the public, without discrimination, any article of public necessity. This view gained support in other courts, especially after 1910. But the Supreme Judicial Court of Massachusetts, as late as 1903, indicated that it had not abandoned the principles which had been enunciated by the majority.[75]

Municipal water works were everywhere regarded as enterprises in support of which the taxing power could be exercised. But the courts displayed far less patience toward municipal enterprises which indirectly aided in the maintenance of an adequate water supply. In *Keen v. Mayor of Waycross*,[76] the Supreme Court of Georgia struck down a city ordinance whereby the municipality attempted to engage in the plumbing business. Strictly construed, the issue pre-

sented for determination was not whether the legislature could grant
to the city the authority to embark in such a business but rather
whether it had, in fact, done so. The judges in their opinion disclosed, however, that they were not prepared to admit that a municipal plumbing enterprise would serve a public purpose. If they
had been favorably disposed toward the ordinance, they could have
sustained it as being in pursuance of legislative authorization to
maintain and establish water works. The court itself admitted that
the plaintiff, a plumber, had enjoyed a monopoly of that business
before the ordinance was passed, and counsel for the city had presented evidence showing that the plaintiff had done faulty work.
Nevertheless, the court took a narrow view of the matter and declared that the ordinance was *ultra vires*. Although it denied that
the plaintiff, as a plumber, could claim any remedy, the court cited
Dillon's *Municipal Corporations* to show that the plaintiff, as a
citizen and taxpayer, was entitled to relief.[77] This distinction, made
in a large number of cases, was obviously more formal than real.

During the first decade of the twentieth century a few municipalities sought to establish publicly owned and operated ice plants
to supply the needs of their citizens. The first case in which the
constitutionality of such an enterprise was tested was *Holton v.
Camilla*,[78] decided by the Supreme Court of Georgia in 1910. The
court approved the project on the arresting ground that the municipalities could furnish their inhabitants with water in either a liquid
or a solid state.[79] This view was sharply criticized four years later by
the Supreme Court of Louisiana in *Union Ice and Coal Co. v.
Ruston*.[80] Speaking through Judge Provosty, the court intimated that
it would sustain the constitutionality of taxes laid for the purpose
of maintaining municipal ice plants if it could be shown that ice was
a by-product of the municipal water and electric works. This situation did not prevail here, however, and the court declared that the
taxing power could not be exercised to sustain the enterprise. Quoting at great length from Cooley's opinion in the *Salem* case and from
other judicial opinions, the court emphasized that custom and usage
constituted a safe, but not an exclusive criterion whereby the nature
of a purpose could be discovered. The judges then proceeded to
quote from Cooley's *Treatise on Taxation* to the effect that the legislature had initially to determine what purposes were public, but the

court hastily added another quotation from the same work to the effect that legislative determination of the question was not conclusive upon the courts.[81] Judge Provosty, on behalf of the court, declared that the legislature had, by authorizing the undertaking, transcended the limits of the taxing power, and he said that the decision in the *Camilla* case was clearly erroneous. Moreover, he rejected the argument that a public character was imparted to the ice business because ice was an article of increasing necessity in modern society. He observed that "this argument of necessity has been so thoroughly pulverized, annihilated, by Judge Cooley in the *Salem* case, that the discussion of it here would be mere waste of time."[82]

It was toward the end of his opinion that Judge Provosty revealed some of the social and economic theories which he and his colleagues entertained. After pointing out that such projects were virtually unprecedented, he observed that such legislation was particularly hurtful to large taxpayers. And he added that the Rock Island Railroad Company paid approximately one-fourth of the taxes which the town received, but it would use only a small part of the ice produced by the proposed plant! Concluding the court's opinion, he said:

For the support of its paupers and indigent sick the municipality may go as deeply as the necessity of the case may require into the pockets of its large taxpayers; but it cannot do so for the purpose of selling ice, or bread, or meat, or drugs, etc., etc., more cheaply to its inhabitants in general than the regular merchants are doing. This would be paternalism pure and simple, a thing foreign to our form of government.[83]

The *Ruston* case was decided in 1914; and, already by that time, the public purpose restriction on the taxing power was undergoing some moderation at the hands of the courts. There were, of course, instances where the judges clung tenaciously to obsolescent ideas, as, indeed, they had done in the *Ruston* opinion. During the period after 1910, the year in which the change in judicial attitudes became perceptible, the Supreme Court of Ohio struck down an ordinance providing for a municipal motion picture theatre,[84] the Supreme Court of California invalidated a law authorizing counties to own cement works,[85] and the Supreme Court of Missouri held unconstitutional the establishment of a municipal ice plant.[86] But these decisions ran against the current of the time. The judges, to be sure, continued to maintain that taxes could be levied and appropriations made only for public purposes. Nevertheless, they interpreted public purpose more broadly than they had previously done. The public purpose maxim was still a valid principle of constitutional law; but, as a result of these liberal decisions, it ceased to serve as a device whereby the courts undertook to enforce laissez faire doctrines upon the popular branches of government and upon the community at large.

The movement away from a rigorous application of the public purpose principle began in the state tribunals, and it soon received the approval of the Supreme Court of the United States. The opinions rendered by the Court in the second and third decades of the twentieth century mark the decline of the public purpose maxim as a judicially enforceable restriction on legislative power.

The Public Purpose Principle in the Supreme Court of the United States

A considerable number of cases involving the public purpose principle came before the Supreme Court of the United States after its decision in *Loan Association v. Topeka*. Almost all these cases concerned the validity of public financial aid to private railroad corporations; and, in view of its earlier decisions, the Court was scarcely in a position to declare measures of this kind unconstitutional. Where such aid was extended to other private enterprises, the result was usually different, however. In *Parkersburg v. Brown*[87] and *Cole v. La Grange*,[88] the Court struck down laws which provided financial assistance to private manufacturers. It was apparent that the justices adhered to the principles enunciated in the *Topeka* case even though they had not many opportunities in which they were able to apply those principles.

The Court indirectly indicated its high esteem for the public purpose principle in two cases which it decided near the turn of the century. The case of *Fallbrook Irrigation District v. Bradley*[89] raised a number of issues, including the question whether or not the creation of an irrigation district was a public purpose for which the taxing power could be exercised. Seven of the nine justices agreed that irrigation of arid lands was a purpose for which taxes could be levied; but they thought sufficiently well of the public purpose restriction to bring it within the scope of due process of the Fourteenth Amendment.[90] Although this development later proved to have no practical ramifications, it did reveal that the justices desired, either consciously or unconsciously, to create a firm constitutional basis for this restriction. Moreover, incorporation of the maxim into the Fourteenth Amendment meant that the judges would not have to resort to extraconstitutional principles in order to support the maxim as a valid proposition of American constitutional law.

Before 1917 the Supreme Court had no opportunity to pass directly upon the constitutionality of taxes levied for the purpose of sustaining state and municipal enterprises. In 1905, however, an opinion in which this question was raised collaterally was filed by the Court. The case of *South Carolina v. United States*[91] involved the validity of a claim made by the state that the sale of liquors by state liquor stores was exempt from federal taxes under the principle of intergovernmental tax immunity.[92] Speaking through Justice Brewer, the Court rejected this claim and held that immunity from federal taxes extended only to those state agencies and instrumentalities which were strictly governmental in character. Although Justice Brewer admitted that the constitutionality of the South Carolina dispensary system had previously been sustained,[93] he intimated that he entertained grave doubts as to either the desirability or the legality of such undertakings. He declared:

There is a large and growing movement in the country in favor of the acquisition and management by the public of what are termed public utilities, including not merely therein the supply of gas and water, but also the entire railroad system. Would the State by taking into possession these public utilities lose its republican form of government?[94]

Brewer made no effort to answer this question. Perhaps it was these doubts, more than concern over the diminution of federal revenues, which led to the decision. At any rate, the Court, by denying tax immunity to state commercial enterprises, refused to encourage such undertakings.

Twelve years after its decision in *South Carolina v. United States* the Court was presented with a case which enabled it to pass directly upon the constitutionality of taxes levied for the purpose of establishing a government in business. But during those twelve years, the atmosphere had changed, and the state tribunals had taken a more liberal view of what constituted a public purpose. Would the Supreme Court follow this new trend or would it turn back the clock and attempt to revitalize the public purpose principle as an important element in laissez faire constitutionalism? It will be recalled that in *Adkins v. Children's Hospital*, the Court had breathed new life into the liberty of contract. Nevertheless, its opinion and decision in *Jones v. Portland*[05] disclosed that it would follow, on matters of taxation, the new judicial current.

The legislature of Maine had, by law, authorized cities and towns of that state to establish fuel yards and to sell, without profit, coal and other heating materials to their inhabitants. The city of Portland attempted to establish such an enterprise. This action was contested by a number of taxpayers who claimed that the law was unconstitutional. In *Laughlin v. Portland*,[06] the Supreme Judicial Court of Maine upheld the legislation. The plaintiffs sued out a writ of error to the United States Supreme Court. Justice Day delivered the Court's opinion sustaining the constitutionality of the law. Citing the *Topeka* case, he declared that taxes could be levied for public purposes only, a limitation which he associated with the Fourteenth Amendment. But he added:

> The attitude of this court towards state legislation purporting to be passed in the public interest, and so declared to be by the decision of the court of last resort of the State passing the act, has often been declared. While the ultimate authority to determine the validity of legislation under the Fourteenth Amendment is rested in this court, local conditions are of such varying character that what is or is not a public use in a particular State is manifestly a matter which local authority, legislative and judicial, has peculiar facilities for securing accurate information.[97]

Reviewing the opinion delivered by the state court, Justice Day emphasized that the establishment of a fuel yard did not differ, in a constitutional sense, from municipal ownership of light plants. In the one case, fuel was sold directly to the inhabitants of the community; and, in the other, fuel was burned at a central station for the purpose of producing electricity which was sold to individual citizens. Heat, he thought, was as important as light and water, and he noted that municipal water and electric plants had long been regarded as legitimate public enterprises. The Court's statement that it would override state legislative and judicial decisions on what constituted a public purpose only in those cases where there was obvious error was significant. The ramifications of the Court's announced respect for local judgment in such matters were fully revealed three years later in *Green v. Frazier.*[98]

The legislature of North Dakota, in pursuance of authority granted by a recent amendment to the state constitution, passed in 1919 a series of measures embarking the state in a number of business activities. The statutes provided for: (1) the creation of an industrial commission authorized to manage, on behalf of the state, certain utilities, industries, and business establishments; (2) the creation of a state bank authorized to lend money to private individuals and corporations; (3) the issuance of bonds in the sum of $2,000,000 to obtain capital for the bank; (4) the issuance of bonds in the sum of $10,000,000 to provide for the replacement of funds employed by the bank in making loans to private persons; (5) the establishment of state warehouses, flour mills, and elevators; (6) the issuance of bonds for the purpose of raising the money necessary to carry on the elevator and flour mill businesses; and (7) state enterprise in the home-building field. Where bonded indebtedness was incurred in carrying out these provisions, the statutes provided that taxes, sufficient to pay interest and principal on such indebtedness, were to be laid.

A number of taxpayers of the state instituted proceedings against the governor and other state officials for the purpose of enjoining them from enforcing the statutes. The state supreme court sustained the constitutionality of the acts and refused to grant the injunction. The complainants then sued out a writ of error to the Supreme Court of the United States. Speaking through Justice Day, the Court delivered a unanimous opinion sustaining the constitutionality of the legislation. It pointed out that due process of the Fourteenth Amendment prohibited taxation for private purposes, but it added:

The taxing power of the States is primarily vested in their legislatures, deriving their authority from the people. When a state legislature acts within the scope of its authority it is responsible to the people, and their right to change the agents to whom they have entrusted the power is ordinarily deemed a sufficient check upon its abuse. When the constituted authority of the State undertakes to exert the taxing power, and the question of the validity of its action is brought before this court, every presumption in its favor is indulged, and only clear and demonstrated usurpation of power will authorize judicial interference with legislative action.[99]

Moreover, the Court emphasized that the legislation had been reviewed favorably by the state supreme court, and it briefly summarized the reasons which the latter tribunal had given for its decision. In conclusion, the Court observed that *Loan Association v. Topeka* involved not a state enterprise but rather public aid to private undertakings.

The opinion of the Court, when considered in the light of the relatively radical character of the statutes involved, is a remarkable example of judicial self-restraint. The Court, it is true, had not repudiated the public purpose maxim as a restraint upon the legislature's power to tax; but it had by deed, as well as by word, indicated that the federal judiciary would not and should not override legislative judgment in these matters.

The decisions in the *Portland* and *Frazier* cases clearly indicated that, so far as the Supreme Court of the United States was concerned, the advocates of laissez faire would henceforth be expected to make their stand against distasteful state taxes and appropriations in the political, rather than the judicial, arena. Although the Court continued to pay tribute to the public purpose maxim as an abstract proposition of American constitutional law, it did not retreat from the position which it had taken in those two cases. The Court was even more emphatic in its refusal to entertain taxpayers' suits against the national government. Three years after its decision in *Green v. Frazier,* the Court, through Justice Sutherland, delivered its unanimous opinion in *Frothingham v. Mellon.*[100] It declared that an individual taxpayer could not expect the Court to restrain public officials from enforcing an allegedly unconstitutional federal statute on the ground that the act would increase present or future taxes. It is true that this principle was somewhat beclouded by the Court's *dicta* in *United States v. Butler,*[101] decided in 1936, but the principles enunciated in this later case were short-lived.

The state courts had already assumed a similar attitude. Although they continued to frown upon public subsidies to private businesses,[102] state tribunals exhibited remarkable tolerance toward new municipal enterprises and toward unusual kinds of public charity. They approved statutes and ordinances which provided for the establishment and operation of public cement works,[103] markets,[104] and gasoline stations.[105] Twenty years earlier, these enterprises most surely would have been regarded as private, and judges would have invalidated public excursions into such fields without much hesitation. By the early 1920's the public purpose principle had ceased to be a major bulwark of property rights. A few state courts, it is true, in exceptional cases made use of the maxim; but, on the whole, it played a minor role during those last years when laissez faire ideas still exercised powerful influence upon the judicial branch of government.

Public Purpose and Laissez Faire

An analysis of the public purpose principle, of the judicial *dicta* which it occasioned, and of the kinds of legislation which failed to meet its test discloses that it, like the liberty of contract, was a constitutional abstraction whereby the economic, political, and social dogmas of laissez faire were read into the fundamental law.

First, the public purpose principle was a response to the belief that governmental powers should not be exercised so as to deprive a person (either natural or corporate) of his property unless he be guilty of a crime or of a civil delinquency or unless he receive some more or less direct compensation for that which was taken from him. The state and federal constitutions had explicitly provided for direct compensation to those persons whose property was taken by the government in the exercise of the power of eminent domain, but no provision had been made for compensatory benefits when property was taken through the avenue of taxation. The courts, relying upon the authority of the publicists, were able to fill in this hiatus in American constitutional law. Running through most of the judicial opinions on public purpose was the idea that the taxpayer must be benefited through the government's expenditure of tax revenues. The judiciary obviously could not insist that every taxpayer receive equal benefits, nor did the judges ordinarily attempt to measure the amount of taxes against the amount of benefit. But the courts did require that the purposes for which taxes were levied and appropriations were made be such that there was a reasonable prospect that some direct benefit would or could accrue to the taxpayer as a member of the body politic.

Second, the public purpose maxim was the constitutional justification for the invalidation of taxes and appropriations which, to the judges, seemed to undermine individual initiative and enterprise. Subsidies to private businesses were declared bad because they upset the natural order of the business community. Free scholarships for needy students were said to be "paternalistic" and were thought to subvert private initiative and ambition. Public charity, according to the courts, could not be extended to the needy in general but only to those who were unable to help themselves.

Third, the courts regarded the public purpose principle as a means whereby the legislature could be prevented from extending benefits to any particular class of persons within the community. The government might, and should, lay down the rules whereby the race for profits and for survival was to be carried on, but it was not to exercise its powers so as to improve the position of any of the contestants. A natural order was declared to prevail. Aid by the government to one person or group worked to the disadvantage of all others. As in their applications of the liberty of contract, the courts emphasized equality—not, however, as an economic and social reality but as a legal abstraction.

Fourth, the public purpose principle was a means whereby the courts circumscribed the legitimate sphere of governmental activity. Government, they said, was instituted to protect private business and not to engage in business. The courts, it is true, rarely, if ever, declared a public business enterprise unconstitutional because some businessman claimed that he could not compete effectively with it. But several opinions disclose that the judges were unwilling to uphold state and municipal excursions into new fields because they felt that the area of private initiative and enterprise would thereby be reduced. For a time it appeared that the courts would approve public business enterprises only where a monopoly existed or where use of public property was necessary for the existence of the business. In some cases the judges went out of their way to emphasize that these were the important considerations—not those having to do with the necessity of the goods and services which such enterprises provided. Later, however, the courts accepted, as legitimate, the argument concerning the necessity of the goods to the community. From that time on, public purpose was a less effective restriction on the power of the government to engage in business activities.

Utilizing the contributions made by Cooley and Dillon to American constitutional jurisprudence, the advocates of laissez faire were able, for nearly fifty years, to impair and inhibit the powers of the legislatures to tax and to spend. The public purpose principle, which these writers had crystallized, was, by no means, their only contribution to laissez faire; but it was a characteristic and important one. And although it might be contended that the principle, in the mouths of the lawyers and the judges, received interpretations which these writers had not foreseen, the fact remains that they were in general sympathy with the economic and social ideas prevailing among the propertied classes and that they had elaborated a constitutional ideology which embraced those ideas. This, in itself, was no mean contribution.

6

The Publicists and Laissez Faire: An Evaluation

WHEN DELIVERING the Storrs Lectures at Yale University in 1892, John F. Dillon declared:

Property, or the full measure of its rightful enjoyment, is also covertly invaded, not by the socialist, but at the instance of a supposed popular demand; in which case the attack is directed against particular owners or particular forms of ownership, and generally takes the insidious, more specious, and dangerous shape of an attempt to deprive the owners—usually corporate owners—of their property by unjust or discriminating legislation in the exercise of the power of taxation, or of eminent domain, or of that elastic power known as the police power,—such legislation resulting, and intended to result, in "clipping" the property or "regulating" the owner out of its full and equal enjoyment and use. Among the peoples of our race the era of the despotism of the monarch or of an oligarchy has passed away. If we are not struck with judicial blindness, we cannot fail to see that what is now to be feared and guarded against is the despotism of the many,—of the majority.[1]

The police power, the power of taxation, and the power of eminent domain—these were the legislative weapons which the proponents of the new constitutional philosophy feared. These were the powers which had to be reconciled with demands for a laissez faire policy beneficial to the captains of industry. And these were the powers which the text writers, as well as the judges and the lawyers, sought to circumscribe.

The over-all influence of the post-Civil War publicists is ascertainable only if reference is made to the more important constitu-

---

[1] For notes to chap. 6, see pp. 198–199.

tional principles utilized by conservatives in their struggle against governmental regulation.

Liberty of contract as a limitation upon the police and commerce powers and public purpose as a requirement for valid exercises of the taxing and spending powers were by no means the only constitutional principles which protected the property rights and privileges claimed by industrial capitalists. During the period from 1870 to 1910 several other principles which restricted legislative powers were developed and applied. Not all this creative work was done by the publicists. Some principles were discovered and elaborated by judges and lawyers.

Of the limitations imposed by the courts upon exercises of the police and commerce powers, liberty of contract was undoubtedly the most characteristic and the most dogmatic. Invoking this abstract doctrine, the judiciary paid tribute to the ideals of liberty and equality. But, in doing so, it arrested legislative attempts, modest though they were, to impart a measure of reality to those ideals. The influence of Cooley and Tiedeman with respect to the origin and growth of the liberty of contract was substantial, but it cannot be said that they alone were responsible for the incorporation of the principle into American constitutional law. Freedom of contract, as a constitutional guarantee, was based upon several ideas, and these ideas did not flow from any one source. The legal foundation upon which the liberty of contract was constructed consisted of the following:

(1) Cooley's interpretation of due process of law as a substantive limitation upon the powers of legislatures.

(2) Cooley's condemnation of partial legislation and his interdiction against the enactment of laws applicable to certain classes only.

(3) The distinction between real and pretended exercises of the police power—a distinction for which the state judges were especially responsible.

(4) Field's and Bradley's defense of economic liberty—the right of everyone *sui juris* to choose and to follow, in all lawful ways, lawful callings.

(5) Tiedeman's formulation, in dogmatic terms, of the implied limitation that the police power could be exercised only to enforce the maxim, *sic utere tuo ut alienum non laedas.*

From these propositions and these sources the right to contract was derived and subsequently elaborated.

The fact that the principles mentioned above were cornerstones of the liberty of contract doctrine accounts for much, however not all, of their importance. They were, in and of themselves, imposing guarantees of property rights. For example, the principle of economic liberty, as developed by Field and Bradley, served the cause of laissez faire in a number of situations where the liberty of contract principle was inapplicable. The latter was a highly specialized weapon with which the proponents of laissez faire resisted legislative attempts to regulate employer-employee relations. But the legislatures, in the exercise of the police power, passed numerous laws which did not materially affect or impair the right of individuals and corporations to negotiate contracts. Such measures obviously could not be challenged as violative of the liberty of contract. Laws outlawing certain businesses,[2] legislation requiring that persons in certain kinds of businesses obtain licenses and fulfill various requirements,[3] and statutes prohibiting the operation of businesses on Sundays[4] were among the measures which the courts scrutinized, not as limitations on the right to make contracts, but as restrictions on the more nebulous and more general right to pursue a lawful calling.

The principle of economic liberty was formulated not so much by the text writers as by the judges and lawyers. Cooley, to be sure, had founded much of his constitutional philosophy upon this principle, but in the early editions of the *Constitutional Limitations* he did not clearly articulate it as a constitutional right. Nevertheless, he made a significant indirect contribution toward the eventual incorporation of economic liberty into federal and state constitutional law. It will be recalled that Field and, to a lesser extent, Bradley emphasized the privileges-and-immunities clause of the Fourteenth Amendment as the guarantee of economic liberty. Their efforts in this direction did not succeed. Rather it was the due-process clause—the provision which Cooley regarded as the major limitation on legislative power—under which the right to choose and follow a lawful calling was eventually subsumed. Here, then, was an instance where the text writers exercised some influence but where that influence was indirect and quite fortuitous.

As was previously stated, the Supreme Court of the United

States, despite the prodding of Field and Bradley, did not immediately accede to the view that economic liberty was guaranteed by
the Fourteenth Amendment. In *Munn v. Illinois*,[5] however, the
Court by implication recognized that the state legislatures possessed
somewhat more authority over businesses "affected with a public
interest" than over businesses in general. Twelve years later, in
Powell v. Pennsylvania,[6] the Court accepted, as a valid proposition
of constitutional law, the principle that the Fourteenth Amendment
protected the right to choose and pursue a calling. But, from the
standpoint of the great entrepreneurs, the general principle of economic liberty was not very meaningful so long as the rule of the
Munn case retained its original import and application. According
to the principles enunciated in this case, businesses which, by virtue
of the magnitude and character of their operations, were affected
with a public interest were subject to more governmental regulation
than were ordinary enterprises. If the *dicta* of the Court in *Powell
v. Pennsylvania* were to be applicable to large business enterprises,
the rule enunciated in the *Munn* case would have to be restricted.
The formulation of a principle which restricted the implications of
the *Munn* decision and which, in doing so, served the interests of
corporate capitalism represents an instance where the text writers
appear to have made no contribution whatsoever.

In *Munn v. Illinois* the Court sustained the constitutionality of
state legislation prescribing the maximum rate which the operators
of elevators and railroads could charge for their services. The power
of the legislatures to prescribe rates was eventually undermined, for
in *Reagan v. Farmers' Loan and Trust Co.* and in *Smyth v. Ames*
the Court declared that the reasonableness of such rates was a matter
into which the judiciary could inquire.[7] Cooley and Tiedeman were
severely critical of the majority opinion in the *Munn* case, but there
is no evidence that the judiciary was much influenced by these
writers when the *Reagan* and *Smyth* cases were decided. Cooley's
attack upon the opinion in the *Munn* case was more direct than was
that of the judges. He argued that the courts should classify businesses as being affected with a public interest only where one or
more of the following conditions prevailed: (1) the business was
pursued as a matter of privilege and not as a matter of right; (2) the
business received special assistance from the government; (3) the

business made use of public property or a public easement; and (4) the business received exclusive privileges from the public in consideration of some special return.[8]

Strict adherence to these criteria of public interest would have completely undermined the rule established in the *Munn* case. The magnitude of a business, its monopolistic character (where no special privileges or advantages were given to it by the public), and its importance to the community would not have been relevant considerations in determining public interest if Cooley had had his way. But the ideas of this writer did not prevail in this instance. Instead of attacking the rule of the *Munn* case directly, the judges engaged in a flanking movement. They held that the reasonableness of the maximum rates which legislatures fixed for businesses affected with a public interest was subject to judicial review. On the surface, the rule established in *Munn v. Illinois* remained undisturbed, but its substance was gradually altered. Large and important enterprises could be regulated, provided that the judiciary agreed that the regulation was reasonable.

The taxing power underwent similar cupellation at the hands of the proponents of the laissez faire constitutional order. As with restrictions on the police power so also with those on the power to tax—some were adduced by the judges and the lawyers and others were developed through the efforts of the text writers. Among the limitations imposed upon the power to tax (and to spend, as well) was the principle that taxation, by its nature, implied a public purpose. This maxim has its roots in the pre-Civil War period, but it did not acquire a firm constitutional status until after the war. In the formulation and development of this principle as a judicially enforceable limitation upon the taxing and spending powers of the legislatures, the writings of Cooley and Dillon were preëminently influential.

Among the other principles which circumscribed the legitimate sphere of taxation was the requirement that taxes be levied equally and uniformly. Most courts interpreted this principle liberally and declared that it was intended to secure equal and uniform taxes on the persons and property made subject to the levy. According to this interpretation, the legislatures were endowed with virtually unlimited discretion in classifying persons and property for the purpose of levying taxes. As a consequence certain types of property could be taxed at a higher rate than other kinds. Only where a classification was palpably unreasonable or capricious would the courts intervene on the ground that the requirement of equality and uniformity was violated. But in a few states the courts went much further. Interpretations of "equality" and "uniformity" were colored by laissez faire ideas. Graduated taxes, especially when made applicable to estates and inheritances, were occasionally invalidated as being contrary to the principle.[9]

Both Cooley and Dillon regarded uniformity and equality as indispensable requirements for valid taxation, but their works were of no special importance in the development and elaboration of the principle.[10] Unlike the public purpose maxim, the requirement that taxes be equally and uniformly apportioned was explicitly stated in most state constitutions. This being so, there was little need to refer to the works of the text writers when the principle was invoked. The eventual perversion of the provision—the incorporation of laissez faire economic and political dogmas into it—was the work of lawyers and judges, and not of the law writers.

The state legislatures had at their disposal three great powers whereby the economic and social life of the country could be regulated and supervised. The police and taxing powers and the power of eminent domain were, in the opinion of the industrial capitalist, sources of great danger. Limitations which hedged in the first two of these powers have already been noticed. It remains to be seen whether or not the power of eminent domain was similarly restricted out of deference to the aspirations of the entrepreneur.

Most state constitutions and the Constitution of the United States contained during the post-Civil War period, as they still do, specific requirements for valid exercises of the power of eminent domain. First, private property may be taken by the government only for public use. Second, when private property is taken by the government in pursuance of this power, the owner is entitled to just compensation. With these provisions at their disposal, the courts were not confronted with the problem of deducing and formulating restrictive principles which had no express constitutional sanction. Nevertheless, a few opportunities for creative work presented themselves. Although the power of eminent domain was seldom exercised so as to affect adversely the property interests of industrialists, there were a few cases in which those interests were so affected and in which the courts invoked new theories in order to preserve property interests.

"Public use" and "just compensation" are general terms and their content is variable. During the age of industrialization these terms were gradually made to reflect the change in the nature of the property right which corporate organization was working. It was the judges, rather than the publicists, who were responsible for the subtle transformation of the public-use and just-compensation clauses into constitutional bulwarks of industrial property rights. For certain purposes property could not be condemned at all.[11] Where property was taken by the government, the courts calculated compensation not upon the basis of the value of the tangible property but upon the basis of the value of property as a "going business."[12]

Cooley, Dillon, and Tiedeman laid varying degrees of emphasis upon the public-use and just-compensation clauses as guarantees of property rights, but these writers did not contribute materially to the laissez faire orientation of these principles.[13] It is true that certain passages from their treatises were frequently quoted by lawyers and judges in cases involving the power of eminent domain, but the ideas set forth in these passages were innocuous and, for the most part, lent support only to the obvious.[14] The amount of creative work whereby laissez faire concepts were read into the law of eminent domain was not great, and it was the judges themselves who were primarily responsible for it.

A review of the laissez faire principles which limited legislative power discloses that some were developed by the publicists and others by judges and lawyers. Due process, economic liberty, freedom of contract, public purpose, equality in the apportionment of taxes, public use, and just compensation: these were some of the materials from which a laissez faire constitutional order was fashioned.

Jacksonian democracy and industrialization had, from the standpoint of the conservative, created a hiatus in American constitutional law. Property rights, it was thought, were endangered for want of adequate constitutional safeguards. In eliminating this hiatus, the judiciary relied upon principles which in turn created a hiatus in legislative power. The power of government was made suspect, and the power of the private entrepreneur was made sacrosanct. The powers of the judiciary expanded at the expense of the powers of the legislature. The great law givers of the last decades of the nineteenth century were not to be found in the state legislatures nor in the Congress. The great law givers were the judges, the lawyers, and the law writers. It was they who dictated the purposes for which government was instituted and the means whereby those purposes could be attained. In doing so, they reflected the fears and aspirations of an industrial oligarchy.

Notes

NOTES TO CHAPTER 1

Conservative Principles and Liberal Reforms
Before the Civil War

(Full facts of publication are supplied in the Bibliography.)

[1] Benjamin F. Wright, Jr., *American Interpretations of Natural Law*, pp. 327–328.
[2] *Ibid.*, pp. 328–329.
[3] *Ibid.*, p. 328.
[4] *Ibid.*, p. 329.
[5] It is significant that Virginia not only adopted the most famous state bill of rights but also produced the author of the Declaration of Independence. Both documents are among the most notable examples of the revolutionary application of the theory of inherent natural rights.
[6] For a concise summary of the political philosophy of the Loyalists, see Leonard W. Labaree, *Conservatism in Early American History*, pp. 125–142.
[7] *Ibid.*, pp. 125–127.
[8] Louis M. Hacker, *The Triumph of American Capitalism*, p. 175.
[9] *Loc. cit.*
[10] *Ibid.*, p. 176.
[11] *Ibid.*, p. 181. As the writer points out, interstate trade barriers had been relaxed somewhat as early as 1783. For a sympathetic treatment of the central government under the Articles of Confederation, see Merrill Jensen, *The Articles of Confederation*.
[12] Charles A. Beard, *An Economic Interpretation of the Constitution of the United States*. Arthur Holcombe, in his recent work, *Our More Perfect Union*, p. 47, suggests that the Constitution was an upper-class document but that ratification was obtained through the support of the rural middle classes.
[13] 2 Dall. 304 (C. C. D. Pa. 1795).
[14] *Ibid.*, p. 310.
[15] *Loc. cit.*
[16] 3 Dall. 386, 387–388 (1798).
[17] During the period 1830–1850 the importance of vested rights declined in both the state courts and the federal courts. See Charles G. Haines, *Revival of Natural Law Concepts*, pp. 97–99. After 1850 there were relatively few cases in which the courts relied primarily upon natural rights. In part this development may be traced to the decline of the doctrine in politics as well as in law. (However, it was revived by both sides in the slavery controversy.) It is not unlikely that the decline was also due to the absorption of the doctrine by specific constitutional provisions. After the Civil War, in one notable case, the United States Supreme Court invoked the doctrine. Speaking through Justice Miller, the Court declared that there were limitations "which grow out of the

essential nature of all free governments. Implied reservations of individual rights, without which the social compact could not exist, and which are respected by all governments entitled to the name." *Loan Association v. Topeka*, 20 Wall. 655, 663 (1874).

[18] 9 Cranch 43 (1815).

[19] 6 Cranch 87 (1810).

[20] *Ibid.*, p. 135.

[21] 7 Cranch 164 (1812).

[22] 4 Wheat. 518 (1819).

[23] Of the judges who decided the case, Justice Story, at least, perceived the importance of the opinion. Charles Warren, *The Supreme Court in United States History*, I, 490.

[24] *Charles River Bridge v. Warren Bridge*, 11 Pet. 420 (1837), discussed below, p. 9 and *Stone v. Mississippi*, 101 U. S. 814 (1880), where the Supreme Court explicitly recognized that the state legislature cannot divest themselves of their police powers when granting corporate charters.

[25] Reservation clauses had been inserted in corporate charters as early as 1805 in Virginia. There were isolated instances of other states including such provisions in charters granted to corporations. In 1831 Delaware adopted a constitution which required that the legislature, in granting charters, reserve the right to revoke them at a later time. This provision seems to have been the first of its kind placed in any state constitution. By 1865 the constitutions of fourteen states included such provisions and other states included reservation clauses in general acts of incorporation. Some states continued to rely upon the older practice of inserting such provisions in charters at the time the legislature granted them. See Benjamin F. Wright, Jr., *The Contract Clause of the Constitution*, pp. 58–60 and 84–85.

[26] 4 Wheat. 122 (1819).

[27] Warren, *op. cit.*, I, 494–496.

[28] 12 Wheat. 213 (1827).

[29] *Ibid.*, p. 346.

[30] *Loc. cit.*

[31] *Ibid.*, p. 347. At another point Marshall declared that "the right to contract is not surrendered with the right to coerce performance. It is still incident to that *degree of free agency which the laws leave* to every individual, and the obligation of contract is a necessary consequence of the right to make it. *Laws regulate this right,* but where not regulated, it is retained in original context." *Ibid.*, p. 350. (Italics mine.)

[32] 11 Pet. 420 (1837).

[33] 4 Pet. 514 (1830). In this case the Court upheld a Rhode Island statute which taxed the capital stock of a bank chartered by that state. The legislation had been assailed as an impairment of the charter although no specific tax exemption had been granted therein. In his opinion, Marshall emphasized the importance of the power of taxation to the existence of the state and concluded that it was not to be assumed, in the absence of a specific provision, that the legislature had intended to relinquish the power. Marshall's opinion is rather interesting because he carefully avoided making any such broad generalization with respect to the police power of the state.

[34] Justice Story, of course, dissented in the *Bridge* case. His views on the opinion of the Court are set forth in a letter written by him to Justice McClean. See William W. Story, *Life and Letters of Joseph Story*, II, 272.

[35] Roscoe Pound, *Spirit of the Common Law,* p. 115.

[36] Sir William Blackstone, *Commentaries on the Laws of England.*

[37] Pound, *op. cit.*, p. 116.

[38] *Ibid.*, p. 117.

[39] John T. Horton, *James Kent: A Study in Conservatism*, pp. 123–231.

[40] James Kent, *Commentaries on American Law*. According to Kent, "in its improved condition in England, and especially in its improved and varied condition in this country, under the benign influence of an expanded commerce, of enlightened justice, of republican principles, and of sound philosophy, the common law has become a code of matured ethics, and enlarged civil wisdom, admirably adapted to promote and secure the freedom and happiness of social life. It has proved to be a system replete with vigorous and healthy principles, eminently conducive to the growth of civil liberty; and it is in no instance disgraced by such a slavish political maxim as that with which the Institutes of Justinian are introduced." *Ibid.*, I, 321–322.

[41] Joseph Story, *Commentaries on the Constitution of the United States*. Referring to the common law, Story wrote that "it has become the guardian of our political and civil rights; it has protected our infant liberties; it has watched over our maturer growth; it has expanded with our wants; it has nurtured the spirit of independence, which checked the first approaches of arbitrary power; it has enabled us to triumph in the midst of difficulties and dangers threatening our political existence; and by the goodness of God, we are now enjoying, under its bold and manly principles, the blessings of a free, independent, and united government." *Ibid.*, I, 141.

[42] John Bouvier, *Institutes of American Law*, I, 41.

[43] Arthur M. Schlesinger, Jr., *The Age of Jackson*, p. 16.

[44] Pound, *op. cit.*, pp. 156–157.

[45] Although the scope of the clause began to diminish at this time, it is not to be presumed that its importance as a basis for litigation diminished simultaneously. Considered from the standpoint of the number of cases in which the obligation-of-contract issue was raised, it continued in ascendancy through the chief justiceship of Morrison R. Waite (1874–1888). Since that time fewer cases have involved application of the clause. It is significant that it reached its zenith at a time when due process had not yet received unqualified approval as a substantive limitation on legislative power. See Wright, *The Contract Clause of the Constitution*, pp. 93–94.

[46] James W. Hurst, *The Growth of American Law*, p. 241.

[47] According to the most sympathetic biographer of John Marshall the only constitutional opinion of the chief justice that was well received was delivered in *Gibbons v. Ogden*, 9 Wheat. 1 (1824). Albert J. Beveridge, *The Life of John Marshall*, IV, 445.

[48] Charles G. Haines, "Judicial Review of Legislation in the United States and the Doctrines of Vested Rights and of Implied Limitations on Legislatures," *Texas Law Review* (April, 1924), 2:286.

[49] Schlesinger, *op. cit.*, pp. 329–330.

[50] *Ibid.*, p. 331. The report of the committee which Story headed was a restrained one in which the members pointed out the value of such a flexible system as that of the common law. They recommended, however, that a partial revision and codification would be feasible. See *Report of the Commissioners on the Practicability of Reducing to a Written and Systematic Code the Common Law of Massachusetts*.

[51] Schlesinger, *op. cit.*, p. 331.

[52] For a lively account of the election of 1840 and of the campaign techniques of the Whigs, see Schlesinger, *op. cit.*, pp. 283–305.

[53] *Ibid.*, pp. 506–507.

[54] According to Hurst, *op. cit.*, p. 240: "At first analysis, surprisingly few of these constitutional enactments of economic policy could be labeled of conservative origin. Most of them were products of the liberal politics of their times, expressing either the

liberal's hopes or his disillusioned reading of experience. The explanation of this 'liberal' background of constitutional legislation lay in the judge-made law of the constitution. Conservatives had their constitutional protection from judges rather than from the specific terms of constitutions. Operating under a few broadly phrased constitutional declarations, judicial review provided the more ready and flexible protections for property. Among the specific constitutional limitations, the notably conservative ones were the limits put on taxation and public expenditure. Even here the picture was confused . . ."

⁵⁵ James D. Richardson, *Compilation of the Messages and Papers of the Presidents, 1789–1897*, II, 483–493.

⁵⁶ Carl R. Fish, *The Rise of the Common Man, 1830–1850*, p. 36.

⁵⁷ Hacker, *op. cit.*, p. 230.

⁵⁸ *Loc. cit.*

⁵⁹ *Ibid.*, p. 231. Cf. Fish, *op. cit.*, p. 37.

⁶⁰ Ernest L. Bogart, *Economic History of the American People*, pp. 327–328.

⁶¹ *Loc. cit.*

⁶² Joseph Dorfman, *The Economic Mind in American Civilization*, II, 621.

⁶³ Fish, *op. cit.*, pp. 55–56. The writer points out that although the bulk of the nation's business was still handled through partnerships and individual enterprises, corporations were needed to carry out business activities which the state governments no longer wished to undertake.

⁶⁴ *Ibid.*, pp. 54–55.

⁶⁵ *Ibid.*, pp. 56–57.

⁶⁶ Schlesinger, *op. cit.*, p. 188. See also, Dorfman, *op. cit.*, p. 621, and Fish, *op. cit.*, p. 57. The first of these laws was passed in 1836 by the legislature of Connecticut. New York had passed a law of this kind in 1811 but it was not a permanent measure, nor was it so regarded at the time of its enactment.

⁶⁷ Dorfman, *op. cit.*, p. 621.

⁶⁸ "To the Jacksonians, their corporations, if allowed at all, should be as free as themselves. The very thought of supervision was inharmonious with the spirit of the age, and not even a corporate individuality, bloated to superhuman size, however much it might anger, could really frighten the self-confident American." Fish, *op. cit.*, p. 59.

⁶⁹ Although Schlesinger maintained that Jacksonian laissez faire permitted governmental intervention in private business activities on behalf of the people, there is not much evidence to support this view. That Jacksonians sought to abolish special privileges for the business community, none can deny, but the individualism of the era generally precluded governmental regulation of the economy. See Dorfman, *op. cit.*, p. 601.

⁷⁰ Fish, *op. cit.*, pp. 33–35. Like the Federalists, the Whigs defended the United States Bank, a protective tariff, and a land policy conducive to speculative investments. All these proposals favored the propertied classes.

⁷¹ *Ibid.*, p. 267.

⁷² Arthur C. Cole, *The Irrepressible Conflict, 1850–1865*, p. 161.

⁷³ 13 N. Y. 378 (1856).

⁷⁴ Hacker, *op. cit.*, p. 20.

⁷⁵ Bogart, *op. cit.*, p. 418.

⁷⁶ Hacker, *op. cit.*, p. 192.

⁷⁷ Bogart, *op. cit.*, p. 387.

⁷⁸ *Ibid.*, p. 425.

[79] *Ibid.*, p. 604.

[80] Schlesinger, *op. cit.*, p. 134. Workingmen also urged abolition or reform of the militia system, equal taxation on all property, adoption of a laborers' lien law, and separation of church and state.

[81] In *People v. Fisher*, 14 Wend. 9 (N. Y. 1835), Chief Justice Savage of New York declared that a trade union formed to raise wages was a conspiracy indictable under the laws of the state. Although admitting that the legislature had repealed the common law upon the subject, the judge proceeded to interpret the statute in accordance with common-law standards. The opinion is a notable one because it was based not only upon the "restraint of trade" principle but also upon an embryonic liberty of contract doctrine.

[82] 4 Metcalf 111 (Mass. 1842). Chief Justice Shaw, speaking for the Supreme Court of Massachusetts, held that "associations may be entered into, the object of which is to adopt measures that may have a tendency to impoverish another, that is, to diminish his gains and profits, and yet so far from being criminal or unlawful, the object may be highly meritorious and public spirited. The legality of such an association will therefore depend upon the means to be used for its accomplishment." *Ibid.*, p. 134.

[83] Fish, *op. cit.*, p. 273. See also, Hacker, *op. cit.*, pp. 271–272.

[84] Fish, *op. cit.*, p. 273.

[85] Bogart, *op. cit.*, p. 435. He attributes the good wages to the fact that the country was then prosperous, and access to western lands relieved competition for factory employment.

[86] Fish, *op. cit.*, p. 273.

[87] In 1847 New Hampshire forbade employment of children under fifteen for more than ten hours per day in factories. Pennsylvania enacted a similar law the following year, and Maine passed a ten-hour law for children under sixteen. The laws of these and other states could be readily evaded by negotiation of specific contracts, however. Bogart, *op. cit.*, p. 433. The author also states that a ten-hour law for women was passed in New Hampshire in 1847. *Ibid.*, p. 601.

[88] John R. Commons and Associates, *History of Labour in the United States*, I, 575–577.

[89] Bogart, *op. cit.*, p. 438.

[90] Cole, *op. cit.*, pp. 149–150. See also, Bogart, *op. cit.*, p. 437.

[91] Hacker, *op. cit.*, pp. 200 and 250.

[92] *Ibid.*, p. 315.

[93] *Ibid.*, p. 373.

[94] *Loc. cit.* See also, Bogart, *op. cit.*, p. 487.

[95] Edward S. Corwin, "The Doctrine of Due Process of Law Before the Civil War," *Harvard Law Review* (March and April, 1911), 24:366–385, 460–479. For a shorter account, see Edward S. Corwin, *Liberty Against Government*, pp. 90–115. A somewhat different version of the early development and application of due process is presented by Rodney L. Mott, *Due Process of Law*, pp. 87–178.

[96] Charles M. Hough, "Due Process of Law—Today," *Harvard Law Review* (January, 1919), 32:223.

[97] 19 How. 393, 450 (1857).

[98] John R. Commons, *Legal Foundations of Capitalism*, p. 21.

[99] *Ibid.*, p. 32. According to a more recent writer on the subject, "The development of the protection of the property right from the doctrine of vested rights and obligation-of-contracts clause to the doctrine of liberty of contract, which involved both liberty and property, has reflected the change in the nature of property as a legal right

at the basis of a capitalistic economy. In the first part of the nineteenth century the property right was a comparatively static right of possession and use, whereas with increasing combination of capital and absentee ownership, made possible by business expansion and industrial collectivization, property became more and more intangible, changing from material *things* into economic *power* which conferred liberty of choice and action upon its legal owner." Benjamin R. Twiss, *Lawyers and the Constitution,* p. 257.

[100] Haines, *Revival of Natural Law Concepts,* pp. 116–117. See also his *American Doctrine of Judicial Supremacy,* p. 411.

NOTES TO CHAPTER 2

Liberty of Contract:
Genesis and Development

[1] 261 U. S. 525, 568 (1923).

[2] 16 Wall. 36 (1873).

[3] Justice Sutherland made this comment in the majority opinion in the *Adkins* case, 261 U. S. 525, 546.

[4] Ray A. Brown, "Due Process of Law, Police Power, and the Supreme Court," *Harvard Law Review* (May, 1927), 40:945. The writer discloses that between 1868 and 1920 more than 180 cases involving applications of the due-process clause to police regulations came before the United States Supreme Court. In only thirteen of these cases were laws invalidated.

[5] For my discussion of vested rights and of the contract clause of the federal Constitution, see pp. 5–9.

[6] 119 Fed. 294 (C.C.A. 7th 1902).

[7] *Ibid.,* p. 299, as quoted by Commons in *Legal Foundations of Capitalism,* p. 18.

[8] Roscoe Pound, "Liberty of Contract," *Yale Law Journal* (May, 1909), 18:455–456. Dean Pound's article is the most comprehensive summary of state decisions in which freedom of contract was the principal consideration. It sheds considerable light on the sources of the doctrine and on the reasons for its development in the United States.

[9] *Ibid.,* p. 456.

[10] *Loc. cit.*

[11] *A Treatise on the Constitutional Limitations Which Rest upon the Legislative Powers of the States of the American Union.*

[12] The first five editions, 1868 to 1883, were the work of Cooley himself and the last three—those of 1890, 1903, and 1927—were edited by other persons.

[13] Sir William Blackstone, *Commentaries on the Laws of England,* ed. by Thomas M. Cooley, I, 123. Cooley listed as "natural" rights the following: (1) life, (2) liberty, (3) formation of family relations, (4) acquisition and enjoyment of property, and (5) making of contracts. That he regarded the last of these as possessing great importance is indicated by his description of it: "This is a right essential to government, essential to society, essential to the acquisition of property and to domestic relations. But here also limitations and restraints are imperative. Unenlightened nature might prompt to many contracts which would be immoral or indecent, or which would tend directly to the defeat of the purposes of government. The law must forbid these while it recog-

nizes the right generally." The last sentence closely parallels Sutherland's *dictum* "liberty is the rule, restraint the exception," and it is the first in which any text writer explicitly set forth the liberty of contract as a fundamental right. Cooley, it is true, had nearly done so five years before in his *Treatise on the Law of Torts . . .* , page 276, where he said: "Every person *sui juris* has the right to make use of his labor in any lawful employment on his own behalf, or to hire it out in the service of others. This is one of the first and highest of civil rights."

[14] Thomas M. Cooley, *A Treatise on Constitutional Limitations . . .* , p. 393. In the second edition Cooley appended to the above passage a significant remark which anticipated later developments in judicial review of police regulations. The new statement, which was retained in subsequent editions also, is as follows: ". . . and those who should claim a right to do so ought to be able to show a specific authority therefor, instead of calling upon others to show how and where the authority is negatived." *Const. Lim.* (2d ed.), pp. 434–435. Although Cooley admitted that a presumption prevails in favor of a law's constitutionality (*Const. Lim.*, 1st ed., pp. 184–185) the above statement implies that in certain cases, at least, the defenders of a law must bear the burden of proof. Liberty was the rule and restraint the exception.

[15] *Ibid.* (1st ed.), p. 355.

[16] The most cited chapter of Cooley's work is entitled "Protection to Property by 'The Law of the Land.'" Therein he set forth his ideas on the invalidity of both partial and arbitrary laws. He seems to have been the first writer to comprehend fully the substantive meaning of due process of law. His emphasis upon the clause may have been due to the nature of his work. He was undoubtedly seeking some constitutional provision under which might be subsumed all of those limitations on legislative power which he had formulated or discovered. In that he was concerned with constitutional limitations in a large number of different states he required, for purposes of generalization, a provision which occurred in most state constitutions and which, at the same time, was so worded that it might be interpreted as a prohibition against all arbitrary exercises of power. The due-process (or its equivalent, law-of-the-land) clause was the only provision which satisfied these requirements. Therefore, Cooley laid particular emphasis upon it.

[17] 16 Wall. 36, 80.

[18] *Ibid.*, p. 81.

[19] Edward S. Corwin, "The Doctrine of Due Process of Law Before the Civil War," *Harvard Law Review* (April, 1911), 24:477.

[20] *Loc. cit.*

[21] 15 Fed. Cas. 649, No. 8,408 (C. C. D. La. 1870).

[22] *Ibid.*, p. 652.

[23] *Loc. cit.*

[24] *Slaughter-House Cases*, 16 Wall. 36 (1873).

[25] For a penetrating analysis and a comprehensive summary of Campbell's argument, see Benjamin R. Twiss, *Lawyers and the Constitution*, pp. 42–62.

[26] 16 Wall. 36, 68–72.

[27] *Ibid.*, p. 72.

[28] *Ibid.*, p. 74.

[29] There is only one instance in which the clause has been successfully invoked by a litigant appearing before the Supreme Court of the United States. In *Colgate v. Harvey*, 296 U. S. 404 (1935), the Court invoked the privileges-and-immunities clause and declared unconstitutional a tax law of the State of Vermont. But this decision was specifically overruled in *Madden v. Kentucky*, 309 U. S. 83 (1940).

[30] There has been, in recent years, a renewed effort by certain justices to incorporate constitutional guarantees of private rights into the privileges-and-immunities clause. These efforts have invariably failed, but in *Adamson v. California,* 332 U. S. 46 (1947), the Court divided five to four on the issue.

[31] 16 Wall. 36, 87.

[32] *Ibid.,* p. 101.

[33] *Ibid.,* pp. 109–110.

[34] *Ibid.,* p. 110.

[35] *Loc. cit.* The passage that Field quoted occurs in *Wealth of Nations,* Bk. I, chap. 10, part 2.

[36] 16 Wall. 36, 122.

[37] It will be recalled, however, that Chief Justice Taney gave a substantive interpretation to property due process of the Fifth Amendment in *Scott v. Sanford,* 19 How. 393, 450 (1857).

[38] 16 Wall. 36, 127. Although Justice Swayne thought that the law violated due process, he defined due process of law as "the application of the law as it exists in the fair and regular course of administrative procedure."

[39] *Loc. cit.* Swayne's idea that the right to pursue a calling was necessary for subsistence (that is, for life itself) and that a deprivation of economic liberty was tantamount to a deprivation of life without due process carried over into *In re Jacobs,* 98 N. Y. 98, 104 (1885), discussed below, pp. 50–55, and into *In re Tiburcio Parrott,* 1 Fed. 481, 498, 507 (C. C. D. Calif. 1880).

[40] 109 Mass. 315 (1872). Another case involving the validity of legislation prohibiting the slaughter-house business in certain areas was *Taylor v. State,* 35 Wis. 298 (1874). There also the law was upheld as valid, but the court emphasized that the legislature could not prohibit innocuous trades under the guise of police regulation.

[41] 109 Mass. 315, 319.

[42] *Loc. cit.*

[43] 70 Ill. 191 (1873).

[44] *Ibid.,* pp. 194–195. The quoted passage is as follows: "All contracts and all right, it is held, are subject to this power [the police power], and regulations which affect them may not only be established by the State, but must also be subject to changes, from time to time, with reference to the well being of the community, as circumstances change, or as experience demonstrates the necessity." *Const. Lim.* (1st ed.), p. 574. (The court incorrectly cited the passage as appearing at page 57.)

[45] 70 Ill. 191, 195. For the passage from Cooley to which the court referred, see below, p. 52.

[46] *Ibid.,* 200. The statement of Cooley occurs in *Const. Lim.* (1st ed.), p. 595.

[47] 70 Ill. 191, 202. The dissenters merely paraphrased the following statement from Cooley: "Although these charters are to be regarded as contracts, and the rights assured by them inviolable, it does not follow that these rights are at once, by force of the charter-contract, removed from the sphere of State regulations . . . the rights and privileges which it confers are only thereby placed upon the same legal footing with other rights and privileges of the citizen in respect to proper rules for their due regulation, protection, and enjoyment." *Const. Lim.* (1st ed.), pp. 576–577.

[48] 120 Mass. 383 (1876).

[49] *Ibid.,* p. 384.

[50] *Ibid.,* p. 385.

[51] Maximum-hours laws for women were approved in the following cases: *State v. Buchanan,* 29 Wash. 602 (1902); *Wenham v. State,* 65 Neb. 394 (1902); and *State v.*

Muller, 48 Oreg. 252 (1906). Similar laws were struck down in *Ritchie v. People*, 155 Ill. 98 (1895), discussed below, pp. 80–84, and in *People v. Williams*, 189 N. Y. 131 (1907). These latter decisions were, for all practical purposes, subsequently overruled in *Ritchie and Co. v. Wayman*, 244 Ill. 509 (1910), and in *People v. Charles Schweinler Press*, 214 N. Y. 395 (1915).

[52] *Wynehamer v. People*, 13 N. Y. 378 (1856), contains the clearest statement of the substantive interpretation of property due process made by any court before the Civil War.

[53] 74 N. Y. 509 (1878).

[54] *Ibid.*, p. 515.

[55] *Loc. cit.* The identification of property with power reveals the change which industrialization and corporate organization were then working in the concept of property. See above, pp. 24–25.

[56] 55 Md. 74 (1880).

[57] Statutes of this kind, popularly called "scrip" laws, were enacted in a number of states during the last two decades of the nineteenth century. Such legislation gave rise to much litigation in which the liberty of contract was invoked; and, in most states, the courts invalidated such laws. Decisions adverse to the constitutionality of such enactments were rendered in the following cases: *Godcharles v. Wigeman*, 113 Pa. St. 431 (1886); *State v. Goodwill*, 33 W. Va. 179 (1889); *Frorer v. People*, 141 Ill. 171 (1892); *State v. Loomis*, 115 Mo. 307 (1893); *State v. Haun*, 61 Kan. 146 (1899); *In re Scrip Bill*, 23 Col. 504 (1897); and *State v. Missouri Tie and Timber Co.*, 181 Mo. 536 (1904). All these cases, except the last two, are discussed either in this chapter or in chapter iii. Statutes of this kind received judicial approval, for a variety of reasons, in *Hancock v. Yaden*, 121 Ind. 366 (1890); *State v. Peel Splint Coal Co.*, 36 W. Va. 802 (1892); *Harbison v. Knoxville Iron Co.*, 103 Tenn. 421 (1899); and *Dayton Coal and Iron Co. v. Barton*, 103 Tenn. 604 (1899). The Tennessee decisions were upheld by the United States Supreme Court at 183 U. S. 13 (1901) and 183 U. S. 23 (1901). Although the statutes considered in the above-named cases differ considerably in detail, their purpose was the same—to prevent exploitation of the worker by prescribing, either directly or indirectly, the media for payment of wages.

[58] 55 Md. 74, 80.

[59] *Ibid.*, pp. 80–81. The statement by Cooley which the court quoted was from his *Const. Lim.* (4th ed.), p. 492. This passage corresponds exactly to that appearing on page 393 of the first edition. See above, p. 31.

[60] 75 Mo. 340 (1882).

[61] *Ibid.*, p. 353.

[62] *Loc. cit.* The passage quoted by the court occurs at page 391, *Const. Lim.* (1st ed.). See below, p. 56.

[63] 75 Mo. 340, 354–355.

[64] 110 Ill. 590 (1884).

[65] *Ibid.*, p. 591. Cooley's *Blackstone* (3d ed.), it will be remembered, contained the first explicit formulation of the liberty of contract as a fundamental, natural right. (See above, n. 13.) It appears, however, that this edition was not available to counsel for Jones because they relied upon a relatively innocuous passage from an earlier edition which merely stated that the right to use and enjoy property was a fundamental right. The brief and argument of Wilderman and Hamil, counsel for the appellant, is summarized in 110 Ill. 590–591.

[66] *Loc. cit.* Counsel cited the *Const. Lim.* (5th ed.), pp. 485–487. See above, p. 31, where I have quoted the passage referred to here.

[67] 110 Ill. 590, 593–594.

[68] 94 U. S. 113 (1876).

[69] For the arguments of counsel I have relied upon the Court's summary which immediately precedes the opinion, 94 U. S. 113, 119–122. The arguments and authorities utilized by counsel for the plaintiffs in error are ably analyzed by Twiss in his *Lawyers and the Constitution*, pp. 70–92.

[70] In support of this contention pages 290 and 350 *et seq.* of the *Const. Lim.* (1st ed.) were cited by counsel. The first reference was completely inapplicable to the issues raised by the case and the second referred to the author's entire chapter on due process of law.

[71] The citation was to *Const. Lim.* (1st ed.), p. 393, where Cooley made his familiar class legislation statement. See above, p. 31.

[72] The reference was to *Const. Lim.* (1st ed.), p. 577, where the writer emphasized that the police power may be exercised only in pursuance of the maxim, *sic utere tuo ut alienum non laedas,* and that the power may not be exercised so as to deprive a corporation of essential rights and privileges held under the terms of the charter.

[73] 94 U. S. 113, 136 *et seq.*

[74] *Ibid.*, p. 143.

[75] See especially, *Reagan v. Farmers' Loan and Trust Co.*, 154 U. S. 362 (1894), and *Smyth v. Ames*, 169 U. S. 466 (1898).

[76] 96 U. S. 97 (1878).

[77] *Ibid.*, pp. 103–104.

[78] *Ibid.*, p. 102. The idea that the legislature had no power to transfer property from A to B had long been associated with the doctrine of vested rights. See above, pp. 4–6. By indicating that such legislation was not due process of law, the Court had accepted, in one extreme instance, the substantive interpretation of the due-process clause. On the other hand, it is fairly clear that such legislation is defective from a procedural standpoint also. The so-called procedural and substantive interpretations of the due-process limitation overlap somewhat, and legislation of this kind violates both.

[79] *Ibid.*, p. 107.

[80] 111 U. S. 746 (1884).

[81] *Ibid.*, p. 750.

[82] *Ibid.*, p. 757.

[83] *Ibid.*, p. 765.

[84] Of the justices who participated in the decision in the *Slaughter-House Cases* only two, Field and Bradley, remained on the Court after Miller's death in 1890. Recent replacements included David Brewer, Rufus Peckham, and Melville Fuller—all aggressive advocates of laissez faire.

[85] *Jones v. People*, 110 Ill. 590 (1884). See above, pp. 44–45.

[86] *Shaffer v. Union Mining Co.*, 55 Md. 74 (1880). See above, pp. 42–43.

[87] 98 N. Y. 98 (1885).

[88] See Twiss, *Lawyers and the Constitution*, pp. 99–106. The court summarized the arguments of opposing counsel (Peter Olney for the state, and William Evarts for Jacobs) in 98 N. Y. 98, 99–102.

[89] 98 N. Y. 98, 104.

[90] *Loc. cit.*

[91] *Ibid.*, p. 105. As Dr. Twiss suggested, the statement is compatible with the Darwinian theory of the survival of the fittest. See his *Lawyers and the Constitution*, p. 106.

[92] 98 N. Y. 98, 105.

⁹³ *Loc. cit.*

⁹⁴ *Ibid.*, p. 106. *Pumpelly v. Green Bay Co.*, 13 Wall. 166 (1871), was a civil action instituted against a private company which, under the color of a Wisconsin law, had constructed a dam which caused certain lands of the plaintiff to be overflowed. The common and necessary use of the property was seriously interrupted and plaintiff demanded just compensation. It was generally admitted that the statute had authorized construction of the dam for the public benefit. The Court held that the principles of remote and consequential injury were inapplicable and that the plaintiff should recover. The *Wynehamer* case, 13 N. Y. 378 (1856), concerned the validity of a state law which prohibited the sale of alcoholic beverages. Wynehamer was convicted of selling such beverages and his conviction was sustained in the lower appellate court. The New York Court of Appeals reversed the decision of the lower court partially on the ground that the statute violated the due-process clause of the state constitution because it failed to differentiate between liquor owned before passage of the act and that acquired after the act went into effect. The judges generally admitted that sale of liquor acquired after the enactment of the law could be prohibited, but they held that such a prohibition made applicable to liquor acquired prior to the enactment violated one of the essential attributes of the property right—the right of sale—without due process of law.

⁹⁵ 98 N. Y. 98, 106–107.

⁹⁶ *Ibid.*, p. 107.

⁹⁷ *Ibid.*, p. 108. The quotation is from *Const. Lim.* (4th ed.), p. 719.

⁹⁸ 98 N. Y. 98, 110.

⁹⁹ *Loc. cit.*

¹⁰⁰ The court's consideration of the question whether or not the law was, in fact, a police regulation is at 98 N. Y. 98, 112–114. The above paragraph is a summary of the court's reasoning on the issue.

¹⁰¹ *Ibid.*, pp. 114–115. The statement clearly reveals the court's bias against economic legislation of any kind.

¹⁰² 99 N. Y. 377 (1885).

¹⁰³ 117 Ill. 294 (1886). Contrary to general supposition, this was the first state case in which the liberty of contract constituted a ground for invalidation of a law. Decided June 12, 1886, it preceded the decision in *Godcharles v. Wigeman* by nearly four months. Dean Pound incorrectly mentions the latter as being the first liberty of contract case in his "Liberty of Contract," *Yale Law Journal* (May, 1909), 18:471.

¹⁰⁴ Wilderman & Hamil, *Abstract and Brief for Appellants: Millett v. People*, pp. 17–18. Counsel said: "Could a provision be more arbitrary? Could the Legislature more unduly or unreasonably interfere with man's inherent right of making contracts about their own private business in their own way? The right of the individual to make contracts for the use and enjoyment of property is a right of property which consists in the free use, enjoyment, and disposal of all his acquisitions, without any control or diminution, save only by the law of the land." In support of this sweeping assertion counsel cited Cooley's *Blackstone*, I, 137, and quoted the *Const. Lim.* (5th ed.), pp. 485–487. (For the text of the latter passage, see above, p. 31.) At page 20 of the brief the attorneys said: "When rights connected with the flowing from property are either abridged or destroyed, the value of the tangible, physical thing is destroyed." Here again they cited the *Const. Lim.* (5th ed.), p. 477. The same work, pages 737 and 739, was also cited to show that coal mining was not a business "affected with a public interest."

¹⁰⁵ 117 Ill. 294, 301. The citation was to *Const. Lim.* (1st ed.), pp. 352–353.

[106] 117 Ill. 294, 301–302. The quotation used by the court is from page 391 of the *Const. Lim.* (1st ed.). The court apparently followed counsel who had quoted the same passage from the fifth edition, pp. 485–487.

[107] 117 Ill. 294, 302–303. In the two decades following the decision in the *Millett* case a number of state tribunals considered the constitutionality of laws requiring that coal be weighed in a certain manner and the weight be credited to the individual workman. The courts were generally hostile to such laws, but there were exceptions. Weighing laws were invalidated in *Ramsey v. People*, 142 Ill. 380 (1892); *Harding v. People*, 160 Ill. 459 (1896); *Commonwealth v. Brown*, 8 Pa. Superior Ct. 339 (1898); and *In re Preston*, 63 Ohio St. 428 (1900). In addition, the Colorado Supreme Court advised the legislature that such an enactment could not be sustained in *In re House Bill No. 203*, 21 Col. 27 (1895). Similar laws were approved, however, in *State v. Peel Splint Coal Co.*, 36 W. Va. 802 (1892), which see below, pp. 70–72, and in *State v. Wilson*, 61 Kan. 32 (1899). The United States Supreme Court declared such a statute constitutional in *McClean v. Arkansas*, 211 U. S. 539 (1909).

[108] 117 Ill. 294, 303. Among the cases cited were *Watertown v. Mayo* (see above, pp. 39–40), *In re Jacobs* (see above, pp. 50–55), and *People v. Marx* (see above, p. 55).

[109] 113 Pa. St. 431 (1886).

[110] *Ibid.*, p. 436.

[111] P. L. Hackenberg and Associates, *Paper Book, Brief for Plaintiffs in Error: Godcharles v. Wigeman*, p. 36.

[112] 113 Pa. St. 431, 437.

[113] Twiss, *Lawyers and the Constitution*, p. 129.

[114] Christopher G. Tiedeman, *A Treatise on the Limitations of Police Power in the United States* and *A Treatise on State and Federal Control of Persons and Property in the United States.*

[115] *Lim. of Pol. Pow.*, pp. vii–viii. Tiedeman elaborated upon these views fourteen years later in his *Cont. of Pers. and Property*, I, ix–x.

[116] "So use your own as not to injure another." Tiedeman, *Lim. of Pol. Pow.*, p. 2. Cooley also regarded the enforcement of this maxim as the principal basis for exercises of the police power; but his attachment to the principle was less pronounced than was Tiedeman's. See *Const. Lim.* (1st ed.), pp. 573 and 577.

[117] Tiedeman, *Lim. of Pol. Pow.*, pp. 5–8. (References to Tiedeman's works, as to those of Cooley, are to pages, not sections, unless otherwise indicated.)

[118] *Ibid.*, pp. 12–13.

[119] *Ibid.*, p. 10.

[120] *Ibid.*, p. 239 (italics mine). Cooley, on the other hand, accepted usury laws although he did so with some reluctance. See Cooley's *General Principles of Constitutional Law*, p. 235.

[121] Tiedeman, *Lim. of Pol. Pow.*, p. 241.

[122] To justify this distinction Tiedeman relied upon his fundamental hypothesis that the police power must be exercised only in enforcement of the maxim, *sic utere tuo ut alienum non laedas*. Consequently, a personal vice, constituting neither a trespass upon nor a proximate injury to the rights of others would not be subject to regulation. *Ibid.*, pp. 150–153, 301–302.

[123] *Ibid.*, pp. 310–311.

[124] *Ibid.*, pp. 294–295. At least one tribunal, the Supreme Court of Washington, came within a hair's breadth of accepting Tiedeman's views on such legislation. Dividing three to two, the court approved a territorial law prohibiting the smoking of opium.

Justices Scott and Stiles dissented on the ground that the statute permitted no judicial inquiry into the question whether or not such smoking was, in fact, injurious to health. Although Tiedeman was not quoted by the dissenters, the brief for the accused is replete with references to his treatise. See *Ab Lim v. Territory,* 1 Wash. 156 (1890), particularly 166 *et seq.*

[125] Tiedeman, *Lim. of Pol. Pow.,* pp. 224–226. Tiedeman argued that a protective tariff violated the due-process clause of the Fifth Amendment as well as other provisions of the federal Constitution.

NOTES TO CHAPTER 3

Liberty of Contract:
Application by State Tribunals and Acceptance by the Supreme Court of the United States

[1] The present chapter deals almost exclusively with cases involving the validity of statutes which regulated these relations. In addition to these cases there were a few in which liberty of contract was invoked by attorneys to impeach the validity of state laws regulating the insurance business. See *Dugger v. Insurance Co.,* 95 Tenn. 245 (1895); *Hooper v. California,* 155 U. S. 648 (1895), discussed below, p. 87; *Allgeyer v. Louisiana,* 165 U. S. 578 (1897), discussed below, pp. 88–89; *Orient Insurance Co. v. Daggs,* 172 U. S. 557 (1899); and *Niagara Fire Insurance Co. v. Cornell,* 110 Fed. 816 (C. C. D. Neb. 1901).

[2] 33 W. Va. 179 (1889).

[3] *Ibid.,* p. 181.

[4] *Ibid.,* p. 182.

[5] *Ibid.,* p. 183.

[6] 118 U. S. 356 (1886).

[7] 33 W. Va. 179, 184. (Italics mine.)

[8] *Loc. cit.*

[9] *Ibid.,* p. 185. For my analysis of *Mugler v. Kansas,* see below, pp. 85–86. The reference to the *Const. Lim.* is apparently to the fourth edition, page 719. See above, p. 52.

[10] 33 W. Va. 179, 186.

[11] 33 W. Va. 188 (1889).

[12] *Ibid.,* p. 189.

[13] *Ibid.,* p. 190.

[14] *Ibid.,* p. 191.

[15] 155 Mass. 117 (1891).

[16] 141 Ill. 171 (1892). See above, chap. ii, n. 57, for cases involving similar laws.

[17] *Ibid.,* p. 181. For the text of the quoted passage, see above, p. 31. The court apparently followed the suggestion of counsel in using this quotation. See George S. House, *Argument for Appellants: Frorer v. People,* pp. 15, 18–19.

[18] 141 Ill. 171, 182. See above, p. 31, for text of Cooley's statement which the court quoted.

[19] *Ibid.,* p. 187. Compare Tiedeman's *Lim. of Pol. Pow.,* pp. 571–572, where the writer emphasized the political equality existing between workman and capitalist. This

equality, he asserted, was the reason for prohibiting legislation which afforded protection to the laboring classes. If the franchise were restricted, such legislation, according to this writer, would then be justified.

[20] See *Adkins v. Children's Hospital,* 261 U. S. 525, 553, where Justice Sutherland, speaking for the majority, said: "In view of the great—not to say revolutionary—changes which have taken place since that utterance [referring to the *Muller* case], in the contractual, political, and civil status of women, culminating in the Nineteenth Amendment, it is not unreasonable to say that these differences [that is, between men and women] have now come almost, if not quite, to the vanishing point."

[21] 36 W. Va. 802 (1892).

[22] *Ibid.,* p. 811. See Tiedeman, *Lim. of Pol. Pow.,* p. 7.

[23] 36 W. Va. 802, 811–812. The court quoted Tiedeman as follows: "It is only in extraordinarily abnormal cases that any one man can acquire this power over his fellow-men, unless he is the recipient of a privilege from the government or is guilty of dishonest practices. The remedy for the first case in a constitutional government is to withhold dangerous privileges, or, if the grant of them is conducive to the public welfare, to subject their enjoyment to police regulation, so that the public may derive the benefit expected, and receive no injury." *Lim. of Pol. Pow.,* p. 242.

[24] 36 W. Va. 802, 820.

[25] *Loc. cit.*

[26] Besides the *Shaffer* and the *Peel Splint* cases the following involved the liberty of contract as a corporate right and privilege: *State v. Brown and Sharpe Mfg. Co.,* 18 R. I. 16 (1892); *Leep v. Railway Co.,* 58 Ark. 407 (1894); *Re Ten Hour Law,* 24 R. I. 603 (1902); *State v. Haun,* 61 Kan. 146 (1899); and *Braceville Coal Co. v. People,* 147 Ill. 66 (1893). In all these cases, except the last two, the courts upheld the challenged law either because the state constitution or a general state statute reserved to the legislature the power to amend and repeal corporate charters or because the magnitude of the corporation and its physical power seemed to justify special regulation. In the *Braceville* and *Haun* cases, discussed below, pp. 74–75 and pp. 75–76, the courts refused to apply these principles.

[27] 36 W. Va. 802, 841–842. The quotation was from Cooley's *Const. Lim.* (1st ed.), pp. 575–577. See above, p. 52.

[28] 36 W. Va. 802, 844.

[29] *Ibid.,* pp. 847–848. The passage from Tiedeman's work which Judge English quoted is: "But the corporation is no more subject to arbitrary regulations than is the individual. In order that the regulation of a corporation may be within the constitutional limitations of police power, it must have reference to the welfare of society, by the prevention or control of those actions which are calculated to inflict injury upon the public or the individual. As in all other cases of the exercise of the police power, the police regulations of corporations must be confined to the enforcement of the maxim, *sic utere tuo ut alienum non laedas,* subject to the observance of which every corporate charter must be supposed to have been granted. Any attempt, under the guise of police regulations, to repeal or amend the charter, or to abridge any of the corporate rights and privileges, would of course, be unconstitutional and void. The property of the corporation can not be confiscated under the pretense of being a police regulation, without payment of compensation." *Lim. of Pol. Pow.,* p. 584.

[30] 115 Mo. 307 (1893).

[31] *Ibid.,* pp. 314–315. See above, p. 31.

[32] *Ibid.,* p. 315.

[33] *Ibid.,* p. 316.

[34] *Ibid.*, p. 320.

[35] 147 Ill. 66 (1893). In two previous cases state courts had considered the validity of payment laws similar to the one challenged in the *Braceville* case. The Court of Appeals of Texas invalidated such a law in *San Antonio Railway Co. v. Wilson*, 19 S. W. 910 (1892), but the Supreme Court of Rhode Island sustained a weekly payment law in *State v. Brown and Sharpe Mfg. Co.*, 18 R. I. 16 (1892). The Rhode Island tribunal emphasized the reserved authority of the legislature to amend corporate charters, but it seemed to imply that the law would be constitutional if applicable to natural persons also. Later decisions determining the fate of payment laws were: *Commonwealth v. Isenberg*, 4 Pa. Dist. Rep. 579 (1894); *Opinion of the Justices*, 163 Mass. 589 (1895); and *Republic Iron and Steel Co. v. State*, 160 Ind. 379 (1903). In the Massachusetts case (which was advisory only) the court received the law favorably; in the other cases the courts struck down the legislation. A case involving the validity of a somewhat different kind of law was decided by the Supreme Court of Arkansas. That tribunal, in *Leep v. Railway Co.*, 58 Ark. 407 (1894), reviewed favorably legislation requiring railroad companies to pay discharged workers on the day of discharge. The court, in an opinion replete with extended quotations from Cooley's and Tiedeman's treatises, indicated that such legislation constituted an arbitrary infringement of the liberty of contract and that, if applicable to natural persons, it would be void. But the court sustained the law as a valid exercise of the legislature's power to repeal and amend corporate charters. The United States Supreme Court eventually sustained a wage payment law in *Erie Railroad Co. v. Williams*, 233 U. S. 685 (1914).

[36] 147 Ill. 66, 71–72. See above, p. 31.

[37] *Ibid.*, p. 75.

[38] 61 Kan. 146 (1899).

[39] *Ibid.*, pp. 155–156. For the texts of those passages from the *Const. Lim.* quoted by the court, see above, p. 31 and p. 56.

[40] *Ibid.*, pp. 163–164. "Laws, therefore, which are designed to regulate the terms of hiring in strictly private employments, are unconstitutional, because they operate as an interference with one's natural liberty, in a case in which there is no trespass upon private right, and no threatening injury to the public. And this conclusion not only applies to laws regulating the rate of wages of private workmen, but also any other law, whose object is to regulate any of the terms of hiring, such as the number of hours of labor per day, which the employer may demand. There can be no constitutional interference by the state in the private relation of master and servant except for the purpose of preventing frauds and trespasses." Tiedeman, *Lim. of Pol. Pow.*, p. 572.

[41] 129 Mo. 163 (1895). Similar decisions were rendered in *State ex rel. Zillmer v. Kreutzberg*, 114 Wis. 530 (1902), see below, p. 77; *Gillespie v. People*, 188 Ill. 176 (1900); *Coffeyville Vitrified Brick Co. v. Perry*, 69 Kan. 297 (1904), see below, p. 77; and *People v. Marcus*, 185 N. Y. 257 (1906). The Supreme Court of the United States struck down a similar state law in *Coppage v. Kansas*, 236 U. S. 1 (1915). The outcome of that case had been anticipated by the decision in *Adair v. United States*, 208 U. S. 161 (1908), where the Court invalidated congressional legislation of this kind. The *Adair* case is analyzed below, pp. 91–92. For a discussion of the constitutionality of laws prohibiting the employer from blacklisting discharged employees see *State ex rel. Scheffer v. Justus*, 85 Minn. 279 (1902), where the court approved the law. But see also *Wallace v. Georgia, Carolinian and Northern Ry.*, 94 Ga. 732 (1894), where the court invalidated a statute requiring employers to furnish discharged employees with letters setting forth the reasons for discharge.

[42] 188 Ill. 176 (1900).

[43] 114 Wis. 530 (1902).

[44] *Ibid.*, p. 534, citing Cooley's *Torts* (1st ed.), p. 278, and Tiedeman's *Cont. of Pers. and Prop.*, II, 939.

[45] 114 Wis. 530, 536. The text of the quotation from Cooley's work is as follows: "It is part of every man's civil rights that he be left at liberty to refuse business relations with any person whomsoever, whether the refusal rests upon reason, or is the result of whim, caprice, prejudice, or malice." *Torts* (1st ed.), p. 278. Tiedeman was quoted as follows: "Every man has a natural right to hire his services to anyone he pleases, or refrain from such hiring; and so, likewise, it is the right of every one to determine whose services he will hire. . . . Governments, therefore, cannot exert any restraint upon the action of the parties." *Cont. of Pers. and Prop.*, II, 939.

[46] 114 Wis. 530, 542, 545, 546. See Tiedeman, *Cont. of Pers. and Prop.*, I, 5, 332, 424.

[47] 69 Kan. 297 (1904).

[48] *Ibid.*, p. 301. The text of the quotation from Cooley's *Torts* (1st ed.), p. 278, is shown in n. 45, above. The passage from Tiedeman's *Cont. of Pers. and Prop.*, appearing in the same note, was also quoted in this case.

[49] 85 Cal. 274 (1890).

[50] George M. Holton, *Brief for Petitioner in the Matter of Habeas Corpus on Behalf of J. C. Kuback.*

[51] *Loc. cit.*

[52] *Loc. cit.*

[53] 85 Cal. 274, 276. This passage is from *Const. Lim.* (5th ed.), p. 745. It does not occur in earlier editions, but it was retained in subsequent ones.

[54] In the following cases the courts struck down laws or municipal ordinances purporting to prescribe either maximum hours or minimum wages for workers on municipal projects when those projects were undertaken by private contractors: *People ex rel. Rodgers v. Coler*, 166 N. Y. 1 (1901); *Street v. Varney Electrical Supply Co.*, 160 Ind. 338 (1903); *People v. Orange County Road Co.*, 175 N. Y. 84 (1903); and *People ex rel. Cossey v. Grout*, 179 N. Y. 417 (1904). Legislation of this kind won judicial approval in *People ex rel. Warren v. Beck*, 10 Misc. N. Y. 77 (1894), and in *In re Broad*, 36 Wash. 449 (1904). The Supreme Court of the United States upheld a law of this character in *Atkin v. Kansas*, 191 U. S. 207 (1903).

[55] 41 Neb. 127 (1894). The courts, in general, reacted favorably to maximum-hours laws applicable to occupations which were especially dangerous or unhealthful; however, that was by no means an invariable rule. Thus the Supreme Court of Rhode Island sustained a ten-hour law for conductors and motormen in *In re Ten Hour Law*, 24 R. I. 603 (1902), and the Court of Appeals of New York, by a majority of one vote, upheld the constitutionality of a ten-hour law for bakers (*People v. Lochner*, 177 N. Y. 145 (1904), affirming 76 N. Y. Supp. 396). On the other hand, the Supreme Court of Colorado advised the legislature of that state that an eight-hour law for workers in mines, factories, and smelters would be unconstitutional (*In re Eight-Hour Bill*, 21 Col. 29 (1895)). The Colorado tribunal adhered to this view four years later in *In re Morgan*, 26 Col. 415 (1899), where it struck down an eight-hour law for workers in mines and smelters, although the Supreme Court of the United States had previously sustained a very similar statute enacted by the Utah legislature. *See Holden v. Hardy*, 169 U. S. 366 (1898), analyzed below, pp. 89–90. The Supreme Court of Nevada, however, accepted the principles of the *Holden* case in *Ex parte Boyce*, 27 Nev. 299 (1904), and in *Ex parte Kair*, 28 Nev. 127, 425 (1905). Later the United States Supreme

Court itself undermined, if not the case itself, at least many of the progressive principles of *Holden v. Hardy* by its decision in *Lochner v. New York,* 198 U. S. 45 (1905),
discussed below, pp. 90–91.

[56] 41 Neb. 127, 135.

[57] *Ibid.,* p. 136.

[58] *Ibid.,* pp. 137–138.

[59] 155 Ill. 98 (1895). For references to cases involving maximum-hours laws for
women see above, chap. ii, n. 51. As indicated previously child-labor laws (enacted by
the states) were invariably sustained. Opinions to this effect were rendered in *State
v. Shorey,* 48 Oreg. 396 (1906), and in *Starnes v. Albion Mfg. Co.,* 147 N. C. 556
(1908).

[60] Moran, Kraus and Mayer, *Brief and Argument for Plaintiffs in Error: Ritchie v.
People.* Cooley was either cited or quoted by counsel seven times. *Ibid.,* pp. 28, 33, 37,
47, 48. Tiedeman was quoted twice. *Ibid.,* pp. 42, 47. Among the passages from
Cooley's work which were quoted was, as usual, his remark on class legislation.

[61] John W. Ela and Andrew Bruce, *Brief and Argument for the People: Ritchie v.
People,* p. 32.

[62] See *Ritchie and Co. v. Wayman,* 244 Ill. 509 (1910), where the court upheld a
ten-hour law for women.

[63] 155 Ill. 98, 108. See above, p. 31, for text of Cooley's statement.

[64] *Ibid.,* p. 113.

[65] *Ibid.,* p. 115. The quoted passage is from Tiedeman's *Lim. of Pol. Pow.,* pp. 199–
200.

[66] 26 Col. 415 (1899).

[67] 169 U. S. 366 (1898). See below, pp. 89–90.

[68] 26 Col. 415, 423–424. The court cited Cooley at page 208 of the *Const. Lim.*
(6th ed.), and quoted several lengthy passages from Tiedeman's *Lim. of Pol. Pow.*

[69] 26 Col. 415, 424–425. The passage quoted was from *Const. Lim.* (6th ed.), p. 208.

[70] 26 Col. 415, 445–446. See *Lim. of Pol. Pow.,* pp. 199–200, 572.

[71] 26 Col. 415, 446. For text of the passage quoted by the court, see above, p. 31.

[72] *Ibid.,* pp. 446–447. The passage quoted by the court appears above, pp. 78–79.

[73] *Ibid.,* p. 447. For text of this quotation, an excerpt from Cooley's *Torts,* see
above, chap. ii, n. 13.

[74] *Loc. cit.* The passage quoted by the court was the following: "Every man controls
his own property as he pleases, puts it to such use as he pleases, improves it or not,
as he may choose, subject only to the obligation to perform, in respect to it, the duties
he owes to the state and to his fellows. The state cannot substitute its judgment for
his as to the use he should make of it for his own advantage." Cooley's *Torts* (2d ed.),
p. 337.

[75] 123 U. S. 623 (1887).

[76] *Ibid.,* p. 661.

[77] 127 U. S. 678 (1888).

[78] *Ibid.,* p. 684. (Italics mine.)

[79] *Ibid.,* p. 687 et seq.

[80] 155 U. S. 648 (1895).

[81] *Ibid.,* p. 658.

[82] 157 U. S. 160 (1895).

[83] *Ibid.,* pp. 165–166. (Italics mine.)

[84] 165 U. S. 578 (1897).

[85] *Ibid.,* p. 591.

[86] 169 U. S. 366 (1898).

[87] 198 U. S. 45 (1905).

[88] *Ibid.*, p. 59.

[89] *Ibid.*, p. 61.

[90] 208 U. S. 161 (1908).

[91] *Ibid.*, p. 172.

[92] *Ibid.*, p. 173. For the text of the passage from Cooley's work which the Court quoted see above, note 45. This is one of the few references which the Court made to Cooley's works in the liberty of contract cases decided by that tribunal. Moreover, there are relatively few references to the works of Cooley and Tiedeman in briefs filed before the Court in this category of cases. Whereas the influence of the publicists on the state courts was direct and obvious, their influence upon the Supreme Court of the United States was indirect and less perceptible. But it seems reasonable to assume that the indirect influence of these writers upon the Court was substantial, although less so than upon the state tribunals. In both the *Lochner* and *Adair* cases the Court mentioned several state opinions in which the works of Cooley and Tiedeman were important citations. Thus, in *Adair v. United States,* Harlan mentioned such cases as *State v. Julow, Gillespie v. People,* and *State v. Kreutzberg,* all of which are discussed in this chapter and in all of which the works and ideas of either Cooley or Tiedeman, or both, were utilized.

[93] 208 U. S. 161, 174.

[94] *Ritchie and Co. v. Wayman,* 244 Ill. 509 (1910), and *People v. Charles Schweinler Press,* 214 N. Y. 395 (1915).

[95] Freund's relative coolness toward laissez faire dogmas was indicated in his preface, where he referred to the right to contract and the right to pursue an occupation as having "an uncertain status." See *Pol. Pow., Public Policy and Const. Rights,* p. iv. When discussing the maxim—*sic utere tuo ut alienum non laedas*—the enforcement of which Tiedeman and, to a lesser extent, Cooley regarded as the principal, if not the sole, justification for police regulations, Freund remarked that "no community confines its care of the public welfare to the enforcement of the principles of the common law." *Ibid.,* p. 6. Some of the extreme applications of the liberty of contract he criticized rather severely. Thus, when discussing the principles of *Ritchie v. People* (see above, pp. 81–84), he said that that opinion "can hardly command unqualified assent either in the light of reason or authority." *Ibid.,* p. 298. Something of the novelty of Freund's view may be gathered by contrasting it with Tiedeman's respectful treatment of the *Ritchie* opinion. See *Cont. of Pers. and Prop.,* I, 336.

[96] William Stead, *Brief and Argument for Appellant: Ritchie and Co. v. Wayman,* pp. 24, 26, 40–44, 57, 60, 65.

[97] 208 U. S. 412 (1908).

[98] See *Adkins v. Children's Hospital,* 261 U. S. 525, 559–560.

[99] In *Chicago, Burlington & Quincy R. R. v. McGuire,* 219 U. S. 549 (1911), the Court sustained a law of the state of Iowa which prohibited employer-employee contracts limiting the right to recover damages at common law. The Court approved a federal statute which abolished, in part, the common-law rules in regard to contributory negligence, fellow servants, and assumption of risk in the *Second Employers' Liability Cases,* 223 U. S. 1 (1912). The statute, as amended, applied to relations between common carriers and their employees while both were engaged in interstate commerce. The Adamson Act, a federal statute establishing an eight-hour day for employees of carriers engaged in foreign and interstate commerce, was approved by the Court in *Wilson v. New,* 243 U. S. 332 (1917). The justices voted five to four in

favor of the law. In *Bunting v. Oregon*, 243 U. S. 426 (1917), the Court sustained a ten-hour law for workers in mills, factories, and manufacturing establishments. The law provided that employees might work overtime up to three hours if paid for the overtime "at the rate of time and one-half of the regular wage." In all these cases liberty of contract was an important consideration; nevertheless, the statutes were upheld. That the principle retained more than formal vitality during this period was evidenced in *Coppage v. Kansas*, 236 U. S. 1 (1915), where the Court struck down a state statute prohibiting yellow-dog contracts. In doing so, the Court relied largely upon the precedent established in the *Adair* case.

[100] Charles M. Hough, "Due Process of Law—Today," *Harvard Law Review* (January, 1919), 32:233.

[101] For comment upon Cooley's influence on Sutherland, see Joel F. Paschal, *Mr. Justice Sutherland*, pp. 16–20.

[102] 300 U. S. 379 (1937). The Court specifically overruled the *Adkins* case and, by implication and in effect, overruled its decision in *Morehead v. New York ex rel. Tipaldo*, 298 U. S. 587 (1936).

NOTES TO CHAPTER 4

The Public Purpose Limitation on the Taxing Power: Origin and Early Development

[1] For example, many state constitutions contain clauses requiring that taxes be levied in accordance with the principle of uniformity. Such provisions have given rise to a considerable amount of litigation, and, in some states, these clauses received a laissez faire interpretation. But, on the whole, the requirement of uniformity in taxation did not serve the cause of laissez faire as satisfactorily as did the implied requirement that taxes be laid for public purposes only.

[2] 35 Va. 120 (1837).

[3] *Ibid.*, pp. 150–154. The majority opinion, delivered by Judge Tucker, follows the dissent.

[4] 24 Wend. 65 (N. Y. 1840).

[5] See particularly, Breck P. McAllister, "Public Purpose in Taxation," *California Law Review* (January and March, 1930), 18:139–140.

[6] 21 Pa. St. 147 (1853).

[7] *Ibid.*, pp. 176–188. In *Commonwealth v. M'Williams*, 11 Pa. St. 61 (1849), the Pennsylvania Supreme Court had sustained, in no uncertain terms, the power of the legislature to enact a law authorizing township supervisors to subscribe to the stock of a turnpike company. The court, in that case, followed the principles which Judges Woodward and Knox enunciated in the *Sharpless* case, but in the four years intervening between these two cases a majority of the judges on the court had moved in the direction of holding that the public purpose requirement was judicially enforceable as against the legislature.

[8] 21 Pa. St. 147, 158–159.

[9] For my discussion of the precarious financial condition of the states during the 1840's and 1850's, see above, pp. 13–14.

[10] 21 Pa. St. 147, 159.

[11] *Ibid.*, p. 168. Chief Justice Black was here following the language used by the Supreme Court of Kentucky in *Cheaney v. Hooser*, 48 Ky. 330, 345 (1849).

[12] 21 Pa. St. 147, 169.

[13] 13 N. Y. 378 (1856). See above, chap. ii, n. 94.

[14] 39 Pa. St. 73 (1861).

[15] 13 Iowa 388 (1862).

[16] The Iowa court, in *Dubuque County v. Dubuque and Pacific R. R.*, 4 Greene 1 (Iowa, 1853), decided that the legislature had authorized counties to subscribe to the stock of private railroad companies. Later this decision was overturned in *Stokes v. Scott County*, 10 Iowa 166 (1859). A comparison of these two opinions, although both dealt primarily with questions of statutory interpretation, indicates growing judicial hostility toward municipal aid to railroads, whether such aid was authorized by the legislature or not.

[17] 13 Iowa 389, 394.

[18] *Ibid.*, pp. 400–404.

[19] *Ibid.*, pp. 412–413.

[20] See, for example, *Booth v. Woodbury*, 32 Conn. 118 (1864), and *Brodhead v. Milwaukee*, 19 Wis. 624 (1865). The Supreme Judicial Court of Massachusetts, however, struck down a provision in a bounty law whereby the towns were authorized to repay individuals, who, through the expenditure of their own money, had induced others to enter military service in their place. The court declared, in *Freeland v. Hastings*, 10 Allen 570 (Mass. 1865), that such an object was not public, and that the provision was, for that reason, unconstitutional.

[21] Robert S. Blackwell, *A Practical Treatise on the Power to Sell Land for the Non-Payment of Taxes* (2d ed., 1864), p. 1. The first edition of this work appeared in 1855.

[22] *Const. Lim.* (1st ed.), p. 479.

[23] *Ibid.*, p. 487.

[24] *Loc. cit.*

[25] *Ibid.*, p. 488.

[26] *People v. Salem*, 20 Mich. 452 (1870), is analyzed below, pp. 116–119.

[27] *Const. Lim.* (1st ed.), p. 488.

[28] *Ibid.*, p. 494.

[29] 65 Pa. St. 146 (1869).

[30] *Ibid.*, p. 157. The distinction between general and local purposes was an important element in the broader concept of public purpose. According to this rule, the state could lay a general tax provided that the object thereof was both public and general. A municipality could levy a special (or local) tax if the purpose were public and local.

[31] 24 Wis. 350 (1869).

[32] *Ibid.*, pp. 354–355.

[33] 27 Iowa 28 (1869).

[34] The first edition appeared in 1872, and the second, third, and fourth editions (each consisting of two volumes) were published in 1873, 1881, and 1890, respectively. The fifth and last edition, in five volumes, appeared in 1911. Each edition was prepared by Dillon himself.

[35] 27 Iowa 28, 41.

[36] *Ibid.*, p. 42.

[37] *Ibid.*, p. 45.

[38] *Loc. cit.*

[39] *Loc. cit.* Dillon cited the *Const. Lim.* (1st ed.), pp. 479, 487, and 521. The first two citations were to Cooley's definition of taxes which, of course, embodied the public

purpose requirement. The third reference was to the following passage: "Wherever a tax is invalid because of excess of authority, or because the requisites in tax proceedings which the law has provided for the protection of the taxpayers are not complied with, any sale of property based upon it will be void also. The owner is not deprived of his property by 'the law of the land,' if it is taken to satisfy an illegal tax. And if property is sold for the satisfaction of several taxes, any one of which is unauthorized, or for any reason illegal, the sale is altogether void."

[40] 27 Iowa 28, 47.

[41] *Loc. cit.* The quotations were from pages 479 and 487 of *Const. Lim.* (1st ed.). Judge Dillon also quoted from the *Encyclopedia Britannica;* Webster's *Dictionary; The New American Encyclopedia; Pray v. Northern Liberties,* 31 Pa. St. 69 (1850); *Camden v. Allen,* 2 Dutch. 398 (N. J. 1857); and *Matter of Mayor of New York,* 11 Johns. 77 (N. Y. 1814).

[42] 27 Iowa 28, 50.

[43] *Ibid.,* p. 51.

[44] *Ibid.,* p. 59.

[45] For all practical purposes *Hanson v. Vernon* was overruled in *Stewart v. Supervisors of Polk County,* 30 Iowa 9 (1870). Chief Justice Dillon had by that time resigned from the Iowa bench to become a United States judge.

[46] 25 Wis. 167 (1869).

[47] 51 Barb. 312 (N. Y. 1868). In this case the Supreme Court of New York for the Fourth Judicial District struck down a law authorizing a town to issue bonds for the purpose of raising money to be donated to a private railroad company. The court objected to that feature of the law which authorized donations, but it observed that laws authorizing municipalities to subscribe to the stock of railroad companies were constitutional. The New York Court of Appeals did not review the decision, nor did it subsequently consider, in any other case, the precise issue which *Sweet v. Hulbert* had raised.

[48] 25 Wis. 167, 186–187.

[49] *Ibid.,* p. 187. Dixon cited the *Const. Lim.* (1st ed.), p. 214.

[50] 25 Wis. 167, 193–194.

[51] *Ibid.,* p. 195. The court quoted from the *Const. Lim.* (1st ed.), p. 531.

[52] 25 Wis. 167, 210.

[53] 20 Mich. 452 (1870).

[54] *Ibid.,* p. 473.

[55] *Ibid.,* p. 474.

[56] *Loc. cit.*

[57] *Loc. cit.*

[58] *Ibid.,* p. 477.

[59] *Ibid.,* pp. 483–484.

[60] *Ibid.,* pp. 484–485.

[61] *Ibid.,* p. 485.

[62] *Ibid.,* pp. 502–522.

[63] It may be suggested that judicial efforts in this direction ran counter to the immediate interests of conservatives and that the public purpose principle, as applied by Cooley and Dillon in the *Salem* and *Hanson* cases, was designed to protect the property of the average citizen and taxpayer from the ravages of big business. Even though such decisions frustrated the aspirations of private railroad corporations, the principles which Cooley and Dillon utilized tended, in the long run, to serve conserva-

tive and corporate interests. Not only was community support to private enterprises denied; but, on the basis of the same principles (when applied to a different set of facts), the property of private enterprise could not be distributed, through the exercise of the taxing power, for community use and service. The versatility of the public purpose maxim will become more apparent in the following chapter which treats the various applications of the principle.

[64] Iowa in *Hanson v. Vernon,* 27 Iowa 28 (1869); Wisconsin in *Whiting v. Sheboygan & Fond du Lac R. R. Co.,* 25 Wis. 167 (1869); and Michigan in *People v. Salem,* 20 Mich. 452 (1870). In addition the Court of Appeals of New York invalidated a state law *requiring* a town to subscribe to the stock of a private railroad company. See *People ex rel. D. W. & P. R. R. Co. v. Batchellor,* 53 N. Y. 128 (1873).

[65] The *Hanson* case was virtually overruled in *Stewart v. Supervisors of Polk County,* 30 Iowa 9 (1870). The *Whiting* decision, although not overruled, was badly undermined by the court's decisions in *Rogan v. Watertown,* 30 Wis. 259 (1872); *Lawson v. Milwaukee Ry.,* 30 Wis. 597 (1872); and *Oleson v. Green Bay Ry.,* 36 Wis. 383 (1874). In these cases the court sustained laws authorizing cities and counties either to loan their credit to railroad companies or to subscribe to the stock of such companies.

[66] The Michigan court reaffirmed the principles of the *Salem* case in *Bay City v. State Treasurer,* 23 Mich. 499 (1871), and in *Thomas v. Port Huron* 27 Mich. 320 (1873). In 1899 the court refused to overrule these decisions in *Attorney-General ex rel. Barbour v. Pingree,* 120 Mich. 550.

[67] See *Olcott v. Supervisors,* 16 Wall. 678 (1872), and *Railroad Company v. Otoe,* 16 Wall. 667 (1872), where the United States Supreme Court upheld state legislation authorizing municipalities to issue bonds to be donated to railroad companies. One of the most exhaustive summaries of cases wherein municipal aid to railroads was upheld appears in *Commissioners of Leavenworth County v. Miller,* 7 Kan. 479, 503–506 (1871). But scores of decisions on the question of railroad aid were rendered later.

[68] For example, see *Commissioners of Leavenworth County v. Miller,* 7 Kan. 479, 499, 509, 540 (1871); *Walker v. Cincinnati,* 21 Ohio St. 14, 44 (1871); and *Stockton & Visalia R. R. Co. v. Council of Stockton,* 41 Cal. 147, 197, 201, 202 (1871). The briefs and oral arguments in the *Stockton* case are of particular interest for their extended discussion of the validity of Cooley's views. The attorney-general, John R. McConnell, clearly discerned the importance of Cooley's statements on taxation because the greater part of his oral argument was devoted to an effort to show that those views were not authoritative. See John R. McConnell, "The Constitutionality of Acts Authorizing Subsidies to Railroads," in 172 Calif. Sup. Ct. Rec. 192.

[69] *Mun. Corp.* (1st ed.), pp. 556–557.

[70] Justice Strong in *Olcott v. Supervisors,* 16 Wall. 678, 689 (1872), declared: "It was asserted (what nobody doubts), that the taxing power of a state extends no farther than to raise money for a public use, as distinguished from private, or to accomplish some end public in its nature . . ." Speaking for the majority, he held, however, that aid to railroads was a public purpose.

[71] 20 Wall. 655 (1874).

[72] *Citizens' Savings Ass'n. v. Topeka,* 5 Fed. Cas. 737, No. 2,734 (C. C. D. Kan. 1874). Judge Dillon regarded the case as governed fully by his decision in *Commercial National Bank v. Iola,* 6 Fed. Cas. 221, No. 3,061 (C. C. D. Kan. 1873).

[73] 20 Wall. 655, 660.

[74] *Ibid.,* p. 663.

[75] *Loc. cit.* Miller cited Cooley's *Const. Lim.* (1st ed.), at pp. 129, 175, and 487. In the first and third of these passages Thomas Cooley had stated the public purpose

restriction on the taxing power. And in the second, he discussed the doctrine of implied limitations on legislative power.

[76] The reference to Dillon's *Mun. Corp.* was to that passage in which the writer set forth his definition of taxation. See above, p. 121.

[77] 20 Wall. 655, 664–665.

[78] *Ibid.*, p. 665.

[79] The case came to the Supreme Court from the United States Circuit Court for Kansas. Jurisdiction was based upon the diversity of the citizenship of the parties, and not upon the claim that a federal question had been presented. For that reason, the Court was able to dispose of the case without referring to any specific federal statute or constitutional provision.

[80] *Ibid.*, p. 670.

[81] A second edition appeared in 1886; and in 1903 and 1924 new editions, prepared by other writers, were published.

[82] *Taxation* (1st ed.), pp. 67–103.

[83] *Ibid.*, pp. 83–103.

[84] *Loc. cit.*

[85] *Ibid.*, pp. 86–87.

[86] *Ibid.*, p. 92.

[87] *Ibid.*, pp. 95–96.

[88] *Ibid.*, p. 102.

[89] *Ibid.*, pp. 83–84.

[90] *Ibid.*, p. 90.

[91] Like Cooley and Dillon, Tiedeman accepted the public purpose maxim as a requirement for valid taxation. However, his treatises were not very influential in the development of the principle. It will be recalled that his most important work, *Limitations of Police Power*, was written in 1886, and by that time the maxim had been firmly established as a valid proposition of American constitutional law. In a few taxation cases this work was cited; but in general, when the public purpose issue was raised, the courts were content to rely upon the treatises of Cooley and Dillon and upon the case law. For Tiedeman's views on the public purpose principle, see his *Lim. of Pol. Pow.*, pp. 474–476.

NOTES TO CHAPTER 5

The Application and Decline of the Public Purpose Maxim

[1] This approximate figure does not include the scores of cases involving city and county aid to railroad companies, nor does it include those cases in which questions of statutory interpretation alone were raised.

[2] The second question, concerning the power of the legislature to authorize cities and towns to engage in manufacturing as a public enterprise, and the court's discussion of it are treated below, p. 145.

[3] *Opinion of the Justices*, 58 Me. 590 (1871).

[4] *Ibid.*, p. 592.

[5] *Ibid.*, p. 593.

⁶ *Loc. cit.* Cf. *People v. Salem*, 20 Mich. 452, 486–487 (1870).

⁷ 58 Me. 590, 593.

⁸ *Ibid.*, pp. 594–595. Cf. *Hanson v. Vernon*, 27 Iowa 28, 45 (1869).

⁹ 60 Me. 124 (1872).

¹⁰ *Ibid.*, p. 129.

¹¹ *Ibid.*, p. 133. (Italics mine.)

¹² 62 Me. 62 (1873).

¹³ *Ibid.*, p. 70.

¹⁴ *Ibid.*, p. 73. The court quoted the *Const. Lim.* (1st ed.), p. 487.

¹⁵ 62 Me. 62, 75.

¹⁶ *Ibid.*, p. 76.

¹⁷ 10 Wis. 242 (1860). In this case the court invalidated a municipal tax law because: (1) by virtue of arbitrary exemptions made in the execution of the law, taxes upon the property of the plaintiff were increased; and (2) the tax was levied for the purpose of abating a nuisance upon the assessed property, that nuisance having been created by the city itself. Apparently the court was groping for some relationship between the purpose of the tax and the granting of exemptions—a relationship which it did not establish very clearly.

¹⁸ 20 Wall. 655 (1874), discussed above, pp. 122–124.

¹⁹ The one case in which a court sustained such aid was *United States v. Realty Co.*, 163 U. S. 427 (1896). In this case the Supreme Court of the United States upheld a law of Congress which appropriated money to pay sugar producers and manufacturers a bounty which had been provided for in earlier legislation and subsequently repealed. The Court refused to determine whether or not the original law was constitutional, but it held that an unconstitutional statute might create a moral obligation which Congress could satisfy through the expenditure of public money.

²⁰ *Weismer v. Douglas*, 64 N. Y. 91 (1876).

²¹ *McConnell v. Hamm*, 16 Kan. 228 (1876).

²² *Ohio Valley Iron Works v. Moundsville*, 11 W. Va. 1 (1877).

²³ *Clee v. Sanders*, 74 Mich. 692 (1889), and *Sutherland-Innes Co. v. Evart*, 86 Fed. 597 (C. C. A. 6th 1898).

²⁴ *United States ex rel. Miles Mfg. Co. v. Carlisle*, 5 App. D. C. 138 (1895); *Michigan Sugar Co. v. Auditor-General*, 124 Mich. 674 (1900); *Dodge v. Mission Township*, 107 Fed. 827 (C. C. A. 8th 1901); and *Minnesota Sugar Co. v. Iverson*, 91 Minn. 30 (1903).

²⁵ *Ferrell v. Doak*, 152 Tenn. 88 (1924).

²⁶ 111 Mass. 454 (1873).

²⁷ *Ibid.*, pp. 460–461.

²⁸ *Ibid.*, pp. 461–462. The constitutional provisions to which Judge Wells referred show, if anything, that the people of the state had invested the legislature with virtually unlimited discretion in the exercise of the taxing and spending powers.

²⁹ *Ibid.*, p. 470.

³⁰ *Loc. cit.* Judge Wells cited the *Const. Lim.* (1st ed.), p. 531.

³¹ 111 Mass. 454, 472.

³² 23 S. C. 57 (1885).

³³ *Ibid.*, p. 62. The court quoted from the *Const. Lim.* (1st ed.), p. 487.

³⁴ 23 S. C. 57, 63.

³⁵ *Ibid.*, p. 65. The court quoted the following passage from Dillon's work: "But it is obvious, from this statement of the grounds upon which the validity of such legislation [aid to railroads] rests, that it furnishes no support for the validity of taxation

in favor of enterprises and objects which are essentially private. We consider the principle equally sound and salutary, that the mere incidental benefits to the public or the State, or any of its municipalities or divisions, which result from the pursuit by individuals of ordinary branches of business or industry, do not constitute a public use in the legal sense which justifies exercise either of the power of eminent domain or of taxation." *Mun. Corp.* (2d ed.), p. 224.

[36] 14 Kan. 418 (1875).

[37] *Ibid.*, pp. 421–422.

[38] *Ibid.*, p. 422.

[39] *Ibid.*, p. 423.

[40] *Ibid.*, p. 427.

[41] 1 N. D. 88 (1890).

[42] 75 Minn. 118 (1898). In this case the court apparently feared that prosperous persons, as well as paupers and prospective paupers, would benefit from the aid. *Ibid.*, p. 123.

[43] *Mayor of Baltimore v. Keeley Institute,* 81 Md. 106 (1895). The court, in its opinion, emphasized the purpose of the law, which was the treatment of drunkards. Had it stressed the character of the immediate recipient, a private medical institution, the result might have been different.

[44] 95 Wis. 153 (1897).

[45] *Ibid.*, p. 157. The court quoted from the *Const. Lim.* (6th ed.), p. 704 and from the *Lim. of Pol. Pow.*, p. 4.

[46] 95 Wis. 153, 157–158.

[47] 118 Wis. 129 (1903).

[48] *Ibid.*, p. 139. The court quoted from Cooley's *Taxation* (2d ed.), pp. 103–105, and from his *Const. Lim.* (6th ed.), p. 608. It also quoted from Dillon's *Mun. Corp.* (4th ed.), pp. 573, 895, 897. In each of these passages is stated the familiar principle that a public purpose inheres in all valid exercises of the taxing power.

[49] 143 Mo. 287 (1898).

[50] According to Breck P. McAllister, "Public Purpose in Taxation," *California Law Review* (January and March, 1930), 18:138, n. 2, nine state constitutions provide that "All taxes shall be levied and collected for public purposes only." He listed the following: Ariz. Const. (1912), art. ix, sec. 1; Ky. Const. (1891), sec. 171; Minn. Const. (1857), art, ix, sec. 2, amend. of 1906; Mo. Const. (1875), art. x, sec. 3; Mont. Const. (1889), art. xii, sec. 11; N. D. Const. (1889), art. xi, sec. 176; Okla. Const. (1907), art. x, sec. 14; Okla. Bill of Rights, sec. 1; S. D. Const. (1889), art. xi, sec. 2, amend. of 1912; and Texas Const. (1876), art. viii, sec. 3. All these clauses were adopted after Cooley and Dillon had popularized, within their profession, the public purpose principle as an implied restriction on the power of the legislatures to tax.

[51] 143 Mo. 287, 314.

[52] *Ibid.*, pp. 322–323.

[53] *Ibid.*, pp. 325–326. The court quoted as follows from Cooley's work: "To justify taxation for the purpose of education, the rules under which the people shall be admitted to the privileges given must not be invidious and partial, but must place all parties on a plane of practical equality. The rule is substantially the same here that applies in the apportionment of taxes; equality must be the aim of the law, and it must be assumed that the State has no special favors to bestow upon privileged classes. . . . It would not be competent to single out some one class of the community and exclude them from the benefits of the public schools on arbitrary grounds." *Taxation* (2d ed.), p. 121.

[54] 75 Ohio St. 114 (1906).

[55] *Ibid.*, p. 132.

[56] *Ibid.*, p. 133.

[57] *Ibid.*, p. 134. The court cited the *Const. Lim.* (6th ed.), p. 207.

[58] 75 Ohio St. 114, 135.

[59] In *Trustees of Brooke Academy v. George*, 14 W. Va. 411 (1878), the court invalidated, as violative of the public purpose requirement, a law which transferred from the Virginia Literary Fund to the trustees of the academy rights to a bequest made by a private individual. The Supreme Court of Kansas struck down legislation appropriating money to a private agricultural association in *Blain v. Riley County Agricultural Society*, 21 Kan. 558 (1879). A municipal ordinance providing for the erection of a public library and memorial hall was held void in *Kingman v. Brocton*, 153 Mass. 255 (1891). The judges found the ordinance particularly objectionable because it provided that the G. A. R.—a private association—was to be entitled to space in the new building. A special tax on fire-insurance companies to raise money for the aid of disabled and superannuated firemen was declared unconstitutional in *Aetna Fire Insurance Co. v. Jones*, 78 S. C. 445 (1907). The fact that the statute provided that the revenue from the tax was to be turned over directly to firemen's associations and was to be administered by them apparently convinced the court that the purpose was private. A special muncipal tax, authorized by the state legislature and approved by a majority of the city voters, for the support of a museum, open to the public but managed by a department of a private university, was invalidated by the Supreme Court of Missouri in *State ex rel. Museum of Fine Arts v. St. Louis*, 216 Mo. 47 (1909). Here again the tax was struck down because the court chose to emphasize the nature of the recipient rather than the character of the purpose. It should be added that the courts cited the works of the publicists in all these opinions except in that delivered in *Blain v. Riley County Agricultural Society*.

[60] *Opinion of the Justices*, 58 Me. 590 (1871). The judges also considered the question whether or not the legislature could authorize cities and towns to subsidize private manufacturers. The part of the court's opinion dealing with this issue is discussed above. See pp. 129–131.

[61] *Ibid.*, p. 597.

[62] *Ibid.*, p. 598.

[63] 41 S. C. 220 (1894).

[64] *Ibid.*, p. 254.

[65] *Ibid.*, p. 245.

[66] *Ibid.*, p. 248.

[67] *Ibid.*, p. 249.

[68] *Loc. cit.*

[69] *Ibid.*, p. 254. The court cited the *Treatise on Taxation* (2d ed.), p. 764.

[70] 42 S. C. 222 (1894).

[71] *Ibid.*, pp. 246–247.

[72] *Opinion of the Justices*, 155 Mass. 598 (1892).

[73] *Opinion of the Justices*, 150 Mass. 592 (1890).

[74] 155 Mass. 598, 602–603.

[75] *Opinion of the Justices*, 182 Mass. 605 (1903). The questions presented here were somewhat more elaborate but, in substance, not very different from those raised in 1892 and answered in 155 Mass. The court made one interesting observation which indicated its laissez faire bias. It declared: "Until within a few years it generally has been conceded, not only that it would not be a public use of money for the govern-

ment to expend it in the establishment of stores and shops for the purpose of carrying on a business of manufacturing or selling goods in competition with individuals, but also that it would be a perversion of the function of government for the State to enter as a competitor into the field of industrial enterprise, with a view either to the profit that could be made through the income to be derived from the business, or to the indirect gain that might result to purchasers if prices were reduced by governmental competition. . . ." 182 Mass. 605, 607. The Supreme Court of Michigan in *Baker v. Grand Rapids,* 142 Mich. 687 (1906), followed the Massachusetts court and declared that cities could not establish and operate fuel yards, but the court conceded that municipalities could sell coal to their inhabitants if a serious shortage were either existent or imminent. On the other hand, the Supreme Court of the United States upheld the power of the legislature to authorize muncipalities to establish and operate such businesses in *Jones v. Portland,* 245 U. S. 217 (1917).

⁷⁶ 101 Ga. 588 (1897).

⁷⁷ *Ibid.,* p. 593. The court cited *Mun. Corp.* (3d ed.), II, 916–917.

⁷⁸ 134 Ga. 560 (1910).

⁷⁹ *Ibid.,* p. 567. The court also contended that, as a matter of law, there was no difference between a municipal fuel enterprise and a municipal ice plant. In its opinion public money could be spent for the establishment and maintenance of either.

⁸⁰ 135 La. 898 (1914).

⁸¹ *Ibid.,* pp. 915–916. See Cooley's *Taxation* (2d ed.), pp. 103, 104, 105, for the passages quoted by the court.

⁸² 135 La. 898, 924.

⁸³ *Ibid.,* p. 926.

⁸⁴ *State ex rel. Toledo v. Lynch,* 88 Ohio St. 71 (1913). In this case, however, the court's principal ground for invalidating the ordinance appropriating money for the establishment of the theater was not the public purpose restriction but rather the strict interpretation which the judges gave to the "Home Rule" amendment to the state constitution.

⁸⁵ *Los Angeles v. Lewis,* 175 Cal. 777 (1917).

⁸⁶ *State ex rel. Kansas City v. Orear,* 277 Mo. 303 (1919).

⁸⁷ 106 U. S. 487 (1882).

⁸⁸ 113 U. S. 1 (1885).

⁸⁹ 164 U. S. 112 (1896).

⁹⁰ *Ibid.,* pp. 156, 161. The language of Justice Peckham, who wrote the majority opinion, leaves much to be desired. He used the terms "public use" and "public purpose" interchangeably; and, for that reason, the incorporation of the public purpose principle into due process of law of the Fourteenth Amendment cannot unreservedly be ascribed to the opinion in the *Fallbrook* case.

⁹¹ 199 U. S. 437 (1905).

⁹² The state, it will be recalled, established the dispensary system in the 1890's. See above, pp. 146–148.

⁹³ *Ibid.,* p. 454. The Supreme Court of the United States upheld the constitutionality of the South Carolina dispensary system in *Vance v. Vandercook Company, No. 1,* 170 U. S. 438 (1898). The Court, in this case, was primarily interested in certain provisions of the revised dispensary law as they affected interstate commerce. The public purpose requirement was not considered in the Court's opinion.

⁹⁴ 199 U. S. 437, 454.

⁹⁵ 245 U. S. 217 (1917).

⁹⁶ 111 Me. 486 (1914).

[97] 245 U. S. 217, 221.

[98] 253 U. S. 233 (1920).

[99] *Ibid.*, p. 239.

[100] 262 U. S. 447 (1923). Another case, *Massachusetts v. Mellon,* involving the constitutionality of the same law, the "Maternity Act" of 1921, was decided simultaneously. Before decision in these cases, the Court had had one or two opportunities to determine whether or not the public purpose principle was applicable to the congressional taxing power. The Court had declined to make its position on this question clear, however. See *United States v. Realty Co.,* 163 U. S. 427 (1896).

[101] 297 U. S. 1 (1936).

[102] See, for example, *Ferrell v. Doak,* 152 Tenn. 88 (1924), in which the Supreme Court of Tennessee invalidated legislation extending public financial aid to a box manufacturer.

[103] *Eakin v. South Dakota Cement Commission,* 44 S. D. 268 (1921). This decision had been anticipated by the ruling given in *Opinion of the Judges,* 43 S. D. 648 (1920).

[104] *Bank v. Bell,* 62 Cal. App. 320 (1923). The state supreme court declined to review the judgment of the appellate tribunal.

[105] *Standard Oil Co., v. Lincoln,* 114 Neb. 243 (1926), affirmed by the United States Supreme Court in 275 U. S. 504 (1927), a *per curiam* opinion. But in 1925 the Supreme Court of South Dakota declared unconstitutional a law establishing the state in the gasoline business. *White Eagle Oil Co. v. Gunderson,* 48 S. D. 608 (1925).

NOTES TO CHAPTER 6

The Publicists and Laissez Faire: An Evaluation

[1] John F. Dillon, *The Laws and Jurisprudence of England and America,* pp. 204–205.

[2] In addition to the cases in which the validity of antiliquor statutes was challenged, there were cases involving the constitutionality of laws which prohibited the operation of other businesses. Usually the businesses which the legislatures condemned were of such a character that the legislation received judicial approval. But laws prohibiting the operation of some businesses were of more doubtful constitutionality. In *State v. Addington,* 77 Mo. 110 (1882), and in *Powell v. Commonwealth,* 114 Pa. St. 265 (1887), the courts sustained laws which prohibited the sale of oleomargarine. But the New York Court of Appeals declared a similar law unconstitutional in *People v. Marx,* 99 N. Y. 377 (1885). See above, p. 55.

[3] There were numerous cases involving laws of this kind. Illustrative of the reasoning of the courts where licensing laws were invalidated are the opinions in *State v. Moore,* 113 N. C. 697 (1893), and *Ex parte Whitwell,* 98 Cal. 73 (1893). In the first of these the court invalidated a law imposing a license fee of $1,000 on persons engaged in the business of hiring workers for service outside the state. The Supreme Court of California, in the *Whitwell* case, struck down a law requiring the licensing and inspection of privately owned insane asylums. The court found that the legislation was void because it imposed unreasonable standards for the location and construction of such institutions.

[4] See *Ex parte Westerfield,* 55 Cal. 550 (1880); *Ragio v. State,* 86 Tenn. 272 (1888); and *Eden v. People,* 161 Ill. 296 (1896).

⁵ 94 U. S. 113 (1876).

⁶ 127 U. S. 678 (1888).

⁷ 154 U. S. 362 (1894) and 169 U. S. 466 (1898).

⁸ *Const. Lim.* (4th ed.), p. 746.

⁹ The Supreme Court of New Hampshire invalidated a state statute imposing a tax of 1 per cent on estates bequeathed to collateral relatives and to nonrelatives on the ground that the tax was not uniform and equal when applied to these persons only. See *Curry v. Spencer,* 61 N. H. 624 (1882). The Supreme Court of Minnesota declared unconstitutional a statute requiring, as a condition precedent to probate proceedings for the settlement of estates, the payment to the county treasurer of specified sums prescribed with reference to the value of the estate. See *State ex rel. Davidson v. Gorman,* 40 Minn. 232 (1889). In *State ex rel. v. Ferris,* 53 Ohio St. 314 (1895), the Supreme Court of Ohio invalidated a law imposing a graduated tax on inheritances exceeding $20,000. Like most state tribunals, the Supreme Court of the United States never acceded to the view that the requirement for uniform taxation was violated by graduated taxes. But Justice Field, in his concurring opinion in *Pollock v. Farmers' Loan and Trust Co.,* 157 U. S. 429 (1895), argued that the income tax law was void because, by exempting incomes of less than $4,000, it was not uniform. *Ibid.,* p. 595.

¹⁰ *Const. Lim.* (1st ed.), pp. 495–517. *Mun. Corp.* (1st ed.), pp. 562–574.

¹¹ For example, see *Matter of Eureka Basin,* 96 N. Y. 42 (1884), where the New York Court of Appeals declared that private property could not be condemned for wharves or basins which were to be privately owned and in which the public was to have no interest. A number of courts denied that the power of eminent domain could be invoked for the purpose of establishing private roads. See *Varner v. Martin,* 21 W. Va. 534 (1883).

¹² Commons, *Legal Foundations of Capitalism,* pp. 186–188.

¹³ *Const. Lim.* (1st ed.), p. 523 *et seq. Mun. Corp.* (1st ed.), pp. 438–474. *Lim. of Pol. Pow.,* pp. 379–391, 420–422.

¹⁴ Twiss, however, suggests that Cooley's ideas influenced the judges in their interpretations of the public use requirement for exercises of the power of eminent domain. See·his *Lawyers and the Constitution,* p. 25. But the principles enunciated by Cooley were not new, and his views, at best, did little more than reënforce ideas prevailing at that time.

Bibliography

DOCUMENTARY MATERIALS

Federal and State Reports. For specific cases see pp. 213 ff.

Report of the Commissioners on the Practicability of Reducing to a Written and Systematic Code the Common Law of Massachusetts. Boston: Dutton and Wentworth, 1837. 46 pp.

Ela, John, and Andrew Bruce. *Brief and Argument for the People: Ritchie v. People.* Supreme Court of Illinois, Southern Grand Division, n. p., n. d. 59 pp.

Hackenberg, P. L., and Associates. *Paper Book, Brief for Plaintiffs in Error: Godcharles v. Wigeman.* Supreme Court of Pennsylvania. Milton, Pa.: Meltonian Print, 1886. 39 pp.

Holton, George M. *Brief for Petitioner in the Matter of Habeas Corpus on Behalf of J. C. Kuback.* California State Archives: File 11094, Case No. 20680. 9 MS pp.

House, George S. *Argument for Appellants: Frorer v. People.* Supreme Court of Illinois, Central Grand Division. Chicago: Barnard and Gunthrop, 1891. 22 pp.

McConnell, John R. "The Constitutionality of Acts Authorizing Subsidies to Railroads." Oral Argument on Behalf of Respondents in *Stockton & Visalia R. R. v. Council of Stockton.* 172 California Supreme Court Records 192.

Moran, Kraus, and Mayer. *Brief and Argument for Plaintiffs in Error: Ritchie v. People.* Supreme Court of Illinois, Southern Grand Division, n. p., n. d. 62 pp.

Richardson, James D. *Compilation of the Messages and Papers of the Presidents, 1789–1897.* 53d Cong., 2d sess., H. Misc. Doc. No. 210. Washington: Government Printing Office, 1896–1899. 10 vols.

Stead, William. *Brief and Argument for Appellant: Ritchie and Co. v. Wayman.* Supreme Court of Illinois. Springfield: Journal Co., 1909. 67 pp.

Thorpe, Francis N. (ed.). *The Federal and State Constitutions, Colonial Charters and Other Organic Laws.* 59th Cong., 2d sess., H. Doc. No. 357. Washington: Government Printing Office, 1909. 7 vols.

Wilderman & Hamil. *Abstract and Brief for Appellants: Millett v. People.* Supreme Court in Illinois, Southern Grand Division, n. p., n. d. 28 pp.

GENERAL AND SPECIAL WORKS:
HISTORIES, BIOGRAPHIES, AND
TREATISES

Beard, Charles A. *An Economic Interpretation of the Constitution of the United States.* New York: Macmillan, 1913. 330 pp.

Beveridge, Albert J. *The Life of John Marshall.* Boston: Houghton Mifflin, 1916–1919. 4 vols.

Black, Henry C. *Handbook of American Constitutional Law.* St. Paul: West Publishing Co., 1895. 627 pp.

Blackstone, Sir William. *Commentaries on the Laws of England.* Oxford: Clarendon Press, 1765–1769. 4 vols.

————. Rev. ed. by Thomas M. Cooley. Chicago: Callaghan. Editions of 1876 and of 1884. 2 vols.

Blackwell, Robert S. *A Practical Treatise on the Power to Sell Land for the Non-Payment of Taxes.* 2d ed. Boston: Little, Brown, 1864. 668 pp.

Bogart, Ernest L. *Economic History of the American People.* 2d ed. New York: Longmans, Green, 1935. 891 pp.

Bouvier, John. *Institutes of American Law.* Philadelphia: Robert Paterson, 1851. 4 vols.

Brannon, Henry. *Treatise on the Rights and Privileges Guaranteed by the Fourteenth Amendment.* Cincinnati: W. H. Anderson, 1901. 526 pp.

Cole, Arthur C. *The Irrepressible Conflict, 1850–1865.* (*A History of American Life,* ed. A. M. Schlesinger and D. R. Fox, Vol. VII.) New York: Macmillan, 1903. 468 pp.

Collins, Charles Wallace. *The Fourteenth Amendment and the States.* Boston: Little, Brown, 1912. 220 pp.

Commons, John R., and Associates. *History of Labour in the United States.* New York: Macmillan, 1926. 2 vols.

————. *Legal Foundations of Capitalism.* New York: Macmillan, 1924. 394 pp.

Cooley, Thomas M. *The General Principles of Constitutional Law.* Boston: Little, Brown, 1880. 376 pp.

————. *Michigan, A History of Governments.* (*American Commonwealths,* ed. Horace Scudder.) Boston: Houghton Mifflin, 1885. 376 pp.

————. *A Treatise on the Constitutional Limitations Which Rest upon the Legislative Power of the States of the American Union.* Boston: Little, Brown, 1868. 720 pp.

————. 2d ed. 1871. 781 pp.

————. 3d ed. 1874. 827 pp.

————. 4th ed. 1878. 883 pp.

————. 5th ed. 1883. 886 pp.

————. 6th ed. by Alexis C. Angell. 1890. 885 pp.

————. 7th ed. by Victor H. Lane. 1903. 1036 pp.

––––––. 8th ed. by Walter Carrington. 1927. 2 vols.

––––––. *A Treatise on the Law of Taxation Including the Law of Local Assessments*. Chicago: Callaghan, 1876. 741 pp.

––––––. 2d ed. 1886. 991 pp.

––––––. 3d ed. by Alfred P. Jacobs. 1903. 2 vols.

––––––. 4th ed. by Clark A. Nichols. 1924. 4 vols.

––––––. *A Treatise on the Law of Torts or the Wrongs Which Arise Independent of Contract*. Chicago: Callaghan, 1879. 755 pp.

––––––. 2d ed. 1888. 899 pp.

––––––. 3d ed. by John Lewis. 1906. 2 vols.

Corwin, Edward S. *Liberty Against Government*. Baton Rouge: Louisiana State University Press, 1948. 210 pp.

––––––. *The Twilight of the Supreme Court*. New Haven: Yale University Press, 1934. 237 pp.

Dillon, John F. *The Laws and Jurisprudence of England and America*. Boston: Little, Brown, 1894. 431 pp.

––––––. *The Law of Municipal Bonds*. St. Louis: G. I. Jones, 1876. 63 pp.

––––––. *Removal of Causes from State Courts to Federal Courts*. St. Louis: Central Law Journal, 1875. 138 pp.

––––––. *Treatise on the Law of Municipal Corporations*. Chicago: Cockcroft, 1872. 808 pp.

––––––. *The Law of Municipal Corporations*. 2d ed. New York: Cockcroft, 1873. 2 vols.

––––––. *Commentaries on the Law of Municipal Corporations*. 3d ed. Boston: Little, Brown, 1881. 2 vols.

––––––. 4th ed. 1890. 2 vols.

––––––. 5th ed. 1911. 5 vols.

Dorfman, Joseph. *The Economic Mind in American Civilization*. New York: Viking, 1946–1949. 3 vols.

Dwarris, Sir Fortunatus. *A General Treatise on Statutes,* ed. by Platt Potter. Albany: William Gould, 1871. 693 pp.

Fairman, Charles. *Mr. Justice Miller and the Supreme Court, 1862–1890*. Cambridge: Harvard University Press, 1939. 456 pp.

Fish, Carl R. *The Rise of the Common Man, 1830–1850*. (*A History of American Life,* ed. A. M. Schlesinger and D. R. Fox, Vol. VI.) New York: Macmillan, 1929. 391 pp.

Freund, Ernst. *Administrative Powers over Persons and Property*. Chicago University Press, 1928. 620 pp.

––––––. *Legislative Regulation*. New York: Commonwealth Fund, 1932. 458 pp.

––––––. *The Police Power, Public Policy and Constitutional Rights*. Chicago: Callaghan, 1904. 819 pp.

––––––. *Standards of American Legislation*. Chicago University Press, 1917. 327 pp.

Gabriel, Ralph H. *The Course of American Democratic Thought*. New York: Ronald Press, 1940. 452 pp.

Gray, James M. *Limitations of the Taxing Power Including Limitations upon Public Indebtedness*. San Francisco: Bancroft-Whitney, 1906. 1316 pp.

Groat, George G. *Attitude of American Courts in Labor Cases* (Columbia University Studies in History, Economics, and Public Law, XLII). New York: Longmans, Green, 1911. 400 pp.

Guthrie, William D. *Lectures on the Fourteenth Article of Amendment to the Constitution of the United States*. Boston: Little, Brown, 1898. 265 pp.

Hacker, Louis M. *The Triumph of American Capitalism*. New York: Simon and Schuster, 1940. 460 pp.

Haines, Charles G. *The American Doctrine of Judicial Supremacy*. 2d ed. Berkeley: University of California Press, 1932. 705 pp.

———. *The Revival of Natural Law Concepts*. Cambridge: Harvard University Press, 1930. 388 pp.

———. *The Role of the Supreme Court in American Government and Politics, 1789–1835*. Berkeley: University of California Press, 1944. 679 pp.

Hofstadter, Richard. *Social Darwinism in American Thought, 1860–1915*. Philadelphia: University of Pennsylvania Press, 1945. 191 pp.

Holcombe, Arthur. *Our More Perfect Union*. Cambridge: Harvard University Press, 1950. 460 pp.

Horton, John Theodore. *James Kent: A Study in Conservation, 1763–1847*. New York: Appleton-Century, 1939. 354 pp.

Hurst, James W. *The Growth of American Law. The Law-Makers*. Boston: Little, Brown, 1950. 502 pp.

Jensen, Merrill. *The Articles of Confederation*. Madison: University of Wisconsin Press, 1940. 284 pp.

Kent, James. *Commentaries on American Law*. New York: O. Halstead, 1826–1830. 4 vols.

King, Willard L. *Melville Weston Fuller*. New York: Macmillan, 1950. 394 pp.

Knowles, Lillian C. A. *Economic Development in the Nineteenth Century*. London: Geo. Rutledge & Sons, 1932. 368 pp.

Labaree, Leonard W. *Conservatism in Early American History*. New York University Press, 1948. 182 pp.

Lewis, John. *A Treatise on the Law of Eminent Domain*. Chicago: Callaghan, 1888. 926 pp.

McCloskey, Robert G. *American Conservatism in the Age of Enterprise*. Cambridge: Harvard University Press, 1951. 193 pp.

McIlwain, Charles H. *Constitutionalism, Ancient and Modern*. Ithaca: Cornell University Press, 1947. 180 pp.

Miller, Samuel F. *Lectures on the Constitution of the United States*. New York: Banks & Bros., 1891. 765 pp.

Mills, Henry E. *A Treatise upon the Law of Eminent Domain*. St. Louis: F. H. Thomas Law Book Co., 1879. 404 pp.

Mott, Rodney L. *Due Process of Law*. Indianapolis: Bobbs-Merrill, 1926. 702 pp.

Nevins, Allan. *The Emergence of Modern America, 1865–1878. (A History of American Life*, ed. A. M. Schlesinger and D. R. Fox, Vol. VIII.) New York: Macmillan, 1927. 446 pp.

Nichols, Philip. *The Power of Eminent Domain*. Boston: Boston Book Co., 1909. 560 pp.

Paschal, Joel F. *Mr. Justice Sutherland: A Man Against the State*. Princeton University Press, 1951. 267 pp.

Pomeroy, John Norton. *An Introduction to the Constitutional Law of the United States*. New York: Hurd and Houghton, 1870. 549 pp.

Pond, Oscar L. *A Treatise on the Law of Public Utilities Operating in Cities and Towns*. Indianapolis: Bobbs-Merrill, 1913. 954 pp.

Pound, Roscoe. *The Spirit of the Common Law*. Boston: Marshall Jones, 1921. 224 pp.

Prentice, W. P. *Police Powers Arising under the Law of Overruling Necessity*. New York: Banks & Bros., 1894. 516 pp.

Randolph, Carman F. *The Law of Eminent Domain in the United States*. Boston: Little, Brown, 1894. 462 pp.

Redfield, Isaac F. *A Practical Treatise upon the Law of Railways*. 2d ed. Boston: Little, Brown, 1858. 823 pp.

Reed, George I. (ed.). *The Bench and Bar of Michigan*. Chicago: Century, 1897. 586 pp.

Russell, Alfred. *The Police Power of the State*. Chicago: Callaghan, 1900. 204 pp.

Schlesinger, Arthur M. *The Rise of the City, 1878–1898. (A History of American Life*, ed. A. M. Schlesinger and D. R. Fox, Vol. X) New York: Macmillan, 1933. 494 pp.

Schlesinger, Arthur M. Jr. *The Age of Jackson*. Boston: Little, Brown, 1945. 577 pp.

Sedgwick, Theodore. *A Treatise on the Rules Which Govern the Interpretation and Application of Statutory and Constitutional Law*. New York: John Voorhies, 1857. 712 pp.

Smith, Adam. *An Inquiry into the Nature and Causes of the Wealth of Nations*. 8th ed. London: Strahan and Cadell, 1796. 3 vols.

Spencer, Herbert. *Justice*. New York: Appleton, 1895. 465 pp.

———. *Social Statics*. New York: Appleton, 1865. 523 pp.

Story, Joseph. *Commentaries on the Constitution of the United States*. Boston: Hilliard, Gray, 1833. 3 vols.

———. 4th ed. by Thomas M. Cooley. Boston: Little, Brown, 1873. 2 vols.

Story, William W. *Life and Letters of Joseph Story*. Boston: Little and Brown, 1851. 2 vols.

Swisher, Carl B. *Stephen J. Field, Craftsman of the Law*. Washington: Brookings Institution, 1930. 473 pp.

Taylor, Hannis. *Due Process of Law and the Equal Protection of the Laws*. Chicago: Callaghan, 1917. 988 pp.

Tiedeman, Christopher G. *A Treatise on Equity Jurisprudence*. St. Louis: F. H. Thomas Law Book Co., 1893. 858 pp.

———. *A Treatise on the Law of Municipal Corporations in the United States*. New York: Banks & Bros., 1894. 839 pp.

———. *A Treatise on the Limitations of Police Power in the United States*. St. Louis: F. H. Thomas Law Book Co., 1886. 662 pp.

———. *A Treatise on State and Federal Control of Persons and Property in the United States*. St. Louis: F. H. Thomas Law Book Co., 1900. 2 vols.

———. *The Unwritten Constitution of the United States*. New York: Putnam, 1890. 165 pp.

Trimble, Bruce R. *Chief Justice Waite, Defender of the Public Interest*. Princeton University Press, 1938. 320 pp.

Tucker, John R. *The Constitution of the United States,* ed. by Henry St. George Tucker. Chicago: Callaghan, 1899. 2 vols.

Twiss, Benjamin R. *Lawyers and the Constitution*. Princeton University Press, 1942. 271 pp.

Warren, Charles. *The Supreme Court in United States History*. Rev. ed. Boston: Little, Brown, 1937. 2 vols.

Watson, D. K. *The Constitution of the United States*. Chicago: Callaghan, 1910. 2 vols.

Willoughby, W. W. *The Constitutional Law of the United States*. New York: Baker, Voorhis, 1910. 2 vols.

Wilson, Francis Graham. *The American Political Mind*. New York: McGraw-Hill, 1949. 506 pp.

Wright, Benjamin Fletcher Jr. *American Interpretations of Natural Law*. Cambridge: Harvard University Press, 1931. 360 pp.

———. *The Contract Clause of the Constitution*. Cambridge: Harvard University Press, 1938. 287 pp.

ARTICLES, NOTES, AND COMMENTS

"Effect of Joining Tax and Appropriation Measures in Same Act—The Colorado Old Age Pensions," *Yale Law Journal*, XLV (February, 1936), 729–731.

"Limiting the Right to Contract," *American Law Review*, XXVI (May and June, 1892), 404–405.

"State and Municipal Excursions into Business Enterprise as Public Purposes Under the Taxing Power," *Harvard Law Review*, XLI (April, 1928), 775–779.

Albertsworth, E. F. "From Contract to Status," *American Bar Association Journal,* VIII (January, 1922), 17–20.

Blunk, Clifford. "Ernst Freund," *Annual Report of the Illinois State Bar Association.* Springfield: Hartman-Jefferson, 1933. Pp. 247–249.

Brown, Ray A. "Due Process of Law, Police Power and the Supreme Court," *Harvard Law Review,* XL (May, 1927), 943–968.

Commager, Henry S. "Constitutional History and the Higher Law," *Pennsylvania Magazine of History and Biography,* LXII (January, 1938), 20–40.

Cooley, Thomas M. "The Constitutional Limits to the Power of Taxation," *Western Jurist,* II (April, 1868), 69–81.

Corwin, Edward S. "The Basic Doctrine of American Constitutional Law," *Michigan Law Review,* XII (February, 1914), 247–276.

———. "The Doctrine of Due Process Before the Civil War," *Harvard Law Review,* XXIV (March, 1911), 366–385; (April, 1911), 460–479.

———. "The 'Higher Law' Background of American Constitutional Law," *Harvard Law Review,* XLII (December, 1928), 149–185; (January, 1929), 365–409.

———. "The Spending Power of Congress-Apropos the Maternity Act," *Harvard Law Review,* XXXVI (March, 1923), 548–582.

———. "The Supreme Court and the Fourteenth Amendment," *Michigan Law Review,* VII (June, 1909), 643–672.

Cushman, Robert E. "John Forrest Dillon," *Dictionary of American Biography* (New York: Scribner's, 1930), V, 311.

Frankfurter, Felix. "Hours of Labor and Realism in Constitutional Law," *Harvard Law Review,* XXIX (February, 1916), 353–373.

Gregg, Phillip E. "The Supreme Court's Interpretation of the Taxing and Spending Powers of Congress," *Rocky Mountain Law Review,* VIII (February, 1936), 145–151.

Haines, Charles G. "Judicial Review of Legislation in the United States and the Doctrine of Vested Rights and Implied Limitations on Legislatures," *Texas Law Review,* II (April, 1924), 257–290; (June, 1924), 387–421; III (December, 1924), 1–43.

Hough, Charles M. "Due Process of Law—Today," *Harvard Law Review,* XXXII (January, 1919), 218–233.

Hubbard, Harry. "John F. Dillon," *American Bar Association Journal,* XIV (1928), 77–79.

Jones, Dana T. "Does the United States Constitution Inhibit State Laws Limiting Hours of Private Daily Employment?" *Central Law Journal,* LIII (November 15, 1901), 384–390.

Judson, Frederick N. "Liberty of Contract Under the Police Power," *American Law Review,* XXV (November and December, 1891), 871–898.

———. "Public Purposes for Which Taxation Is Justifiable," *Yale Law Journal,* XVII (January, 1908), 162–169.

Kent, Charles A. "Thomas McIntyre Cooley," *University of Michigan Memorial Discourses* (1899), pp. 3–28.

Knowlton, Jerome C. "Thomas McIntyre Cooley," *Michigan Law Review,* V (March, 1907), 309–325.

McAllister, Breck P. "Public Purpose in Taxation," *California Law Review,* XVIII (January, 1930), 137–148; (March, 1930), 241–254.

McBain, Howard L. "Due Process of Law and the Power of the Legislature to Compel a Municipal Corporation to Levy a Tax or Incur Debt for a Strictly Local Purpose," *Columbia Law Review,* XIV (May, 1914), 407–428.

McLaughlin, Andrew C. "Thomas McIntyre Cooley," *Dictionary of American Biography* (New York: Scribner's, 1930), IV, 392–393.

Myrick, O. H. "Liberty of Contract," *Central Law Journal,* LXI (December 22, 1905), 483–496.

Pingrey, D. H. "Limiting the Right to Contract," *Central Law Journal,* XXXIV (January 29, 1892), 91–96.

Pound, Roscoe. "Common Law and Legislation," *Harvard Law Review,* XXI (April, 1908), 383–407.

———. "Liberty of Contract," *Yale Law Journal,* XVIII (May, 1909), 454–487.

Shattuck, Charles E. "The True Meaning of the Term 'Liberty' in Those Clauses in the Federal and State Constitutions Which Protect 'Life, Liberty, and Property,' " *Harvard Law Review,* IV (March, 1891), 365–392.

Sturgis, Roger F. "Demands of Labor and the Fourteenth Amendment," *American Law Review,* XLI (July and August, 1907), 481–497.

Summer, Lionel M. "Christopher Gustavus Tiedeman," *Dictionary of American Biography* (New York: Scribner's, 1936), XVIII, 531.

Tucker, John. "The Law School of the University of the City of New York," *Intercollegiate Law Journal,* I (December, 1891), 43–49.

Williston, Samuel. "Freedom of Contract," *Cornell Law Quarterly,* VI (May, 1921), 365–380.

Table of Cases

TABLE OF CASES

Index

INDEX

Articles of Confederation, 3–4

Blackstone, Sir William: influence of his *Commentaries on the Laws of England*, 9; Cooley's editions of the *Commentaries*, 44, 56, 176 n. 13, 179 n. 65

Boucher, Jonathan, 3

Brandeis, Louis D., 94

Calvin, John, 2

Campbell, John A.: argument in *Slaughter-House Cases*, 32, 35; influences Justice Field, 36

Class legislation, 27, 32; condemned by Cooley, 31; and United States Supreme Court, 46, 91; in state courts, 43–44, 49, 54, 55, 56, 57–58, 66–67, 68, 69–70, 72–73, 74–75, 76, 77, 81, 82; as element of liberty of contract, 96, 161

Codification of law, 12

Common law: conservative character of, 9–11: fails to provide conservatives desired protection, 11; and due process, 21; and legal incapacities, 31, 70, 91

Company stores, judicial consideration of laws concerning, 57–58, 69–70. *See also* Scrip laws

Constitutional Convention, 4

Constitutional Limitations, Cooley's, 22, 26–27; reasons for popularity, 29–30; conservative bias, 30; key passages in, 31; invoked as authority by state courts, 40, 43, 44, 52, 56, 67, 69, 70, 72, 73, 74, 75–76, 76–77; in United States Supreme Court, 46, 49, 85, 188 n. 92; question of use in *Godcharles v. Wigeman,* 58; character of, compared with Tiedeman's works, 59–60, 83; used in yellow-dog contract cases, 76–77; used in cases involving maximum-hours

laws, 79–80, 81, 82, 83, 84; and public purpose, 106–109; used in taxation cases, 113, 115–116, 123, 125, 133, 134, 136, 137, 140, 141, 143, 190 n. 39; and rate-fixing, 163–164

Contract clause: judicial applications of, 5, 6–9; and reservation clauses, 7, 21, 172 n. 25; failure as guarantee of property rights, 11, 20, 21; after Civil War, 25, 48, 173 n. 45

Cooley, Thomas M., 22, 26–27; biographical sketch, 27–29; publishes *Constitutional Limitations,* 29; opinion in *People v. Salem,* 116–119. *See also* Blackstone; Class legislation; Due process; Economic liberty; Implied limitations; Natural rights; Public improvements: Public use. See also *Constitutional Limitations; Taxation, Treatise on; Torts, Treatise on*

Corporations, controversy over status of, 14–16

Custom and usage, criterion for valid exercises of taxing power, 118, 123, 141, 143, 149, 150

Dillon, John F., 22; biographical sketch, 111–112; judicial opinions of, 112–114, 122. See also *Municipal Corporations*

Divine law, 2

Due process, 21–22, 27; and economic liberty, 24, 162; and class legislation, 31, 32, 74; emphasized by Cooley, 32, 177 n. 16, 190 n. 39; development before Civil War, 33, 99, 181 n. 94; interpretation by United States Supreme Court, 33, 35, 38, 45–49 *passim;* interpreted by state tribunals, 42, 50–55 *passim;* and screening laws, 72; and scrip laws,

221